WOMAN'S PLACE

A GUIDE TO SEATTLE

AND KING COUNTY

HISTORY

Mildred Tanner Andrews

GEMIL PRESS
Seattle, Washington

Cover photo: Women's Place? The sky's the limit!
(Courtesy of Whatcom Museum of History and Art)

Supported by the
King County Cultural Development Fund
Hotel/Motel Tax Revenues for Arts and Heritage

Library of Congress Catalog Card Number: 93-079116
ISBN 0-9640239-0-3

Published by

GEMIL PRESS
851 NE 56th Street
Seattle, WA 98105
(206) 524-1426

CONTENTS

v

FOREWORD

There has been a revolution in the way we do history in this country. This has served to "democratize" the field in ways that were unimaginable only a few decades ago. Regional history is no longer the exclusive province of a few professionals and academics. It belongs to everyone, affects everyone, and is open to the creative participation of everyone. It is not just about the lifestyles of the rich and famous, or about the traditional concentration and exercise of power in the hands of a few. It is about cultural diversity--about every community preserving, enriching and passing on its traditions, values and wealth of material culture to succeeding generations. We are--all of us--the inheritors and stewards of the legacy provided for us by persons and generations who have gone before.

Mildred Tanner Andrews is in the vanguard of those authors whose work has opened our eyes and has helped us to understand and acknowledge the women who were pioneers, builders and sustainers of our communities. Her books WASHINGTON WOMEN AS PATHBREAKERS and SEATTLE WOMEN: A LEGACY OF COMMUNITY DEVELOPMENT are invaluable guides to neglected but essential aspects of our heritage. This new work focuses on historic sites and landmarks which are not only significant to local history but to the very fabric of state and regional history. This guide is a delight to read and it will reward its users with many new insights into the built environment and cultural legacy of King County. With the publication of this guide, Mildred continues her pioneering work in regional studies. I recommend it highly.

Charles Payton
Community Museum Advisor
King County Cultural Resources Division

From headquarters in Seattle's Arcade Building, the Washington Equal Suffrage Association distributed colored posters to members who displayed them in conspicuous spots. 1910. (Courtesy of Special Collections Div., Univ. of Washington Libraries, Asahel Curtis #19943)

PREFACE

The power of historic sites helps define communities by giving us a sense of continuity. Yet, like traditional histories of the American West, most of our landmarks commemorate men who were leaders in government, the military and our major industries.

WOMAN'S PLACE, A GUIDE TO SEATTLE AND KING COUNTY HISTORY provides fresh insights into our cultural heritage by exploring more than 250 sites where you can walk in the paths of spirited women and sense the significance of their struggles and achievements. Included are theaters, art schools, homesteads, farms, Tribal centers, schools, libraries, museums, hospitals, factories, mansions, clubhouses, parks, brothels, union halls, airports, churches, businesses and judges' chambers to name a few. Sites selected are at least 25 years old or connected with significant activities that began prior to 1970.

This guidebook is intended for anyone who wants to know what could be called the real story about how we came to be what we are. What emerges is a historical tapestry of grassroots, human tales that interweaves past and present lives. While the book includes notable women, it also emphasized unsung heroes--wives, mothers, wage earners and clubwomen of diverse urban and rural, ethnic, religious, economic and social backgrounds.

Take it with you on your daily rounds and discover interesting stories connected with sites close to home. Why not pack up your family, friends or out-of-town visitors for a drive and few hours of learning about King County's rich and colorful past? Each tour offers spectacular viewpoints with inviting spots for a picnic and areas where you might prefer to walk.

You can start at any point, or chart your own route, combining sites from the eleven different tours. Maps are provided with numbers identifying each site, along with detailed written directions in the text. If you or your group choose to explore a thematic perspective--such as environmental preservation, the arts, politics, or women and paid work--use the index and the table of contents to custom design your own tour.

Is all of this important? Yes! In our fast-paced, computer-driven society, where the lines between male and female rights and responsibilities grow increasingly blurred, we can learn from past generations of King County women whose concerns were often similar to our own:

- In the 1870s and again in the 1890s, Susan B. Anthony crusaded for woman suffrage in Seattle and galvanized support for related causes, including "Equal Pay for Equal Work."

- The University of Washington School of Nursing refused to admit Maxine Pitter Haynes because she was Black, then later responded to Black students demands and recruited her to serve on the faculty.

- Auburn's Women's Christian Temperance Union worked to prevent drug and alcohol abuse and established the public library as an alternative to saloons.

- In the 1920s Seattle Mayor Bertha Landes cracked down on corruption with a policy of "municipal housekeeping." It echos the stance of many of today's elected women who maintain that the personal is political and the political is personal.

- Clubwomen were among the first to sound the environmentalists' alarm.One of their legacies is Federation Forest State Park near Enumclaw.

- As single parents, Kate Dougherty of Duvall, Cheng Hiang and Dorothy Bullitt of Seattle, and Mathilda Olson of Maple Valley suddenly had to take over management of the family business. While caring for their children and participating actively in their communities, each of them earned the respect of the predominantly male business establishment.

One of my most difficult challenges in writing this book was deciding what to leave out. I could not possibly include the legacies of every woman's club or stories of women's experiences in every home and at every work place. My selection is based to a large extent on diversity in hopes that the reader will be able to find examples in the text that relate to other sites and women's activities connected with them. I invite you to join me in the effort to rescue additional women from historical oblivion.

To credit everyone who has guided me in this project would be almost as impossible as compiling a complete history of women in King County. For the past twelve years, I have combed state and county archives and listened to hundreds of stories, sometimes in the form of lengthy interviews and sometimes a casual conversation, that have helped shape my interpretation. I am grateful to the interviewees and to writers of academic and community histories, many of whom are cited in the text.

I also appreciate the assistance of archivists, librarians, and historians who have helped me find elusive records and who guided me in the selection of photographs. Among them are: Richard Engeman, Carla Rickerson and Karyl Winn at the University of Washington's Manuscripts and Special Collections Division; Carolyn Marr and Rick Caldwell, Museum of History and Industry; Eleanor Toews, Seattle Public Schools Archives; Elaine Miller, Washington State Historical Society, Tacoma; Charles Payton and Mary Matthews of the King County Department of Parks, Planning and Resources; Beth Chave,Seattle Landmarks Commission; Margaret Riddle, Everett Public Library; Ross Rieder, Pacific Northwest Labor History Association; Sister Rita Bergamini and Loretta Greene, Sisters of Providence Archives; Pat Matheny White, Chicano Archives, the Evergreen State College; Barbara Krohn, Women in Communication's, Inc.; Edith Johnson, Daughters of the Pioneers of Washington; Dorothy Cordova, Filipino American National Historical Society; Audrey Schroeder and Judy Kelley, Fall City Historical Society; Ray Fowler and Marcie Williams, Marymoor Museum; Patricia Cosgrove and Linda Van Nest, White River Valley Historical Museum, Auburn; Marie Folkins, Gilman Town Hall Museum, Issaquah; Linda Yelm, Issaquah City Historian; Lisa Alfien, Bellevue Art Museum and Pacific Northwest Arts and Crafts Fair; Toni Nagel, Whatcom Museum of History and Art; Esther Mumford, Black Heritage Society of Washington; Marianne Forsblad, Nordic Heritage Museum; Vicki Stiles and Barbara Monks, Shoreline Historical Museum; Greg Watson, Snoqualmie Valley Historical Museum; Ethel Telban and Bea Mathewson, Renton Historical Museum; Linda Smith, Federal Way Historical Society; Ann Steiert and Bob Eaton, Black Diamond Historical Museum; Clay Eals, West Seattle Historical Society;

Ranger Steve McBee, Federation Forest State Park; Gayle Palmer, Washington State Library, Olympia; Lillian Chappell, American Indian Women's Service League; Barbara Loomis, Kirkland Historical Society; Tove Burhen, Duvall Historical Society; Isabel Egglin and Kay Reinartz, Queen Anne Historical Society; Grace Speers, Junior League of Seattle; Melanie Draper, Greater Des Moines-Zenith Historical Society; Alan H. Archambault, Fort Lewis Military Museum; Tyler Devlin, a friend of Lady Willie Forbus; Ruth Vincent and Priscilla Chong Jue, Wing Luke Asian Museum; Eric Taylor, Taylor'd Exhibits; and Rod Slemmons, Seattle Art Museum.

This project was made possible by a grant from the King County Cultural Development Fund Hotel/Motel Tax Revenue. My very special thanks to Charles Payton, Museum Advisor of the King County Cultural Resources Division, who monitored my progress and who was the first to read an early draft of the entire manuscript. His knowledge of county history and landmarks records provided invaluable guidance, and his critique of content and style guided me through revisions. I am also grateful to Jill Wiske, Shirley Yee, Esther Mumford, Ethel Telban and Marie Folkins, each of whom read and criticized all or parts of the work. In the process, we have had some stimulating conversations, comparing my findings with their knowledge and insights.

Many thanks also to Johnny Wakely, a skilled transcriber with an understanding of the intracacies of computer programs and an eye for detail. He meticulously transcribed my manuscript and formatted the text.

Finally, my husband George has been the best of companions, giving me his unflagging and good-humored encouragement. He contributed many an hour to draw the twelve maps and design the book's cover. I lovingly dedicate this book to him and to my mother, Mildred Chargois Tanner, whose moral support knows no bounds.

Mildred Tanner Andrews
Seattle

WOMAN'S PLACE

A GUIDE TO SEATTLE

AND KING COUNTY

HISTORY

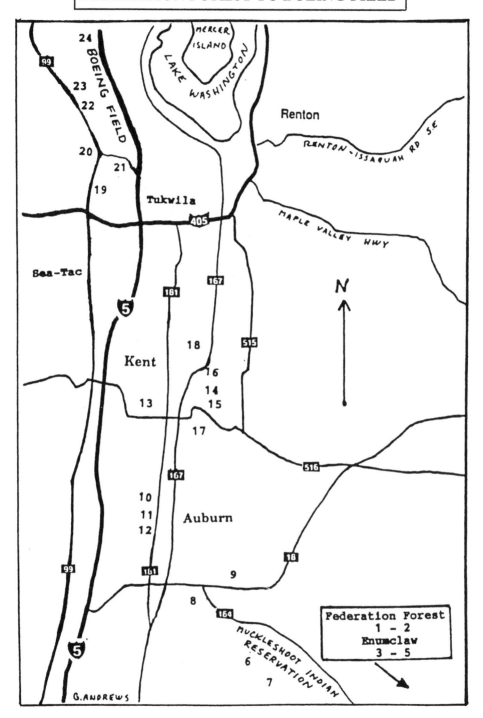

I. FORESTS TO FARMS TO FACTORIES
Federation Forest to Boeing Field

This tour begins in Federation Forest State Park, located on scenic Chinook Pass Highway (SR-410). With stunning views of Mount Rainier, you descend along the raucous White River to the peaceful farming community of Enumclaw. From there take the Enumclaw-Auburn Highway (SR-164) through King County's only treaty lands, the Muckleshoot Reservation, with a stop at tribal headquarters. Then follow directions to sites in the Green River and Duwamish Valleys. Bicyclists and hikers may choose to take the historic Interurban Trail or the serpentine Green River Trail, mapping out alternative routes to sites of interest.

Many of King County's first settlers pioneered in the fertile valley that later attracted significant numbers of Japanese, Italian and Filipino immigrants. Beginning in 1883, railroads and Interurban rail lines linked the valley and its abundant agricultural produce to Seattle. The automobile and improved highways brought the once dominant Interurban to a halt in 1928, causing several small station towns to disappear and leaving only Pacific, Algona, Auburn, Kent and Tukwila as valley commercial centers. When the Howard Hanson Dam was constructed in 1962 to control the annual Green River floods, it ironically spelled the demise of the bucolic farmscape. As developers moved onto the dry land, cities and factories sprawled across former dairies and truck farms, leaving only vestiges of an earlier way of life. The tour that follows the rivers from the mountains through the valley concludes at Boeing Field where the Duwamish nears the end of its journey into Puget Sound.

1. Federation Forest State Park
On State route 410, 17 miles east of Enumclaw

As president of the Washington State Federation of Women's Clubs, Elvira Marquis Elwood addressed the 1902 convention: "It seems to many, perhaps, an unnecessary precaution to sound the note of alarm regarding the destruction of trees by forest fires and the lumberman's ax when our Evergreen state is so richly endowed with magnificent forests . . ." Clubwomen lobbied the legislature for highway beautification and protection of endangered species of wildlife, while giving strong support to the movement to establish Olympic National Park. In response, Governor Meade appointed Elwood to the State Conservation Commission.

In the 1920s under the leadership of President Esther Stark Maltby, the federation negotiated with Snoqualmie Falls Lumber Company, a Weyerhaeuser subsidiary, to arrange purchase of a 62-acre tract of virgin forest on the western slope of Snoqualmie Pass. Sporting "Save a Tree" buttons, members canvassed their communities to raise funds. When "sold" for $100, a tree would be marked with a metal commemorative plate engraved according to the wishes of the purchaser. Contributions came from far and wide. The Seattle Soroptimists and the State Federation of Colored Women's Clubs proudly purchased trees, while the National Geographic Society signaled its support with a check for $1,000.

In ensuing years logging operations on adjacent lands left the park unprotected. Strong winds toppled several of the giant fir trees. To make matters worse, the state highway department worried about imperiling motorists and wanted to clearcut a 200-foot swath through the park on each side of the highway. Finally, the federation negotiated with the state to sell the original old-growth stand and replace it with a new and larger 600-acre preserve of second growth timber near Chinook Pass. During World War II, when lumber was at a premium, the emphasis was on cleaning up logged-off areas, reforestation, and keeping the natural scenery intact.

More recently, the Catherine Montgomery Interpretive Center was established at the park. It was named in honor of an ardent conservationist and pioneer teacher who willed substantial funds to the federation for park improvements. The Center's purpose is to show the widely diverse contrasts in flora and climate in Washington's seven different biotic or life zones (the entire nation only has ten and few other states can claim more than three). By word, picture and living displays, the Center illustrates Washington's Coast Forest Zone, Mountain Forest Zone, Sub-Alpine Zone, Alpine Zone, Yellow Pine Forest Zone, Bunchgrass Zone, and Sagebrush Zone.

Visitors can explore the forest via two carefully constructed trails, one of which is approximately half a mile and the other a full mile long. Nature trail guidebooks are available at the Interpretive Center.

"The Botany Bunch" studies flora in the Cascades. 1908. Asahel Curtis photo #10770-71. (Courtesy of the Washington State Historical Society, Tacoma)

2.   Naches Trail
Federation Forest State Park

The first wagon road to cross the Cascades passed through Federation Forest State Park along the West Trail, where traces of its existence can still be seen. In 1853 Captain George McClellan investigated the trail across 5,000 foot Naches Pass, which for generations had been used by Native people, but concluded that it was not suitable for a proposed railroad. Puget Sound pioneers in their determination to establish a route through the Cascades formed a volunteer road crew to establish a rough path up their side of the mountains.

When James Longmire heard rumors of the new and shorter road from Walla Walla, he rerouted his caravan of 36 covered wagons. Arriving in the mountains in October, the pioneers found snow and no sign of a road. At the pass, they faced the worst part of their journey--a treacherous drop-off, so steep that they had to lower wagons, people, and supplies by ox-hide ropes. They then followed the White River, laboriously hacking out a path through the dense forest.

At a time when Victorian ethics dictated female submissiveness and when women could neither vote nor serve on juries, they--however reluctantly--were obligated to leave families and friends behind and follow their husbands. Women pioneers, like those in the Longmire party, often made the arduous journey with small children and sometimes gave birth enroute. On the verge of collapse, Mrs. Longmire and Mrs. Light carried a baby and led a three-year-old child out of the forest and into a clearing where Andy Burge, a member of the volunteer road crew, was clearing brush. He exclaimed, "My God women, where did you come from?," gave them all of his food and supplies, and dashed off to summon help.

At the end of their journey, members of the party disbanded to stake claims throughout the Puget Sound Region. Their descendants number in the thousands. One of them is Claire Raaum of Redmond who has organized a popular annual reunion and who is working to preserve the Naches Trail as a landmark. As lower and easier routes were discovered, pioneers rarely crossed Naches Pass. Today it is accessible only by trail.

3.   Danish Hall
1708 Porter Street, Enumclaw
Turn right on Porter

In 1907 the Danish Sisterhood opened the town's first lending library in Danish Hall, built by the men's brotherhood as a center for cultural and community life. Families gathered for holiday celebrations and traditional dances, and children came on Saturdays for Danish school. In 1928 Mary Fell Stevenson Yerxa--Enumclaw's public-spirited founding mother--bequeathed her house on the corner of Myrtle and Wells behind City Hall for the library's new home. By then the sisterhood's collection had grown to more than 750 volumes, 400 of which, not surprisingly, were in Danish.

In her book NEW LAND, NEW LIVES, historian Janet Rasmussen notes that in the first decades of the 20th century, 35 to 50 percent of the 150,000 Scandinavian immigrants coming to the Northwest were women. She says that most were young, unmarried, and "motivated by economic pressures to seek employment overseas." They were "strong, eager, independent, and very self-reliant and were very successful in making the transition to the new life they established here. They were sought after in the job market (often in service occupations like cook or seamstress) so they were able to make a living." Scandinavian women socialized in their churches and ethnic organizations and frequently married someone from their homeland. In communities such as Enumclaw, they maintained beautiful gardens and high standards of neatness.

Several Scandinavian names are listed in the records of the Enumclaw Garden Club, organized in 1923 with a predominantly female membership. The club launched its annual flower show to raise funds for civic beautification. Projects included landscaping and a fish pond on the grounds of the city's handsome Municipal Building, gardens in city parks, and planting the huge Christmas tree that lights up the town square. Enumclaw earned its reputation as "the town beautiful" with visitors marvelling at the near absence of litter.

4.   Enumclaw Community Memorial Hospital
2125 C Street
Continue on Porter; turn right on C Street

In 1944 Vi Cass, a science teacher at the high school and a civic activist, galvanized the community support for a permanent local hospital. She took the lead in sorting out federal regulations for construction and in negotiating a mortgage. Community organizations and individuals pitched in, donating funds, furnished rooms, hand-sewn linens and garments, medical and laboratory equipment, and landscaping. with pride in their self sufficiency, local citizens managed to build and equip their hospital without assistance from the federal government. When it opened in 1949, the first superintendent was Martha Lee, followed by Mary Nolte.

5.   Lyceum Group and Farmer's Picnic
State Route 164 and 228th Avenue SE
Return on Porter; turn right on Griffin which is SR-164

In an era before radio or motion pictures, rural families had to create their own social and cultural life. Joining in the Lyceum movement of the late nineteenth century were farm families on the Enumclaw prairie who came from far and wide to meet at the Firgrove Schoolhouse. On Saturday nights, they held debates, gave literary and poetic readings, and presented musical and dramatic performances.

In August 1892, the Lyceum group celebrated its first anniversary with a picnic, launching an annual event that for the next 40 years rivaled the Fourth of July as a summer highlight. Following the haying season, everyone welcomed the break. Covered buggies and hay wagons filled with families, converged at the picnic site. The women worked for days to prepare the feast of fried chicken, potato salad, cakes and pies. In her book, THERE IS ONLY ONE ENUMCLAW, Louise Poppleton quotes Lena Morris Thompson who took part as a child: "First, there was a program with children singing and speaking pieces learned at school, and a grown up chorus. The Enumclaw Band sent chills up my spine, because the only music we heard was what we made ourselves, usually just singing with no accompaniment. After lunch, we watched horse racing, ran in children's races, cheered the men's tug of war, and a baseball game. In the evening, a crowd went over to J. P. Jones' Store and danced.... No liquor was allowed on the ground, but plenty was bootlegged in, while others sneaked out to find a 'blind pig' in the adjacent woods."

Eventually, the picnickers formed a corporation and purchased a ten-acre site on the Auburn-Enumclaw Road. They built a covered dance pavilion, a bandstand, a caretaker's house, a baseball diamond complete with grandstand, campsites with stoves and tables, and in 1913 a popular moving picture house. To support what became a week-long picnic, they brought in concessions, gambling games and carnival attractions.

As automobiles became commonplace, the picnic grew, attracting huge crowds from all over the state. Poppleton says, "The increasing crowds and carnival concessions spoiled the friendly, rural atmosphere, and parents objected to the large amounts of money spent.... When fire destroyed the pavilion and movie house in 1935, the Association disbanded, and after 44 years, the Picnic came to an end..."

6.   The Muckleshoot Administrative Building
172 SE and 392nd Street SE
Turn south on 172nd SE from SR-164

Located on King County's only treaty land, the Muckleshoot Reservation has a strong tradition of women's leadership. For example, in 1945 Annie Garrison was elected tribal judge; and in 1955 six women and three men served on the tribal council. In 1970, when fire destroyed the old Tribal Hall, Marie Starr was chair of a council made up of five women and four men. With assistance from Green River Community College and the City of Auburn, the council began its multi-year fund-raising project for a new administrative building and community center.

The current council chair is Virginia Cross, who has written several books and articles, including the MUCKLESHOOT INDIAN HISTORY, co-authored with Patricia Noel and published by the Auburn School District for use in its classrooms. As in the past, the elders pass down ancient myths and lore to younger generations, teaching them to live in harmony with the earth and with each other.

While advocating through the courts for Indian and tribal rights, the elders have implemented numerous educational and social service programs. An example is the Muckleshoot Youth Home, located next to the administrative building. Marie Starr served as founding director of the demonstration program, initially funded by HEW to implement

Muckleshoot Chapel. (Courtesy of King County Department of Parks, Planning and Resources)

the Indian Child Welfare Act of 1978. Its purpose was to prevent the removal of Indian children from their natural parents and to keep families together.

In the warm and comfortable building, adult members of the tribe create a temporary home for children, giving their parents needed time to deal with critical problems of their own, such as homelessness, unemployment or alcoholism. Trained staff members work with parents in crisis, involving them as much as possible in their children's lives and ameliorating the transition to their future as a family. The Muckleshoot Youth Home has provided desperately needed services with a program that can function as a model for other tribes.

7. Saint Claire's Indian Mission Chapel
Next to the Administrative Building

Built by Indians of hand-hewn timber in 1870, Saint Claire's Mission Chapel has housed both Catholic and Shaker religions. The Muckleshoots and members of other tribes in King and Pierce Counties have congregated at the chapel for weddings, funerals and other religious and social gatherings. In the 1930s a violent windstorm wrought such severe damage to the building that members nearly abandoned it.

One group that resisted giving up was the Nesika Women's Club which gave a benefit dance to raise funds for renovation. Even though the building was in a state of disrepair, faithful Shakers continued to use it. One of them was Julia Sam who died in 1942, having worshiped there for 68 years. When the church with its moss-covered belfry was finally boarded up, members continued to try to save it. In an interview with the SEATTLE POST INTELLIGENCER on June 6, 1955, Tribal Judge Annie Garrison said, "If I have a special project, it's the old church... Some of us would like nothing more that to see the altar and pews and windows back and hear the bell ringing on a Sunday morning."

Later the church was moved to a heritage village in Federal Way. In 1979 with grant assistance from King County, the Muckleshoot tribe was able to reclaim it and move it back to the reservation.

8.   Auburn Public Library
Auburn Dance and Music Center
Women's Christian Temperance Union
306 Auburn Avenue
State Route 164 becomes Auburn Way S. Turn left on Third NE and go one block to Auburn Avenue

In the anthology, RECLAIMING THE PAST: LANDMARKS OF WOMEN'S HISTORY, historian Gail Dubrow discusses the often-overlooked grassroots significance of the Women's Christian Temperance Union which "exercised profound local influence...and clearly altered the course of American history." She challenges her readers to locate local examples of buildings, suitable for landmark designation, that were founded by the WCTU. Auburn's venerable Carnegie Library meets the challenge!

A major goal of the WCTU was to establish cultural institutions to serve as alternatives to saloons. In 1904 the Auburn unit established the town's first lending library and reading room in a space above the fire hall with Isadora Ayers as librarian. As the book collection grew, so did the need for expanded space. In 1911 the library board made a successful grant application to the Carnegie Foundation. City voters passed a library levy to raise requisite operating and matching funds, while pioneers Arthur and Jane Ballard contributed the building site. In accord with the WCTU's vision, the library became the town's "temple of culture," providing a proper venue for meetings, events, reading or browsing.

The Auburn unit was founded in the 1880s as part of the western Washington WCTU. Delegates attended regional and national meetings, returning home with strategies for direct action. In this significant social and political movement, their mission was to curb vice and make their communities liveable. In the 1890s when Auburn saloonkeepers violated the law and opened on the Sabbath, 60 members of the WCTU marched into their establishments, then confronted the Justice of the Peace and the City Council to demand enforcement.

To improve public sanitation, the local unit raised funds for Auburn's first public drinking fountains. Members regularly contributed cash donations and jars of home-canned produce to the WCTU's White Shield Home for "fallen women" and their children, located in Tacoma. Politically, the local unit did its part in grassroots crusades for woman suffrage and prohibition.

In the 1960s the Auburn Public Library moved into its present modern building at Les Gove Park. In keeping with the WCTU's priorities, the Auburn Dance and Music Center acquired the old Carnegie Library and continues to nurture the community's cultural life. The Center has faithfully restored the building which is listed on the National Register of Historic Places.

9.   White River Valley Historical Museum
918 H Street SE
Go south on Auburn Way S; turn east onto 12th SE; turn left into Les Grove Park

Alarmed because local historical records were being lost and stories forgotten, the Auburn Women's Club in 1952 invited valley residents to the library for a pioneer party to organize the White River Valley Historical Society. Members collected and preserved artifacts and archival materials, while launching a fund-raising drive to construct a museum on the site donated by the city of Auburn. The museum, which opened in 1970, displays interpretive exhibits of the valley's pioneer history and maintains a research library. A notable feature is the mosaic that greets visitors in the foyer. It was created by Doris McIntire Tilden, an Auburn native, who used bits of tile, petrified wood, and tumbled glass to depict some milestones of valley history.

10. Jeffs Home
Children's Home Society of Washington
4338 Auburn Way N

In the 1860s Thomas pioneer, Richard Jeffs, married a part-Klickitat woman named Mary. They developed and cleared their land where they made a fortune raising hops. Unlike many other pioneers, Jeffs did not abandon his native wife as more white women arrived. In his HISTORY OF KING COUNTY, Clarence Bagley who knew Jeffs said, "[He] always maintained that his wife who had stood by him in the difficult days when he had had to wrest a home from the wilderness should reap the rewards along with him when he attained affluence." The Jeffses' rewards were severely diminished by the tragic deaths of their two sons, both of whom were studying law at Stanford University. Since they had no heirs, they bequeathed half of their estate for the "Jeffs Orphan Home."

The orphanage opened in 1928 as part of the Children's Home Society of Washington (CHSW). With a matron in charge, it housed up to 30 boys at a time, age six to sixteen. The valley community responded with an outpour of good will; clubs and organizations planned outings for the boys and brought them gifts, especially during the Christmas holidays. In his book FARMLANDS, Thomas historian Stan Flewelling tells of a group of women who formed the G.T.C. (meaning unknown) to aid the orphanage. Boys who lived in the home maintained high standards of grooming and behavior and everyone pitched in with house and farmwork. Going to school, games, music, reading, sports and bedtime prayers were part of the daily routine.

In accord with the CHWS's mission, a major goal was to arrange suitable adoptions. Joseph Ruttan was a boy who liked the home so much that he resisted attempts to "adopt him out." Because he misbehaved, prospective adoptive parents repeatedly sent him back. He fondly recalled projects with the Future Farmers of America and 4-H, such as building a wading pond or raising Orphan Annie, the pet pig that lived in the basement until her weight threatened to cave in the steps.

In a 1937 issue of the society's WASHINGTON CHILDREN'S
HOME FINDER, Matron Cordelia W. Howland gave a glowing
description of a different scenario:

> The phone rings and a message comes from the office, "Bring
> Georgie in. He is to be placed." The matron calls little ten
> year old George from his play and tells him that there is a
> father and a mother who want him for their boy. "O boy! I'm
> glad! and I'll be good so they will keep me." With an uncanny
> sense of perception the other boys rush up to him and begin,
> "Lucky guy! Wish'st t'was me."

The property was managed by trustees of the Jeffs estate who were
legally bound to maintain it as a working farm. As valley economic
patterns changed, they found it increasingly difficult to make ends
meet. In 1968 they reluctantly decided to close the home, then
granted assets to the CHSW which reopened it as its south King
County branch. In recent years, it has shifted its focus toward
residential treatment, administering aid to homeless, abused or
otherwise troubled youth and their families. The former Jeffs Orphan
Home has been preserved, reminding residents and visitors of an
important part of local history. (Please see Chapter V, Children's
Home Society of Washington for further information.)

11.   Thomas School/Thomas Academy/PTA
8207 S 280th Street
*Continue north on Auburn Way S; turn left on S 280th
Street*

In 1987 St. James School, an interdenominational institution in Kent,
purchased the complex of buildings on the site that had housed the
Thomas School and community center since the 1880s. Determined
to preserve the historic integrity of the 1928 brick building, volunteers
set to work and remodeled it. When the new private school was
dedicated, scores of former grade school students came for the

celebration.

By the late 1920s, almost two-thirds of the children at Thomas School were of Japanese descent. To enable non-English-speaking Issei (first generation Japanese) parents to participate, Matahichi "Mat" Iseri organized a Japanese PTA, then served as translator, enabling it and its English-speaking counterpart to work together. He later learned that he was the first male PTA president to be registered in Washington State. (Please see next item for more about the Iseri family.)

In the 1920s, the Thomas PTA organized a hot lunch program with members volunteering to help in the school kitchen. Much of the produce for the 3¢ lunches was donated by local farmers. For fundraisers the association sponsored dramatic skits put on by school kids and often directed by a creative and dedicated teacher, Myrtle Currie. In 1939 when President Roosevelt introduced the March of Dimes, Currie came up with the idea of covering a continuous tape with coins. The first one measured ten feet, five inches long and was sent directly to the White House, whereupon the idea was adopted nationally.

The World War II evacuation of people of Japanese descent dealt the school a crushing blow. In the post-war period, Currie--then promoted to school principal--did what she could to help the few families who returned. Mat Iseri's daughter, Mae Yamada, vividly remembers a boy at school who punched her son, hollering "Jap, what are you?" Currie intervened, insisted that the boy apologize, and worked steadfastly to quell racist attitudes that children had inherited from their parents.

In the post-war period with no service clubs left in Thomas, the PTA became the major source of community life. It established an annual carnival, hobby fairs, talent shows, potlucks and monthly square dances. When Currie retired in 1962, the PTA set up a scholarship fund in her honor.

12. Matahichi "Mat" and Kisa Iseri Farm (site)

Now the Valley Drive-In Theatre
S 277th Street and Auburn Way N

Mae Iseri Yamada now of Kent was born and raised in a hard-working, public-spirited community that became an economic cornerstone of the White River Valley during the first half of the twentieth century. Despite laws that prohibited the Issei from becoming citizens or owning land, the community took root and prospered, becoming the predominant ethnic group by the 1920s. The only member of her large family to return to the valley after their internment during World War II, Mae is breaking the silence of a people who were wronged and humiliated. In recent years she has shared her story with school children, community groups and media, while serving on the board of the White River Valley Historical Museum.

Mae's father, Mat Iseri, was one of only a few English-speaking Issei and was well-known in the community. In addition to serving as a translator, he was a founding member of the Buddhist Church, the Japanese Association, the Japanese PTA and the Japanese school. Since public life was a traditionally male domain, Mae's mother, Kisa, helped with refreshments or programs, giving her support from behind the scenes.

At home with their two daughters and ten sons, Kisa played a more assertive and often dominant role. While Mat insisted that the children address him in English, Kisa stuck to Japanese, making sure that her family knew their cultural traditions. She was equally insistent that the children complete high school. To supplement their income, Mat worked in an Auburn grocery store and later opened a general store on the family farm. When he delivered groceries, Kisa ran operations on the farm, supervising the children, working with them in the fields, and minding the store.

Despite the rigorous work load, the Iseris always managed to do extra for their family. Every Sunday there was a community picnic for which Kisa made time-consuming sushi and tempura. Mae recalls,

"When the picnic was over everyone came to our house and sang and danced until midnight. I still don't know how we made it to school on Monday morning." The commodious house that the Iseris built was always open to visitors, especially the kids' friends who frequently spent the night.

When Mae was in her teens, her only sister died, leaving her and her mother to do housework, serve tea, care for younger children, wash, iron and mend clothing for her father and ten brothers. Mae still feels grateful to them for their appreciation of "women's work" and for trying to make things a little easier. She treasures the electric sewing machine that her father gave to her mother and also thinks fondly of the mangel that her brothers gave her to ease her endless ironing chores.

The community changed abruptly and permanently with the bombing of Pearl Harbor when President Roosevelt issued Executive Order 9066. On December 7, 1941, at 7:30 p.m., armed soldiers arrested Mat Iseri. When rumor came that he was being held in Seattle, Mae went to investigate. Because she was a girl, the family thought that she would have the best chance. During the five minute visitation time, she was able to reassure him that his family was safe and that they were planting new crops.

Mae and a brother helped register people of Japanese descent. Although they were charged with no crime, they were forced to abandon their homes to be interned at Tulelake. Six months later, Mat was finally allowed to join them. One of Mae's brothers served in the all-Nisei (second generation Japanese) 442nd Regiment and was killed in France, helping rescue members of the Texas 36th Division, also known as the "Lost Battalion." His death and the fact that he never knew that his family was finally set free haunts Mae to this day.

At camp Mae married and had two children. Following the war, she was the only member of her family to return to the farm. With broken hearts, her parents moved to Ontario, Oregon to begin anew. Mat, who had embraced his new country with such vigor, would never again be the optimistic community leader that he once was. Kisa, on the other hand, carried on and when widowed, made the nontraditional vow to never live with any of her children. In Oregon she was again noted for her warm hospitality and for sharing home-grown produce with friends and neighbors. When she died in 1992 at age 104, hundreds of people came to her funeral and the family received more than 800 pieces of mail.

13.   Neely-Soames House
23691 Russell Road, Kent
Continue north; turn left on S James Street to Russell Road S

David A. and Irena Kemp Neely and their two small boys were covered-wagon pioneers who endured the arduous journey over Naches Pass in 1854. When they arrived on a prairie near Enumclaw, they had to stop so that Irena could give birth to a daughter, Salethia. The Neelys then staked their claim of 320 acres on the riverside where they built a log cabin. In 1878 the family--then numbering nine--moved into the spacious home which quickly became a center for community social events. The home remained in the family for three generations. Irena, who lived to the age of almost 100, shared the house with the family of her son David F. Neely, whose daughter Ruby Neely Soames later inherited it. In 1985 Ruby donated it to the City of Kent.

The house is built of lumber that David A. Neely felled on the homestead. Featuring gingerbread trim and an inviting veranda, it is festooned on three sides with lavender wisteria. Irene Neely seems to live on in the old fashioned flower garden where her day lillies, columbine, cynthia, and blue peter continue to bloom.

In 1993 shortly before her death, City Historian Rae Reitan said that the Greater Kent Historical Society hoped to open the home as a city museum. For many years, Kent historians and elders have worked diligently with the White River Valley Historical Society and Museum that was built in Auburn. Some think that historic preservation efforts in rapidly growing Kent would benefit if the city had a museum of its own. The Neely-Soames house is listed on the State Register of Historic Places.

Vice Squad confiscating stills in Kent.
(Courtesy of White River Valley Historical Museum)

14. International Order of Odd Fellows Hall
316 W Meeker Street
Go south on Russell Road; turn left on W Meeker Street

Throughout the West, almost every small town had at least one lodge that served as a meeting place for members and as a gathering place for community events. Kent was no exception. The Odd Fellows and their sister organization, the Rebekkahs, set a lively pace in the hall that was built in 1904. "The opera house," earned its nickname for numerous events that were open to the public, including moving pictures, stage plays, dances, Christmas celebrations, concerts and high school graduation celebrations. During World War I, the

Rebekkahs with cooperation from the Red Cross turned the hall into a hostess house, where they entertained soldiers.

The IOOF Hall was one of several Kent buildings that hosted Music Week performances, a program started in the 1920s by the Kent Music Study Club under the leadership of President Hattie Churchill. A typical Music Week included: Student Night at the City Hall auditorium; School Night at the high school auditorium; Radio Night featuring local musicians on Seattle station KOMO; Church Night at the IOOF Hall presented by the music honorary society, Mu Phi Epsilon of the University of Washington; Band Night on Bowen Field with bands from local and nearby communities; and Home Night with chamber music and soloists in different homes. Music Week was an unqualified success! The idea was quickly adopted by the State Federation of Music Clubs with Churchill appointed as chair and then by the national federation.

In the 1930s, the old IOOF Hall was gutted by fire, then refurbished. In the 1940s as the Odd Fellows' membership declined, the Rebekkahs took over management. Today they continue to hold meetings and special events in the elegant upstairs dining room. To make ends meet, they lease the ground floor to local businesses, one of which is the Kent Cafe.

15.   Kaibara Park
W Meeker Street and 1st Avenue N

In the depths of the Great Depression, Kent proclaimed itself "the Lettuce Capital of the World," celebrating its agricultural heritage and doing its best to bolster public morale. At Kaibara Park, more than 25,000 festival goers consumed "the world's largest salad," made of lettuce and Nalley's mayonnaise and tossed by three young women clad in bathing suits and sterilized rubber boots. Other festival highlights were the grand parade through downtown Kent and the coronation of the Lettuce Queen and her court, some of whom wore formal gowns and others kimonos.

Libby, McNeill and Libby got into the spirit with an ad in the KENT NEWS JOURNAL, proclaiming that the Libby label's "universal distribution" was returning "hundreds of thousands of dollars" to local farmers and noting that Libby employed 250 people in its Kent cannery. In 1937 the community's biggest-ever Lettuce Festival was also its last. Prices for agricultural commodities dropped to new lows. The next spring, Cannery Union members, many of whom were women, marched the picket line in strikes against Libby, McNeill and Libby and other local plants.

16.   Libby, McNeill and Libby
Between 4th and 6th Avenues on W Smith Street (site)
Go north on 1st Street; turn left on W Smith

By the late teens, Kent was an agricultural processing and shipping center. In addition to local laborers, hundreds of seasonal workers-- many of whom were Native American or non-English-speaking immigrants--flocked to the valley during the harvest. In the fields women worked shoulder to shoulder with men and children.

At Libby, McNeill and Libby, which employed more than 500 workers, rows of neatly-uniformed women stood beside conveyor belts, sorting and grading successive crops of berries and vegetables that required quick processing. The state's hard-won minimum wage and hour laws for women did not apply to cannery and agricultural workers who often labored long hours for a pittance.

During World War II, local women and children became the backbone of the agricultural labor force. Public-spirited women responded to the late night whistle at Libby, McNeill and Libby, working a shift to help keep local food production strong. It was important to local business, but was also perceived as a patriotic mission. The sudden evacuation of families of Japanese ancestry had robbed the valley of some of its most productive business people and workers. Further contributing to the labor shortage were men enlisting in the Armed Services and women, attracted to lucrative defense-related jobs at

Kent's Northwest Metal Products Company and at The Boeing Company.

The war-time upheaval was the catalyst for a rapidly changing environment. Valley communities began the shift from an agricultural-based economy to high-tech factory complexes, shopping malls, explosive population growth and consequent urban sprawl. One of the casualties was Libby, McNeill and Libby, which closed its plant in Kent in the 1960s. For decades it had provided one of the few respectable employment options for unskilled and non-English-speaking women workers.

17.   Kent City Hall and Library Complex
4th Avenue S and W Gore Street
Go south to W Gore Street

In 1969 Isabel Hogan became Kent's first female mayor, a post that she held for 16 years during which time the city's population almost doubled. Early in her administration, Kent celebrated the opening of its new four-story city hall and adjacent public library. Later, trees were planted along city streets; parks and recreation facilities were expanded including Russell Road Park, the Kent Commons building for indoor recreation, and beautiful Mill Creek Canyon Earthworks Park which has become a popular gathering place for community events. The new parks and open spaces, along with rezoning statutes to preserve farmlands, have helped maintain the community's time-honored environmental charm, while keeping rampant urban growth in check.

Another priority of Hogan's administration was revitalization of old and deteriorating downtown Kent. Laurel Whitehurst, past member of the King County Landmarks Commission, worked with the mayor and others to plan the popular Saturday Market that draws people into the city and preserves the area's rural heritage. As in the past, farm families vend home-grown fruits, vegetables and flowers from colorful stands. Additional features are musical performers, arts and crafts booths, and guided tours through Kent's restored historic district.

Several of Mayor Hogan's priorities are rooted in the mission of the Women's Improvement Club, founded in 1911 as an auxiliary of the Men's Civic Club. Initially, the WIC organized a city cleanup with school children and adults pitching in. The WIC functioned as an umbrella for several subsidiary clubs including the Music Study Club and the Garden Club. The latter presented the community's first flower show and then took on the responsibility of keeping up the city park with members contributing their time and labor. Another WIC priority was the public library which opened in 1921 with an all-female board of directors.

The Music Study Club (please see above, Odd Fellows Hall) would have welcomed Hogan's boost to the arts, which began when she formed a citizen's group to commission artworks for the new city hall. As part of the Parks and Recreation Department, the Kent Arts Commission pushed through a per capita tax for art in public places. It has funded downtown historical murals, the intriguing earthworks sculpture at Mill Creek Park, concert series, festivals and more.

18.   Leon and Magdelena Mendoza Laigo Farm
SW corner of Valley Road (84th Avenue S) and S 212th Street
Go east on W Gore Street to Central Avenue, then north

In the mid-1930s Magdelena Mendoza Laigo was one of the first Pinays (women from the Philippines) to move to the Green River Valley. The significant bachelor population that worked on farms regarded Pinays with high esteem, since their presence meant homes, families and the beginning of communities. In keeping with their cultural traditions, Magdelena controlled the family purse strings and was her husband's equal in business.

The Laigos leased their farm from their neighbor, Mr. O'Brien. While Leon made daily trips to the Pike Place Market to sell their produce, Magdelena managed the farm. Although they had no children of their own, they opened their home to children of friends and relatives. A niece, Dorothy Laigo Cordova, has fond memories of summers on the farm--slopping pigs, gathering snails for supper, playing in Mr. O'Brien's orchard, and eating sweet vegetables off the vine. Although they were without electricity or running water, her hard-working aunt managed to make life on the farm a joy for children.

Following the World War II evacuation of Japanese farmers, Filipinos who had worked for them sometimes became caretakers in their absence. Others purchased farms at a bargain price. Still others were told by the U.S. government to work as farm managers. The upheaval permanently changed valley demographics with a notable increase in Filipino families.

The Laigos left O'Brien in the 1950s to move to Seattle where Magdelena opened a grocery store at 11th and James--then the heart of the city's Filipino community and now a part of Seattle University.

19.   Joseph and Martha Jane Steele Foster House (site)
Now occupied by the Clubhouse on the Foster Golf Course
Go west on S 212th Street, then north on SR-181 which changes to Interurban Avenue and leads to the clubhouse at 136th Street

In 1864 the Steele family of six adults and three children packed what they could take with them and headed West. The catalyst was the Civil War which by then raged so near their Missouri home that they heard battle cries and cannon blasts. A daughter Martha (age 28), who had paraded on horseback in support of President Lincoln, drove one of the family's three horse-drawn covered wagons all the way across the Oregon Trail. The Steeles homesteaded on the banks of the Duwamish River where they established the first ferry crossing.

In a population with a serious "bachelor problem," few eligible women remained single for long. According to Kay Reinartz's recent history, TUKWILA: COMMUNITY AT THE CROSSROADS, one of the first callers at the Steele home was the Honorable Joseph Foster, a 36-year-old member of the Territorial Legislature. Following a proper courtship, he and Martha celebrated their wedding and moved to his homestead across the river, where they raised dairy cows, pigs, chickens, and a huge garden.

Their home, the largest in the neighborhood, became the center for community gatherings. In 1877 tragedy permanently disrupted their lives when all three of their children succumbed with one week to diphtheria. They later had two more sons and resumed their roles as community leaders in their town named Foster--now part of the city of Tukwila.

Whenever it was possible, Martha accompanied Joseph to legislative sessions in Olympia. A staunch supporter of the suffrage crusade, he had consistently supported legislation to enfranchise women. In 1883 he sponsored the successful bill that finally gave Martha and other Washington women the right to vote and serve on juries.

In cooperation with law-and-order men, women wielded their new-found power to close down saloons and bawdy houses in local communities throughout the territory. As city coffers--often dependent on sin taxes--dwindled, a powerful backlash emerged. Suffrage opponents carried their cause to the Territorial Supreme Court which in 1887 ruled the women's vote unconstitutional. When legislators reenfranchised women at their next session, the justices again overruled the measure. In 1889 when Washington declared statehood, male voters ratified the state constitution, but rejected a proposed woman suffrage amendment by a vote of 35,527 to 16,163. Martha Foster and other Washington women would have to wait until 1910 to again march to the polls as men's equals. (Please see Chapter VII, the Arcade Building for further information)

20. Riverton Hospital
13041 E Marginal Way and 40th Avenue S
Go northwest on Interurban Avenue; turn west on S 133rd Street, then north on 40th Avenue S

To put her husband through the University of Oregon Medical School,

Ella Wadell Nichols ran a boarding house in Portland. Dr. Frederick Nichols and Ella, a trained nurse, moved to Riverton in 1913, where they dedicated their lives to caring for people throughout the valley. Other doctors who lived in the community worked at the Riverton Sanitarium, making Dr. Nichols the only one to practice locally and make house calls.

If the doctor had to perform surgery in a patient's home, Ella went along to assist. Historian Kay Reinartz writes that on foggy nights, Ella sometimes got out of the car with her lantern to lead him down dark laneways. Their rented home doubled as the doctor's office, and if hospitalization was required, Ella moved the patient into a spare bedroom where she provided round-the-clock care. To make ends meet, Dr. Nichols also opened an office in the Cobb Building in Seattle.

By 1918 they had saved enough money to build their three-story combination hospital and home, which Dr. Nichols designed and constructed himself. Patients and neighbors admired the sumptuous rose gardens that were the couple's hobby. An efficient homemaker and administrator, Ella mothered their four adopted children and ran the Riverton Hospital. In many ways the hospital and home were one: her staff members often boarded upstairs with the family, prepared patients' meals in the family kitchen, and combined the hospital and family wash. Newborn babies were cared for in the dining room, the warmest part of the house.

When Ella died in 1929, Dr. Nichols had to close the hospital and struggle to raise their two remaining children alone. He soon married Victoria O. Belaire, a registered nurse from eastern Washington. With Victoria as its capable administrator, the Riverton Hospital reopened for a brief three years. The final closure came in the depths of the Great Depression when most patients could not pay their bills. For another 20 years until his death at age 83, Victoria continued to assist her husband with office management, deliveries, operations, nursing care and maintenance of a comfortable home. In 1962 the Nichols children sold the building that had doubled as their home and a hospital. It was later converted into low-income housing.

21. Ernest and Delia Finucan Merkle House
12244 42nd Avenue S
Go east on S 128th Street, then north on 42nd Avenue S

Born in Ireland, Delia Finucan, a 16-year-old school teacher, emigrated alone to America. In the "land of opportunity," she boarded a train to Iowa to join her sister and find temporary work as a housemaid. At a box social, Ernest Merkle bought her dinner basket and before long the newlyweds were on their way to Puget Sound. In 1908 they moved into their comfortable home on a peaceful bend of the Duwamish River. The five Merkle children and free-roaming farm animals played and grazed on meadows pocked with stumps of giant trees.

As more families and more animals moved into the area, Delia and other mothers grew increasingly concerned about unchecked animal waste and about their children's safety, especially around long-horn steers. A born leader who had probably learned some tricks from her father, an Irish barrister, she drew up a petition for a local Herd Law. Despite protests from dairymen, her cause eventually won voter support and the years of fenceless farms came to an end.

As precinct committee representative from Allentown, Delia initiated numerous other ordinances, but is best remembered for organizing the campaign that established the Duwamish School District in 1911. Thanks to her leadership, grade school children no longer had to make the three-mile trek back and forth to the school in Foster. From 1911 to 1973, the Duwamish School doubled as a community center for dances, lectures, concerts, town meetings, and eventually a first home for the public library. In the 1970s it was torn down and replaced by Duwamish Park.

In an era when local social service agencies were almost non-existent, people took their problems to "Grandma Merkle." In her history of

Tukwila, Kay Reinartz writes: "Many a woman and man sought her out for a private conversation about problems that she or he was facing, ranging from dealing with shortages of money and marital conflicts to depression and loneliness..." Delia Merkle is an outstanding example of a woman with good instincts and altruistic motives who helped build a livable community.

22.   The Boeing Company
Duwamish Plant
Go north on 42nd Avenue S, veer west at the bend of the Duwamish, then northwest on E Marginal Way S

The most dramatic period for women workers at The Boeing Company was World War II. It was big news when the first seven "girl welders" were hired in early 1942. By late 1944 when the company produced its 10,000th B-17 since Pearl Harbor, more than half of the work force at the Duwamish and nearby Renton plants was female.

The beginning of the war triggered a sudden shift in attitudes toward working women who during the Great Depression had had limited job opportunities. Suddenly, government-produced film clips were showing neatly dressed and coifed women coming out of factories where their jobs as welders or machinists were--according to the announcers--no more complicated than baking a cake.

In King County, "Rosie the Riveter" joined the formerly all-male union, working shoulder to shoulder with men on daytime, swing and graveyard shifts. For the first time, Boeing also hired minority women. While motivated in part by their paychecks, women were there for other reasons as well, including patriotism and an unprecedented opportunity to prove that they could handle a "man's job."

Following the armistice, government propaganda suddenly revised its message, showing clips of crying, dirty children,

"Rosies" at The Boeing Company during World War II.
(Courtesy of The Boeing Company Archives)

neglected by moms who would rather work than care for them. Another message was that "men's jobs" should go to returning servicemen. Wives and mothers responded, submitting their resignations. The Boeing Company laid off thousands of others, although some were later recalled because of union seniority.

An exception was red-headed, blue-eyed Bessie Leister Dempsey, who with the stage name Yvonne St. Clair had flourished as a ballerina, vaudeville dancer and Hollywood star. Divorced with custody of her son Mark, she worked her way through the University of California's mechanical engineering program, specializing in aerodynamics and graduating in 1947 in the upper 10% of her class. At age 34 in 1948, she became Boeing's first female engineer, remaining on the job for the next 23 years.

Contrary to popular "Leave It to Beaver" mythology, Bureau of Labor statistics show that more women held jobs outside the home in the 1950s than during the war, and that for the first time, married women outnumbered single women in the work force. At Boeing most were employed in traditionally "female jobs." In the 1960s popular women's magazines, which for years had canonized the "happy homemaker," began to recognize the "trapped housewife."

As stereotypes exploded, King County women joined in national and international crusades for equal rights. For modern activists, Dempsey and her World War II forebears have been valuable role models. While its top executive and board positions are still an exclusively male domain, women employed at The Boeing Company now have unprecedented opportunities and sex-based job classifications are a thing of the past.

23. The Museum of Flight
9404 E Marginal Way S
Southwest corner of Boeing Field

The Museum of Flight is an independent, non-profit organization, dedicated to the preservation of aviation history. Although the industry has been decidedly male-dominated, women have been involved in various ways since the pre-World War I era. One of the exhibits shows seamstresses fabricating airplane wings--a traditionally female job that women continued to hold after the Armistice until cloth wings became a thing of the past. The exhibit is located in the historic "Red Barn," The Boeing Company's original building which was moved to its present location after the Port of Seattle donated it to the museum. Another fascinating exhibit, Northwest Aviators in the Golden Age, features photos, artifacts and stories of Gladys Buroker, Dorothy Hester Stengel, and Mary Riddle (the first Native American woman pilot), who in the 1920s and 1930s barnstormed, wing walked, taught others to fly, and broke records.

A World War II era exhibit shows Women's Air Force Service Pilots (WASPs), delivering aircraft to military bases throughout the United States, sometimes training male pilots, and test-flying aircraft, or towing target sleeves for anti-aircraft practice to free male pilots for combat. Although some of these heroic women volunteers died for their country, they were regarded as part of an experimental program and as such did not receive military benefits. It was 1977 before Congress awarded them retroactive status as Veterans.

Other exhibits show early "stewardesses," daring wing walkers, welders and sheet metal workers during World War II, and more contemporary women astronauts and commercial airplane pilots.

24.   Ruby Chow Park
6265 Stanley Avenue S
Continue northwest on E Marginal Way; turn right on Ellis Avenue S, then right on S Albro Place

In WASHINGTONIANS: A BIOGRAPHICAL PORTRAIT OF THE STATE, Frank Chin writes that the former King County Council member "made it from the bottom, from the lowest, to become the first woman in Chinatown politics, then led the Chinese community to discover itself as a political power in Seattle."

The first of ten children, she was born in 1920 to a Chinese mother from Victoria, B.C., and an immigrant Chinese father, who worked as a dock boss for a Seattle fish company. During the Great Depression, Ruby's formal education came to an end when she had to drop out of Franklin High School to work as a waitress. At age 18 she married, moved to New York City, had two children and then was divorced.

When she returned to Seattle in 1943, she was married to Ping Chow, an actor who had come to the United States on tour with a Chinese opera company. They saved their money until they could purchase an old house at Broadway and Jefferson. While living upstairs, they opened the downstairs in 1948 as Ruby Chows Restaurant. With Ping cooking and Ruby serving customers, Seattle's first Chinese restaurant outside Chinatown was an immediate success. Chin says, "Newspapers regularly front-paged snaps of dignitaries, governors, mayors, and consul-generals walking up the steps toward the moon-gate entrance..." The English-speaking member of the partnership, Ruby managed the business for 31 years, setting up a profitable sideline of frozen foods.

In the 1950s as the Korean War stoked up renewed anti-Asian sentiment, Ruby came up with her first political plan. She went to the powerful Chong Wah Association, the political center of the Chinese community, and made a proposal that the men approved. By introducing Chinese pageantry to the city, Ruby stole the show at the Seafair Parade. It took 100 men to carry the 125-foot dragon, made in Hong Kong, on its undulating dance along the parade route. Ruby also presented the exotic drill team made up of 50 girls whom she had personally selected, trained and costumed. Chin wrote: "Ruby Chow's Chong Wah Chinese girls' drill team was drumming and dinging and marching in parades all over the country and winning prizes." He also noted the political ramifications, as Chinese Americans basked in the glow of good publicity.

Ruby's next political move was in Chinatown itself, where the Chong Wah board was made up entirely of older immigrant men. After years of running the Seafair activities alone, she turned to women friends, asking them to join her Chinese Community Service Organization to support candidates for the forthcoming Chong Wah election. Chin wrote:

> The old stranded generation of the last Wah Kiew "overseas Chinese" has never recovered from the shock of Ruby Chow, who...brought American-born, English-speaking, non-Cantonese, northern Chinese, outsiders and women onto the Chong Wah board. To this day, the only Chong Wah board in the world where women sit with men to make decisions about the community is in Seattle.

In 1970 Ruby was elected to the King County Council where she served for 16 consecutive years. Her distinctive beehive hairdo and arched, darkly-penciled eyebrows made her one of the most recognizable figures in county politics.

Following her mother's example, Cheryl Chow got involved in public service and now serves on the Seattle City Council. Twenty years ago when the Seattle Chinese Athletic Association (SCAA) allowed only boys' basketball teams, Cheryl began coaching and promoting girls' basketball. The sport, like her mother's drill team, was a means of teaching teamwork, culture, equality and assertiveness to adolescent and teen-age girls. Unlike Ruby, who had had to promote her drill team as a benefit to the community, Cheryl could sell girls' basketball because it was good for the girls. Today, the Chinese Girls Drill Team is still going strong and girls make up half of the teams in the SCAA.

Still a community leader, Ruby Chow now has her own consulting firm which advises companies on compliance with federal affirmative action guidelines and which promotes trade between the Pacific Northwest and China.

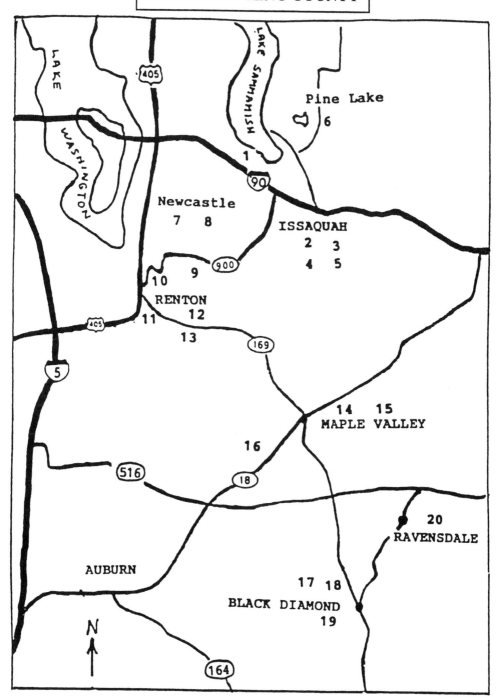

SOUTHEAST KING COUNTY

LAKE

LAKE SAMMAMISH

Pine Lake
6

405

WASHINGTON

1

90

Newcastle
7   8

ISSAQUAH
2   3
4   5

900

9

10

RENTON
12

405

11

13

169

5

14   15
MAPLE VALLEY

16

516

18

20
RAVENSDALE

AUBURN

17 18
BLACK DIAMOND
19

N

164

Page 35

II. COAL DUST LEGACIES

Issaquah to Black Diamond

Your tour begins in the Issaquah area where a treasure trove of restored historic buildings and sites bring to light a heritage of lumbering, coal mining, dairying and community life. From pioneer homesteaders, to a controversial mayor, to pathbreaking school administrators, women's heritage in this community emerges with lasting influence. Continue on to the wooded Newcastle Hills, where Adriena Baima's board and batten house stands as a lone reminder of the once-booming mining town.

Passengers and coal were transported by rail to Renton, your next destination with several visitation points. Located on the south shore of Lake Washington, it was a major industrial and transportation center that brought coal, lumber and agricultural produce from the hinterlands to Seattle. The historical museum and other sites provide links to the past in the city that founded King County's first public school and that is now home to The Boeing Company's second plant, shopping malls and burgeoning housing developments.

From Renton follow State Route 169 to sites in scenic Maple Valley and on to Black Diamond where the museum, historic miners' houses, and other structures provide unique insights into the town's and the region's mining heritage. After a stop at the turn-of-the-century bakery, which now includes a deli, you may want to make a side trip into the spectacular Green River Gorge, a 14-mile conservation area east of Black Diamond that encompasses several state and county parks.

In the late 19th and 20th centuries, miners dug some of the nation's deepest and most hazardous slope mines and tunnel mazes to reach coal deposits along your tour route. Thousands came to work in the mines, including immigrants from Italy, Slovenia, Finland, Wales and other European countries, and black and white Americans from the

East and South. Women--often with large families--took in boarders, started schools for their children, and joined lodges and churches.

Because of labor disputes and mining disasters that periodically closed down the mines, the predominant bachelor population was mobile. Families who found it more difficult to move often weathered the tough times and put down roots. In the 1920s the simultaneously dwindling coal market and escalating miners' strikes rang the death knell for some of the county's largest employers. Company towns including Franklin, Coal Creek and Newcastle disappeared. Issaquah, Renton and Black Diamond managed to survive, relying on community-spirited residents and on other local industries.

1.   Elizabeth Lewis Homestead

Take exit 13 from I-90; go north to Lake Sammamish. The homestead, shaped like an inverted "T," juts into the lake next to the mouth of Lewis Creek

Elizabeth and William Lewis immigrated from a coal-mining town in Wales to Pennsylvania and on to Newcastle in 1883. With the birth of their fifth child, they became homesteaders, filing their claim for the wooded acreage on Lake Sammamish. William's job in the Newcastle mines qualified them for a company house and to supplement his income, Elizabeth took in boarders. Following his death in a mining accident, the company permitted the family to remain in one of Newcastle's largest houses, where she continued to provide board and room for bachelor miners.

Determined to keep their claim, Elizabeth did what was required of homesteaders to "prove up." Every weekend for three years, she walked the six miles from Newcastle to Lake Sammamish and back to make improvements on the property. When someone challenged her claim in court, she was able to satisfy government requirements and emerge the winner. Today, the property remains in the family which from the 1880s to 1992 operated Lewis Hardware in Issaquah.

2.   Alexander House

155 Gilman Boulevard, Issaquah
From I-90 take Issaquah exit #17 and head south; turn right onto Gilman Boulevard for about 150 yards

In recent years the Issaquah Historical Society rescued the house from developers and moved it to its current site, where it serves as the Tourist Information Center. Thomas and Caroline McKivor Alexander built their farmhouse on Lake Sammamish in the early 1900s. Following his death, she turned it into a popular weekend retreat for wealthy Seattleites who came by train to enjoy the lake and her delectable farm-fresh cuisine.

3.   Issaquah City Hall

135 East Sunset Way

Issaquah's most controversial and only female mayor was elected in 1932, only to be recalled a year and a half later. In the depths of the Great Depression, voters rallied to Stella Alexander's campaign promise to reduce the tax levy for new concrete sidewalks. Her troubles began when three newly-elected councilmen refused to serve with a woman mayor. Without legal authority, she promptly appointed replacements. Her troubles came to a head when two sets of councilmen appeared at the next meeting. When she moved to exclude the original group, the motion died unseconded. Pushed to the limit, she hoisted an oak chair and aimed it at the head of the most offensive man, whereupon he beat a hasty retreat. Local residents grew increasingly sensitive about how Seattle dailies were portraying their town and its "petticoat mayor."

Instead of setting out to exploit Issaquah's mayor because she was female, the Seattle press was more likely interested in the bizarre series of events. In any case the SEATTLE POSTINTELLIGENCER asked for Mayor Alexander's side of the story. When asked if she would consider submitting her resignation from the unpaid office, she said that she could not, because she had "the welfare of the town at heart." Instead of placing all of the blame for overt sexism on her male colleagues, she explained to the reporter: "A lot of women are jealous of me--they don't like to see another woman in office." Unlike Alexander, most other elected women of the day counted on strong support from their club sisters.

4.   Gilman Town Hall Museum
165 Southeast Andrews Street
Phone: 392-3500; Open Saturday noon-4 p.m.; Monday 10:30 a.m.-2:30 p.m.

Thanks to the seed planted and nurtured by Harriet Fish, Issaquah has a picturesque historic district, complete with a museum to preserve and interpret local history. The museum is housed in the 1889 Gilman Town Hall, which bears the city's former name. Behind it is a two-cell jail with foot-thick cement walls, built in 1914 as an escape-proof replacement for the former wooden calaboose.

Beginning in the 1950s, Harriet Fish wrote a column for THE ISSAQUAH PRESS, a weekly newspaper, bringing to light colorful and vivid accounts from the community's past and simultaneously sounding the alarm as bulldozers ripped away historic structures. With help from old-timers, she collected artifacts and records which were temporarily stored at Marymoor Museum in Redmond.

In 1972 when Mayor Keith Hanson expressed interest in marking historic sites and raising funds to preserve them, Fish wrote to her readers "...my question to you is: Are you interested enough to help us establish an historical organization in Issaquah to consider, to act, to determine our historical sites and secure funds and markings for them????..." Members of pioneer families and newcomers alike joined her and with the help of the city, they formed the Issaquah Historical Society. Almost immediately, the derelict Gilman Town Hall came on the market, whereupon the City Council voted to purchase it for a museum. Members of the Historical Society and local high school students repaired and cleaned the building and within a year they moved their collection into its own home.

In 1972 Mayor Hansen appointed Fish as the first City Historian. When she later moved to Sequim, the local historic preservation movement and the museum were fueled by community energy and pride. Today, downtown Issaquah's historic buildings are an attraction for out-of-town visitors and residents alike.

5. Issaquah High School Girls Basketball Team, 1913 Masonic Hall
155 W Sunset Way
Go south to Sunset Way; turn right

Although girls' rules clearly made basketball a non-contact sport, Issaquah's first team of six had a different initiation. In his December 5, 1979 article in the ISSAQUAH PRESS, Joe Peterson wrote about this maverick team, quoting one of its members, Minnie Wilson Schomber: "I played many a game with blood streaming down my face from my nose..." With only six players--a team of five and one substitute--the girls had to scrimmage against the boys' squad. According to Minnie, "They resented it and made us play boys' rules. We got roughed up plenty!" Despite increasingly liberal dress codes that opened up the sport to girls, their uniform was still a handicap. It consisted of heavy black serge bloomers, long black stockings, white middy blouses and black ties.

Competition with rival girls' teams in Bothell, North Bend, Preston and Redmond presented another challenge. For a game in Bothell, the girls had to catch the 8:00 a.m. Saturday train in Woodinville, then transfer. When they arrived at noon, their foes met them at the station, took them to a lunch party, and then to dinner in their homes. After the evening game, the girls spent the night with their hosts, then boarded the train, arriving back in Issaquah at 7:00 p.m.

At home enthusiastic crowds flocked to the Masonic Hall for Saturday night double headers--first the girls and then the boys. The first girls to sport royal blue and gold IHS letters on their sweaters were in Minnie's words "...envied and respected by our classmates."

Miners, many of whom were foreign born, gave generously to nuns on "begging tours." Mother Joseph (right) and the Sisters of Providence canvassed mining areas from King County to Montana. (Courtesy of the Sisters of Providence Archives)

6. Providence Heights Sister Formation College Lutheran Bible Institute

Go north on Front Street across I-90, then north for two miles to SE 43rd Way. Turn right and go one mile up the hill past Providence Point to entrance on left

The interconnected ten-building complex is located on a 243-acre site on Pine Lake that seems to be on top of the world. Its central focus is the chapel with stunning stained glass windows designed and executed by Gabriel Loire of Chartres, France. Established by the Sisters of Providence in 1961, the college's pioneering program has been called the most significant movement in Catholic education today.

The Sister Formation Movement grew in response to Pope Plus XII, who in the early 1950s urged better training of parochial school teachers. In the United States, sisters in the Catholic Education Association conducted a survey and were shocked by their findings. Most sisters left their parish schools with minimal education. As teachers, they had to attend summer school for ten to twenty years to complete their training. The same pattern was true for sisters entering nursing, social work and other professions.

The Ford Foundation provided funding for the first nationwide Sister Formation workshop which the Sisters of Providence, headquartered in Seattle, hosted at their hospital in Everett. The outcome was a recommendation of five years of continuous higher education for young sisters. The Sisters of Providence negotiated with Seattle University, a Jesuit-administered coeducational institution, to establish a demonstration program. In 1961 Seattle University's College of Sister Formation moved to its own new campus at Providence Heights.

The concept of the degree requirements proved sound. Today, sisters throughout the nation attend college until they receive a Bachelor of Arts or Science degree to prepare for their intended profession. In 1970 the Sisters of Providence embarked on another path-breaking innovation. They decided to close their demonstration campus, concluding that uncloistered young sisters living in religious communities would benefit more from attending college with other students. As informed scholars, they needed to be exposed to today's world so that they could better prepare to deal with it.

Until 1978, the Sisters of Providence continued to operate the campus as their headquarters and a conference center. They then sold the property to Lutheran Bible Institute.

7. Pacific Coast Company House #75, Baima House

7210 138th Avenue SE, Newcastle

Take I-90 to I-405; turn left on Coal Creek Parkway SE, then left on the Newcastle-Coal Creek Road (133rd Avenue SE), then right on 136th Place SE, and left on 138th Avenue SE

The little board and batten house, a few scattered outbuildings, and dilapidated remnants of a mine adit on the brambled, wooded hillside are all that remain of the town of Newcastle, which at the turn of the century boasted a population of more that a thousand. In 1884 a reporter described the townsite as "Straggling in and out of great dumps of clay and waste that extend like black spurs from the foot of the mountain, the cottages being grouped upon the rocky, stump-infested, forest-bound hillside, without an attempt at order or comeliness."

Pacific Coast Company House #75, a typical one-story, box-like structure, was built in the 1870s by a miner who paid ground rent to the Seattle Coal Company. In 1906 the company rented it to Italian immigrants, Adriene and Bernard "Barney" Baima and their five children. In one of the two small bedrooms, she gave birth to two more sons, Valentino "Val" and John. Large families were typical and immigrant groups developed strong community ties. Songfests were popular at the Baima house where Adriene played her cherished pump organ that she brought with her from the old country.

Lucile and Richard McDonald interviewed Val for their book THE COALS OF NEWCASTLE:

> Marriages held at the little dwelling were filled with music...On the dark side Val remembers his smashed teenage brother, Joe, being moved into the house--a victim of an underground accident that crippled him for life. In this same house Barney Baima died, gasping, choking for air, a victim of mine smoke, powder dust and coal dust. That was in October 1916; Barney had been sick a long time. Val recalled his father's funeral with the horse-drawn hearse, the entire Newcastle band at attention, and a large crowd of relatives

and friends. The slow parade moved through Main Street to the graveyard near Lake Boren.

The youngest son John, now a resident of Newport Hills, was the only boy to complete high school. He considers himself lucky, since his brothers had to quit after the eighth grade to join their father in the mines. Typically, they stayed home, contributing their earnings to the family until their eighteenth birthday. When the oldest son Joe married Ida DeLaurenti, a neighbor, they moved into the smaller board and batten house that still stands next door.

Following her husband's death, Adriene and her sons saved their money and in 1920 she purchased the house from the company. A year later the "Great Strike" and lockout of 1921 dealt a crushing blow to Washington's coal production. The Pacific Coast Company

Baima House. Pacific Coast Company House #75. (Courtesy of King County Department of Parks, Planning and Resources)

at Newcastle limped on until 1929, but then abandoned the town. The Baimas watched as almost all of the buildings were demolished for use as scrap lumber. Adriene's home was spared, only because she owned it. She remained in the house until her death in 1953, along with some of her sons who continued to produce coal as independent miners.

When Pamela and Gary Lee purchased the property directly behind their home and nursery business, they knew that they were acquiring the remaining vestiges of old Newcastle. Recognizing the historic value of the dilapidated Pacific Coast Company House #75, they carefully restored it. The house is a landmark listed on the King County and National Registers and will consequently be preserved from the area's rapidly encroaching urban sprawl. Although it is occupied by renters, visitors can view it from the outside.

8. Thomas Rouse Road
136th Avenue SE, Newcastle
Just south of the Baima house

An official marker designates this historic road as a Community Landmark. Although it is paved and no longer bears the ruts of horse-drawn carriages and miners' carts, it follows the heavily-used route, platted in the 1880s by Thomas Rouse, a miner who doubled as a licensed preacher. One of the road's travelers was his wife, Georgianna Fournier Rouse, the mother of 11 children. As the community midwife, she made house calls to deliver babies and administer home remedies. In pioneer days, she was often the only available source of health care.

The Rouses came West from Illinois in 1877 and homesteaded along Rouse Road. They and three of their children are buried in the Newcastle Cemetery, a King County Landmark near Lake Boren. Today their grandson and his wife reside at the old homestead where they are prime movers in the Newcastle Historical Society.

An especially interesting time to visit Newcastle is on the first Sunday of June when old-timers convene for the annual "Return to

Newcastle" celebration, co-sponsored by the Issaquah Alps Trails Club, King County Parks Division, and the Renton and Newcastle Historical Societies. Along with historical exhibits, there are tours through the woods to fast-disappearing remnants of the past including concrete foundations, railroad grades, mine waste heaps and remnants of adits.

9.   Renton Senior Center

211 Burnett N
Go south on Coal Creek Parkway SE; turn right on NE Sunset Boulevard; turn right on N 3rd Street

Long-term residents along with newcomers congregate for a wide range of activities at the Renton Senior Center. A highlight of the center's soon-to-be-published history by Kay Reinartz is the story of its acclaimed all-female drill team.

In 1980 when June Grube suggested the idea to other members of the Late Bloomers cheering squad, they responded with enthusiasm. The Renton Marine Recruitment Office supplied two sergeants for the first six months to coach some 25 members in precise military routines. Joyce Ness then took over, bringing with her 30 years experience as a trainer of drill teams. Lloyd Martin joined in with his drum, sharing the talent that he had nurtured since his 1920s vaudeville days. Nattily dressed in the patriotic red, white and blue uniforms that members designed and made themselves, the United State's first senior drill team debuted in regional parades, attracting local and national media coverage and winning numerous awards.

In 1985 with members ranging from age 60 to 85, the team received an invitation to compete with some 6,000 teen-age girls in the Miss Drill Team USA International in Los Angeles. Renton's Rotary Club and Veterans of Foreign Wars Chapter made major contributions to fund the $7,000 cost of the trip.

The Renton RECORD-CHRONICLE reported on the event, quoting team president Ann Kooser: "We opened up the pageant. We were the first ones on the performance floor of the Los Angeles Sports Arena. All these kids started screaming so loud we couldn't even hear the commands." Following hours of performances by more than 100 youthful drill teams, the awards ceremony finally began. A crowd of more than 13,000 again erupted into cheers and a standing ovation when the announcer proclaimed: "First prize goes to the Renton Senior Center Drill Team from Washington!"

Today the Drill Team remains a vital source of pride for its members, the Senior Center and the City of Renton. Whenever a member decides to retire, someone else steps in. A difference is that men can now join, as evidenced by the one male that marched with the 1993 team.

10. Jane Duff Building

Corner of S 3rd Street and Williams Avenue S
Go west on N 6th; turn left on Logan Avenue N; turn right on S 3rd Street

At the turn of the century, Jane and Edmond Duff immigrated from Ireland to Renton, then the heart of King County's coal mining region and a vital transportation center with three railroads. The Duffs purchased the Gladstone Hotel which they operated themselves until 1915 when they converted it into commercial building. In 1963 it was destroyed by fire. Jane Duff, by then widowed, and her children erected the new Jane Duff Building on the site. She died at age 90 just days after the opening of their major tenant, the 88¢ Store. Local business people like Jane Duff have prevailed through Renton's dramatic economic evolution from coal mining to Boeing dominance and have contributed to the community's sense of stability.

11. Renton Historical Museum

235 Mill Avenue S
Phone: 255-2330. Open Tuesday 10:00 a.m.-4:30 p.m. and Sunday 2-5 p.m.
Go east on S 3rd Street, then left on Mill Avenue S. Park in the City Hall parking lot

The museum is housed in a depression-era Art Deco Fire Station, erected by the Works Progress Administration and listed on the State Register of Historic Places. Until late 1993 it was operated by an all-volunteer staff, most of whom are dedicated women. They have curated comprehensive exhibits of Renton area history and amassed an impressive archival collection.

The exhibits interpret Renton's industrial transitions from logging, mining and shipping to jet aircraft and high technology. They also bring to light the significance of women's contributions. Through their homes, jobs, churches, and organizations, women have helped stabilize the rapidly-changing community, keeping family and cultural traditions alive.

Visitors will learn about Renton's and King County's first public school. Although there is no marker or remaining physical evidence of the structure, we learn that it was a 14 by 16 foot, rough-hewn shack with rows of rough boards for children's desks and a fireplace built of mud and stone. Cattail mats, made by Indian women, lined the walls to provide insulation. In 1853, teacher Adelaide Andrews, the daughter of early settlers welcomed her first pupils.

12. Gravesites of Jenny and Henry Moses
Mt. Olivet Cemetery, Renton
Go north on Mill Avenue S, turn right on Bronson Way, then left on Sunset Boulevard, then right on NE 3rd Street, then right on Blaine Avenue

Although a Renton swimming pool is named for her son Henry, her tombstone is the only monument to Jenny Moses. In 1937 hundreds of family members and friends gathered at St. Anthony's Church for her Requiem Mass, then followed the hearse to her grave. Beside her is her husband, the highly esteemed Duwamish Chief Henry Moses, who preceded her in death many years earlier when their six sons were still small.

The first white settlers in the Renton area were Diana and Henry

Tobin who staked their claim on the Black River with friendly Duwamish Indians as their neighbors. Following Henry's death, Diana married Erasmus Smithers who purchased the claim adjoining hers. As more settlers acquired property, they and federal agents tried to get the remaining Duwamish to leave, whereupon Diana protested. The Duwamish had not entered into a treaty and had therefore received nothing from the federal government for their ancestral land; they were peaceful and they wanted to stay. Erasmus acceded to Diana's wishes, allowing Indians, including the Moses family, to stay on their property. Diana often said that their presence made her feel protected when her husband was away.

When Chief Moses died, local business people collected 79 silver dollars to give to Jenny who had been left with little money. Not one to complain, she did housework and collected rags which she wove into rugs to sell. As the boys grew older, they worked at odd jobs to help out. Kind and generous, she brought gifts of fresh salmon and trout to her friends who in turn reciprocated. In her home she kept alive ancient teachings, instilling them in her sons. Like their parents, the boys gained the respect of their schoolmates and members of the community. Just before his death, Erasmus Smithers gave Jenny Moses legal title to the acre of land on which she and her family lived. Years later her sons sold it to the Renton School District.

13. Philip Arnold Park
S 7th Street and Jones Avenue South, Renton
Go west on NE 3rd Street, then left on Houser Way N, then left on Main Avenue which becomes Benson Road, then left on Puget Drive, then left on Beacon Way S

In 1947 a group of mothers formed the Renton Hill Community Club. Their purpose was to develop a safe playground for children and a memorial to the boy who was electrocuted while climbing a power transmission line in the neighborhood. They persuaded Puget Power to sell ten acres of hill-top land at a price that was acceptable to city fathers. With help from their children, the women cleared brush from the site. They held bake sales and bazaars to raise funds for picnic tables and playground equipment. During the 1950s, the club organized and paid for the park's annual Fourth of July celebration, complete with fireworks.

14. Maple Valley Historical Museum
23015 SE 216th Way
Phone: 255-7588. Open 1st and 3rd Saturdays 11 a.m.-3 p.m. and by appointment
Return to Houser Way N, then turn right on Maple Valley Highway (State Route 169), turn left onto SE 216th Way. Go .3 mile and turn right. The museum is on the second floor of the Tahoma School District Administration Building

Women volunteers have been mainstays of this museum since its founding in 1979. The collection in the old schoolhouse showcases artifacts and memorabilia from the valley's pioneer history. While preserving the past, the museum has served as a catalyst for community events, including the annual Maple Valley Days celebration.

15. Olof and Mathilda Olson House and Barn Brunton Estate
24206 SE 216th Street, Maple Valley
Continue east on SE 216th Street

Olof and Mathilda Johnson Olson and their children moved to Maple Valley in 1898 to the 80-acre farm that they purchased from Fred and Annie Koch Miegel. The Olsons met the Miegels in Mullan, Idaho, where both men were associated with a mining company. Born in Sweden, Mathilda Johnson immigrated to America at age 18. After working for four years, she married Olof, the son of Norwegian immigrants. With three children and plans for more, the Olsons wanted a country home far away from the rowdy milieu of the mining camp.

In Maple Valley, Mathilda assumed the primary responsibility for raising the children and managing the farm. She planted a large fruit orchard and vegetable garden and also raised ducks, turkeys, chickens, hogs, goats, sheep, horses and dairy cows. Olof, whose specialty was tunnel engineering, was away for long periods of time, designing and supervising construction of tunnels for the Great Northern and Northern Pacific Railroads.

In 1906 with eight children, the family had out-grown the pioneer home where the Miegels had once lived. Using the material he knew best, Olof designed and built their expansive two-and-one-half story house out of solid concrete, then constructed the barn with its unique barrel-vaulted roof. Known as a gracious hostess, Mathilda welcomed friends and neighbors into the lavishly furnished home, making it a center of community life. In 1926 tragedy struck when Olof was killed in an accident. Mathilda remained on their farm, managing it until her death in 1954.

In 1964 Fred and Pat Brunton of Bellevue purchased the estate, where she often hosted fundraising events for the Seattle Opera and the Seattle Symphony. As a member of the King County Arts Commission from 1968 to 1976, and chair from 1971 to 1974, she became the major proponent of the 1% for the Arts Program. She was a member of the Arts Commission's Historical Committee which launched King County's Historic Preservation Program in 1975. Mathilda and Olof Olson's house and barn, also known as the Brunton estate, is a designated King County Landmark.

16. Jacqueline Meadows
Maple Valley
Go southwest from the town of Maple Valley on State Route 18 past 240th Street. The property is on the right between the highway and the next street, Wax Road

Now platted for a housing development, this is the former farm of Joseph and Jacqueline Cotton, where he raised and trained prize-winning horses to race at Longacres. Following his death, Jacqueline sold the farm and all of the horses, save a mare that continues to produce sought-after foals.

In her book, CALABASH, historian Esther Mumford notes that during the 19th century, most of the horse trainers in Kentucky and the southern states were African Americans, but that today "they are barely associated with the industry." She says that King County is one of only a few areas in the nation where black people, such as the Cottons, still own, and groom race horses.

17.　Black Diamond Historical Museum

32627 Railroad Avenue
Phone: 886-1168. Open Saturday and Sunday 12-3 p.m. and Thursday 9 a.m.-4 p.m.
From State Route 169 turn west on Baker Street which ends at the Museum

The Black Diamond Historical Museum is housed in what was once the depot for the Columbia and Puget Sound Railroad. Built in 1886, it was the first permanent building in a tent city that had sprouted around the coal fields. While planning a local celebration of the nation's bicentennial, a committee headed by Ann Steiert formed the Black Diamond Historical Society, then persuaded the city to donate the dilapidated old depot for a museum.

Volunteers restored the building, dug a basement, and added outdoor exhibits including a replica of an underground coal mine, a one-room jailhouse, a blacksmith shop, and an old railroad line complete with timber car and caboose. Inside exhibits give visitors an understanding of coal mining and insights into the town's early home and community life.

Ann has curated displays of local women's hand-sewn elegant dresses and elaborate hats that they donned for lodge and church meetings. There are others that convey the drudgery of early-day housework. Photographs portray families and sometimes women's organizations which included the Rebekkahs, the Pythian Sisters, the Eastern Star, the PTA, and church guilds. Ann recalls that women were intensely loyal to their organizations which presented plays, hosted community picnics and potlucks, and raised funds for local charity. They played an important part in building the community spirit that sustained Black Diamond after the closure of the mines.

Known as the "Thursday Crew," loyal male volunteers continue to join Ann once a week for their day at the museum, where they build new exhibits and maintain the building. They readily interrupt their work to take groups of school children and visitors on guided tours. Wives of members of the "Thursday Crew" arrive at Noon with a delectable lunch--a much appreciated reward for the volunteers' efforts.

18.   Black Diamond Hotels (Sites)
In the area around the Depot/Museum

From the 1880s when the Black Diamond Coal Company began operations, miners' families came and several remained for generations. In BLACK DIAMOND: MINING THE MEMORIES by Diane and Cory Olson, Alice DeWinter Shanks shared memories of her grandparents who came to Black Diamond in the 1890s and built the Jones Hotel:

> It was a boarding house. They had a big family. They probably took in a few boarders and said, "Well, we can handle more." They got more. Grandma said, usually thirty, once in a while forty, were living there. It would depend on how the mines did. There would be two beds in each room. They put up their lunches and cooked their breakfasts and suppers and washed their clothes.

> I think they served family style. Grandma and Aunt Margaret were cooking and baking all the time there. The meat market would carry quarters and halves of meat over, so they'd have it right there. They had a regular little locker room. They had a great big restaurant stove. Grandma had one in the kitchen and one in the wash house for heating the water. They had to haul the water. Later they had pipe water going through the stove, but Aunt Margaret said at first they'd just heat it up on

top. They'd have to wash dang near everything by hand. They washed every day and dried them on the clothesline or hung them on the back porch. The miners showered and changed clothes after they come off work.

Black Diamond Bakery, early 1900s
(Courtesy of Black Diamond Historical Society)

19. Black Diamond Bakery
Railroad Avenue (south of the Depot/Museum)

The Black Diamond Bakery has been tantalizing townsfolk and visitors alike since it opened in 1902. The original brick oven, which is probably the only one in the West still in commercial use, is still fired up daily at Noon with half a cord of wood. Victor Evans and his identical twin brother, Vincent, were born in 1916 to Jack and Aurelia Minaglia Evans. In MINING THE MEMORIES, Vincent shared his recollections:

I was born in the bakery where my father was a baker....To

keep me warm...they laid me down near the baking oven. That old baking oven served as my incubator...My twin brother, Vincent, and I were one of the attractions at the Bakery....it used to keep my mother busy keeping us dressed up and all in shape for all the people coming in to see us. She said it was a real headache....

My father came to Black Diamond in 1910. My mother worked at the Bakery so she had a lot of contact with my father. They were married in 1913. They didn't have any children until 1916. In Black Diamond that was unheard of. Where were the children? It got to be sort of embarrassing. Well it made up for it when the twins came along!

The oven was the same one presently found in the bakery. Pop used to say there was a regular baking routine. He'd fire the oven about 4 o'clock in the morning....He did all the main part of the baking. My mother used to help with some of the chores and with lots of the details like icing the cakes. My Aunt Mary Minaglia used to help when my mother was not available....

Today's visitors can look through the window to see bakers at work, using the historic oven. The bakery and newer delicatessen are open Tuesdays through Fridays from 8 a.m. to 4 p.m. and on weekends from 7 a.m. until 5 p.m.

20.   Gracie Hansen Community Center
27132 SE, Ravensdale
Go northeast on the Black Diamond-Ravensdale Road

Gracie Hansen's Paradise International lives on in Ravensdale. Following the 1962 Seattle World's Fair, Hansen donated the building to the town for a community center. Since its coffers could not meet renovation costs, King County assumed ownership and paid the bills.

Seeking to attract fair-goers tantalized by more than science, state legislators had added Show Street, where Gracie's 700-seat supper club introduced local audiences to Las Vegas-style entertainment and won top billing. In his book MEET ME AT THE CENTER, historian Don Duncan wrote:

> Gracie's show was a hit as much for her own personality and the jewels and feathers and thick eye-makeup she wore as for the 30 statuesque beauties who paraded around the stage.

He relates further that "her previous biggest effort to crash show business had been the Morton, WA., PTA Follies." That she remained true to her Lewis County mining town heritage is evident in Ravensdale, where nobody forgets the darling of the World's Fair press, the hostess with pizazz and a heart of gold.

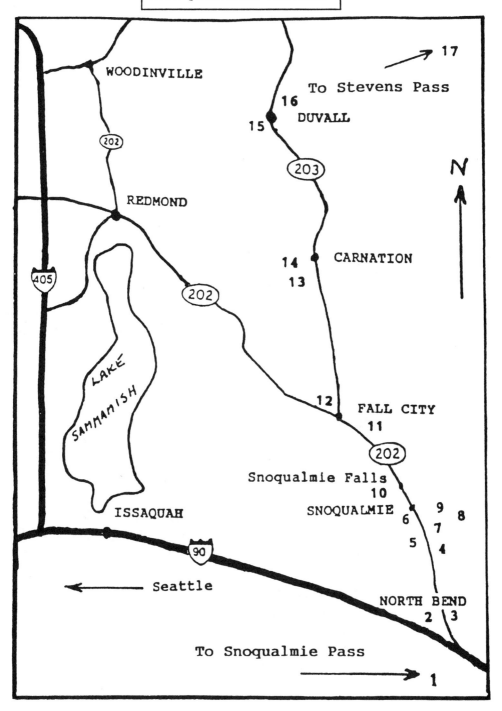

SNOQUALMIE VALLEY

III. THROUGH THE VALLEY OF THE MOON

Snoqualmie Valley to Stevens Pass

If you plan to visit the valley's first designated site, take your hiking boots and follow the path of early mountaineers along rollicking Humpback Creek for a four-mile round-trip trek to pristine Lake Annette. Most will want to begin at the second site, the Snoqualmie Valley Museum, in the alpine town of North Bend. Stop by the Visitor's Center beside the museum for a map and guides to the area's abundant historic and recreational sites. The route continues into the picturesque Snoqualmie Valley, an area rich in logging and farming heritage, where dairy farms still dot the landscape. Don't miss magnificent 268-foot high Snoqualmie Falls, a sacred place for Native Americans that continues to awe visitors with its thundering power and rising mists. Your tour ends as it began, high in the spectacular Cascade Mountains, a paradise for outdoor sports enthusiasts and sightseers alike.

Enroute are communities including North Bend, Snoqualmie, Fall City, Carnation, Duvall and Skykomish where residents take pride in their heritage, as evidenced by the historic buildings and sites that they have carefully restored. The descriptions in this guide provide insights into women's multiple roles in logging communities, rural areas, and small towns. Several stories of Native American women are included, ranging from ancient to modern times, that illustrate their leadership in tribal politics and economics and in cross-cultural relationships.

1.   Annette Lake
Between North Bend and Snoqualmie Pass
Take the Asahel Curtis Campground exit; walk south along the bank of Humpback Creek for about two miles

From the turn of the century, women have been active members of the

Seattle Mountaineers, participating in hiking and camping trips, dances, mountain climbing, etc. Their passion for outdoor recreation and sports went hand in hand with advocacy for the environment and campaigns for designated parks and wildlife preserves. Joining forces with the Federation of Women's Clubs, they launched the state's conservation movement and celebrated the establishment of Mt. Rainier National Park in 1899, as their first major victory. In the 1910s the Seattle Mountaineers leased land from the Forest Service, where they built a lodge on Snoqualmie Pass and helped develop the year-round recreation area with its network of trails. When they discovered unnamed lakes, they named them, often in honor of an ardent member, such as Annette "Annie" Wiestling of Seattle.

2. Snoqualmie Valley Historical Museum
320 North Bend Boulevard S
Take Exit 31 from I-90 into North Bend

Ada Snyder came to the upper Snoqualmie Valley in 1910 to teach at the old North Fork elementary school. She married Eugene Hill, owner of the general store, then transferred to the North Bend Elementary School where she remained for decades. Her pupils included Native Americans, along with children and grandchildren of the valley's early settlers. Through their families, she gained an intimate understanding of the community's roots. For more than 30 years, she listened to stories of pioneer days and wrote them down. Several are published in her book, HISTORY OF THE SNOQUALMIE VALLEY.

In 1939 Hill orchestrated a pageant to commemorate the valley's history and to celebrate Washington state's fiftieth birthday. By then she had collected artifacts, clothing and photographs to use for costumes and props. Valley old-timers searched their attics and barns, finding more treasures to contribute. Following the pageant, she put the collection on display at her school.

In 1960 the Snoqualmie Valley Historical Society organized to develop her collection into a museum for North Bend, Fall City,

Snoqualmie and the rest of the upper valley. In 1979 the museum moved from temporary quarters into its own building. Support has come from several sources, notably the Fall City Study Club, a women's organization that planted the seed for several other east King County museums and libraries.

3.   North Bend Ladies Aid
Community Church
Continue on State Route 202 into town; turn right

In the 1890s, the town of North Bend was rough with brawls and drunkenness, especially at the end of the hop harvest when Indians had money and when whites sold them liquor. Feeling a need for spiritual guidance, the town's solid citizens recruited circuit preachers to hold services, first at the hotel and after it was built, at the schoolhouse. The first minister was Methodist; another who sometimes came from Fall City was Mrs. Smith, a Baptist. In 1903 when the faithful decided to build a church, a group of women formed the North Bend Ladies Aid with the motto: "For the good of the Church and other charitable causes."

As fund-raisers, they sponsored popular baseball games, horse races, egg and spoon races for ladies, bazaars, suppers and box socials. In her book, Ada Snyder Hill quotes a member, Anne Carpenter, who wrote:

> One bazaar and supper brought us $165 with which we papered the Church, revarnished the seats and woodwork, bought two chairs and a carpet for the rostrum, also built on the little room which was used for a Sunday school classroom....Our bazaars and suppers were always held in the old Oddfellow's Hall, upstairs, and oh the work carrying all the wood and water upstairs. Coal oil lamps, no street lights, no sidewalks and those horrible long skirts which had to be held up or pinned up....But we were all willing and had fun along with our work.

4. Tollgate Farm

State Route 202

Continue northwest on SR-202 across the South Fork of the Snoqualmie River. The farm is on the left

Its Native American custodians maintained the ancient prairie for centuries, periodically burning down young trees to let the sun reach patches of earth. Generations of women gathered berries, camas roots, tiger lilies and other medicinal and edible bounty that grew on the fertile land. When settlers claimed the already-cleared land, its native dwellers were perplexed and sometimes provoked to hostility.

In the fall of 1853, Indian war parties from eastern Washington massacred settlers in the White River Valley and set fire to their homes. In January 1856, a war party attacked the tiny settlement of Seattle, only to be beaten back by soldiers. Chief Patkanim led 60 Snoqualmie braves in pursuit of the marauders. When he found two of his captives guilty as ringleaders of the White River Valley massacres, he ordered them hanged. During the same period, soldiers of the Washington Territorial Volunteers built forts throughout King County, but there were no further attacks and the brief war quickly subsided.

In 1860 Lucinda and Gordon Fares moved into the abandoned blockhouse at Tollgate Farm, where she became the valley's first female settler and also its first dairy farmer. A covered-wagon pioneer, she had come West with her parents in 1851 to homestead on the Duwamish River, where she and her mother, Diana Borst Collins, were King County's first female pioneers.

"Lucindy," as she was called, was unable to read or write, but could speak fluently with Duwamish and Snoqualmie Indians in their own complex languages. As a girl she had rescued her neighbor Henry Van Asselt from almost certain massacre by telling the armed war party that he had lead in his body. According to Duwamish beliefs, the lead shot imbedded in his arm rendered him invincible.

Clarence Bagley, who knew the early pioneers, talked with reliable sources that vouched for the tale of Lucinda, who was quite obese, and her trained cows. In his HISTORY OF KING COUNTY, he wrote:

> Lucinda kept thirty cows at one time and would have found it a difficult task to walk around to milk each of them had she not taught them to come to her when she called them by name. She would sit upon a stool....'Come on, Pidey,' she would call out, and Pidey would come over obediently to be milked. When 'Pidey' had given up her milk, she would pass on and then Lucinda would call Mary, and so on, until all thirty cows were milked....

Although the Fares had no children of their own, she adopted a baby boy when his westward-bound parents abandoned him. Eventually, Lucinda and Joseph were divorced, after which she married John Gordon. Her uncle Jeremiah Borst, who had preceded her to the valley and opened it for settlement, bought their farm and she and her new husband returned to her girlhood home at what is now Georgetown. Bagley wrote: "Rough and ready....with a heart of gold, [Lucinda] ranks with Jeremiah Borst as an outstanding person of the pioneer period."

An article in a scrapbook at the Snoqualmie Valley Museum refers to "Lucinda's Mountain," apparently so-called by pioneers before it was officially named Rattlesnake Ridge. Someone erroneously thought he had heard the sound of rattlers, which are foreign to the western Cascades. Kenneth "Greg" Watson, the museum's director, recently made the timely proposal that the "Ridge" across the valley from Mt. Si and overlooking Tollgate Farm be renamed Lucinda's Mountain. It would be the only mountain in King County to be named for a woman.

Later owners of Tollgate Farm built the picturesque house and barn that are still in use on the prairie's oldest dairy farm.

5.   The Swing/Quarry Rock
State Route 202
Continue northwest; the rock is on the left midway between North Bend and Snoqualmie

From generation to generation, members of the Snoqualmie tribe have related ancient stories about the physical and spiritual origins of their people and their valley. One of them, called "The Swing" (Yay-du-od), explains their intimate connection with the moon.

In ancient times before people had a human form, two Snoqualmie sisters plotted their escape from star men who had abducted them from the valley to the sky. The sisters went about their womanly duties, gathering and preserving roots and berries. Eventually, one of them had a baby which they took with them to the meadow. The star men had cautioned them not to dig too deep, but one day they disobeyed since that was the only way to reach the tenderest fern roots. Their digging sticks punctured a hole through which they could see their homeland far below. They carefully replaced the sod, then began to braid cedar ropes into a ladder. When it was finally long enough, they climbed down through the hole, taking the baby with them. Joyful friends and relatives gathered from all over the valley to welcome them home.

The baby grew up to be Snoqualm (the moon). During his travels, he came upon a huge fish weir built by Raven. When he turned it to stone, the water thundered over it in a magnificent waterfall. At Snoqualmie Falls, the site that the tribe considers the center of creation, Snoqualm formed the first woman and man. He also changed other myth beings into animals, plants and earth forms that we know today. One day his star father's scouts came to the valley to lure him back to the sky. The people below still see Snoqualm through the hole that his mother and aunt had dug. A full moon means that it is wide open and a quarter moon shows that it is open just that far.

In ancient times members of the tribe swung back and forth on the ladder which hung down between Rattlesnake Ridge and Mount Si. Evidence is still visible in the canyons on the mountain sides, where they dragged their feet. One night when they forgot to fasten the ladder up and let it hang, Rat chewed through the ropes and it fell to the ground. The huge rock that settlers called the stone quarry is known to the Indians as "the Swing." Tribal elders tell this story which intimately connects their people with the moon, the stars, and the earth.

Picking hops in the Snoqualmie Valley. Photo by Darius Kinsey. (Courtesy of Whatcom Museum of History and Art)

6.   Seafirst Bank

301 River Street, Snoqualmie

In the 1950s this valuable piece of property was known locally as "Peggy's Puddle," a stagnant, mosquito-breeding swamp, owned by Peggy Nelson. She and others appealed to the University of Washington, which helped develop a community revitalization plan. Enthusiastic neighbors turned out in droves to haul away trash and paint dilapidated buildings. Charlotte Paul Groshell (see below, SNOQUALMIE VALLEY RECORD) chaired the local history committee. Nelson appropriately headed the committee to raise funds for a new sewer system to replace collapsed wooden culverts and drain the puddle from the center of town. Today the scenic community with several restored historic buildings is a popular stopping place for weekend tourists from Pugetopolis. Its picturesque railroad depot is listed on the National Register of Historic Places.

7.   Snoqualmie Prairie/Hop Ranch/Meadowbrook
West side of the City of Snoqualmie approaching the Meadowbrook Bridge that crosses the river

Known as the "Father of the Prairie," Jeremiah "Jerry" Borst, settled upriver from Snoqualmie Falls and subsequently acquired much of the surrounding acreage. Little is known about his first wife, except that she was Native American. His second, Mina, was a granddaughter of Chief Betsayoos of the Snoqualmie and the daughter of "the widow," so-called by settlers since she did not remarry after her husband's death. Historian Clarence Bagley interviewed Alice Borst Rachor of North Bend, one of Mina's and Jerry's children who said of her grandmother: "She was very kind to us children and often would tell us that if the Indians came on a raid from east of the mountains she had roots, dried berries and other food stored away so that we could hide." To support herself, "the widow" kept house for the Kellogg family.

Following Mina's death, Jerry married Kate Kanim Smith, a double cousin of Mina and half sister of Chief Jerry Kanim. Kate was bright, witty, enjoyed shopping for fashionable clothes in Seattle stores, and managed a household where other native women worked as her servants. With a knowledge of herbs and traditional cures, she was a was a great help to friends and neighbors when someone was ill.

The Borsts raised bountiful crops of fruit, vegetables, wheat and timothy hay, along with hogs. During the harvest, neighboring Indians worked as hired hands. Kate sometimes accompanied her husband and his retinue on long canoe trips to Seattle where they marketed their produce and bacon. In language reflecting her native sense of time, she told Bagley about one of the trips: "We leave when the salmon berries just begin to bloom. This is about June and when we come back the berries are gone, so we are away a long time." They camped out on the banks of the river, eating wild game and fish. With Indians carrying provisions purchased in Seattle, they returned home afoot.

In 1882 Jerry Borst sold most of his property to the newly formed Hop Growers' Association and the family moved to his niece Lucinda's former home, Tollgate Farm. When he died in 1890, his business dealings were complicated and Kate received little from the estate. Unlike most other Indian wives of white men, she had resources of her own to get by. She moved to Redmond where she tended her beautiful flower garden and participated actively in the community. At one time she was called upon to christen the wooden ship "Snoqualmie" launched in Seattle for the United States Emergency Fleet Corporation. She died in 1938 at age 83 and was buried next to Jerry in the Fall City cemetery.

After the Borsts left Snoqualmie Prairie, the 1500-acre Hop Ranch became the valley's first major business. While immigrants from Europe and Asia made up a portion of the work force, the major pool was Native American families who came by the hundreds during the harvest season to pick the sticky hop cones. The high prairie was an ancient gathering place, where Indians had feasted, played gambling games, traded goods and trinkets, and kept alive traditional stories, songs and dances.

At a time when the Snoqualmies were losing their lands, when their children were being sent to boarding schools, and when Indian agents urged members of the tribe to move to the Tulalip Reservation near Marysville, the hop harvest offered rewards beyond cash income. Indian families gathered to celebrate their culture in the camps on the edges of the fields. Traditionally, picking berries, digging roots, preserving and trading food supplies had been women's work. In the hop fields the majority of the pickers were women, who as always were mainstays in tribal economics. The Hop Ranch thrived for about 15 years until a lice infestation wiped out the crop throughout western Washington.

Today, nothing remains of the Hop Ranch or of the Borst home. The Meadowbrook business district with brick buildings from the 1920s is located on the site and King County has purchased a substantial part of the acreage for a public park to be called Three Forks Park.

8. Snoqualmie Falls Lumber Company (site)
Across the river from the City of Snoqualmie

During World War II "lumberettes" worked in the mill, replacing men who had joined the Armed Forces. Most were residents of the company town of Snoqualmie Falls, complete with school, hospital, community hall, store, tree-lined residential streets, and bachelor dormitories. Built in 1916-17 by the Snoqualmie Falls Lumber Company (Weyerhaeuser), it housed mill workers and their families, who worked in one of the valley's major industries. In 1950 when the company decided to reseed the area with Douglas Fir, it shut down the town, offering its employees their homes for $100 to $175 plus moving costs. More than 60 were moved across the river to a newly-developed tract in Snoqualmie.

9. Snoqualmie Valley Record
102 N Falls Avenue, Snoqualmie

Best-selling author Charlotte Paul skyrocketed to the top of the national best-seller list when she wrote her first book, a peppery autobiography about the trials of raising a family, while writing books and publishing the SNOQUALMIE VALLEY RECORD, a weekly

Workers at the Snoqualmie Mill, where women did "men's jobs"
during World War II.
(Courtesy of Snoqualmie Valley Valley Historical Museum)

community newspaper. Her 1955 success, MINDING OUR OWN
BUSINESS, was followed by a sequel, AND FOUR TO GROW.

The daughter of Seattle pioneers, she grew up locally, graduated from
Wellesley College, then worked as a correspondent for the CHICAGO
TIMES. She married a colleague, Ed Groshell, who moved with her
to Snoqualmie, where they bought the newspaper. After eleven years
and her first five books, including fiction and non-fiction works, they
sold their business and obtained a divorce.

In 1964 she moved to Washington D.C. to accept President Johnson's
appointment to a six-year term on the U.S. Board of Paroles. While
there, she married Robert Reese, then returned with him to their new
home on Lopez Island, where she resumed her writing career in
earnest. When PHOENIX ISLAND, a book about life on Lopez

appeared in 1976, it sold more than a million copies. Several other books followed, the last of which was SEATTLE (1987), a turn-of-the-century novel laced with intriguing characters and events from local history. In 1989 at age 73, Charlotte Paul died of cancer.

10. Snoqualmie Falls Generating Station
Snoqualmie Falls
Continue northwest on State Route 202

In 1980 the American Society of Civil Engineers declared the Northwest's first hydro-electric power plant a National Engineering Landmark. A participant in the ceremony was 83-year-old Dorothy Baker Bond of Kirkland, who at the age of eleven months had flipped the switch to initially turn on the power. Holding her was her father Charles Baker, the designer of the facility that continues to churn out electricity today.

Under the leadership of Karen Boney and other elders, the Snoqualmie Tribe successfully demonstrated in July 1990 against Puget Sound Power and Light Company which had planned to divert more water from the falls to generate electricity. In an August 5, 1990 interview with SEATTLE TIMES, she observed, "For many years our tribal elders tried to avoid conflict. That's over." She noted further: "We are a very matriarchal society and the elders, who are mostly women, keep in contact with everyone in the tribe." From tribal headquarters in the old Eagles Hall in Carnation (across the road from Hjertoos Farm, number 13 in this chapter) the elders continue their fight to preserve the waterfall's spiritual power and to protect fish runs which would suffer from further diversions of the river.

The Cavity Generating Station is listed on the National Register of Historic Places and the Falls Historic District has been determined eligible for the National Register. Puget Sound Power and Light, the owner and operator of the power generating complex, plans to create a museum and visitors center in the plant to be completed in the mid 1990s.

11. Prescott/Harshman House

Fall City Telephone and Switchboard Company
33429 Redmond-Fall City Road

Julia and Newton Harshman moved to Fall City in 1903, where he and a partner ran a sawmill. To keep in touch with their families, they installed a phone line between their homes and the mill. One by one, neighbors asked to be hooked up as subscribers and the fledgling phone company grew into the Harshman family business.

By 1907 Julia was operating the switchboard in their home, while Newton supervised maintenance, installations and repairs. When he died in 1929, the system had grown to 300 phones. She carried on with help from her daughter Gertrude and son-in-law George Saterlee. In 1933 after Julia's death, the Saterlees and their five children moved into the house to take over. In their family everyone had a job. George did installations and repairs; Gertrude was the night operator; and the children by the age of seven or eight each worked a shift. After 16 years, the Saterlees sold the business to Cascade Telephone Company, bringing the years of the home-operated switchboard to a close.

The first telephones played an important part in the development of east King County, linking isolated rural communities including Carnation, Preston, Fall City, North Bend, Newcastle, Coal Creek and Snoqualmie. Both Julia and Gertrude were active members of the Fall City Study Club, the Order of Amaranth, the Eastern Star and other organizations. As telephone operators, they answered numerous questions and kept their neighbors informed.

In her book FALL CITY: IN THE VALLEY OF THE MOON, Margaret McKibbon Corliss reflected on the end of an era when Gertrude laid her switchboard to rest:

> Central [the phone operator] no longer would tell us that it was no use calling Susie at home because this was the day she would be at Card Club at May's, or that someone else had

gone to Seattle for the day!

Listed on the King County Register of Historic Places, the Prescott/Harshman house has been carefully restored with few alterations to its original appearance. Although it no longer contains the original switchboard, it is a reminder of the "homegrown" personalized services associated with the early telecommunications industry.

Prescott/Harshman House. Fall City Telephone and Switchboard Company. (Courtesy of King County Department of Parks, Planning and Resources)

12.   Olive Taylor Quigley Park
Fall City (on the river bank)

Following the 1961 Derby Days Parade, the community convened for official dedication ceremonies of Olive Taylor Quigley Park. The Fall City Study Club in cooperation with the King County Department of Public Works founded the park, named in honor of one of its charter members. Present at the dedication, Quigley was the daughter of David "Doc" and Helen Taylor who homesteaded in the valley in

1872.

The Taylors purchased a lot in Fall City to erect the two-story building that served as their home, store, boarding house and later a hotel. Olive's marriage to Joseph Quigley was cut short when he died just four years after their wedding. With no children she devoted herself to clubs, friends and community service. In addition to the Study Club, she was a member of the Order of the Eastern Star, the Fall City United Methodist Church, the Washington State Pioneers, and the local Garden Club. She died in 1974 at the age of 98.

13.   Hjertoos Farm
31523 NE 40th, Carnation
At Fall City turn right on State Route 203

In 1888 Bergette Jacobson and Bertine Solberg emigrated from Norway. Bertine's brothers, who were clearing their land near Vincent, met them in Seattle. While working as a cook in a boarding house, Bergette studied English and soon passed her citizenship test so that she could take advantage of the Homestead Act. As an American citizen, she filed her claim next to the Solberg brothers.

Andrew Hjertoos, a carpenter and brick mason from Norway, arrived in Seattle in 1889, the day after the great fire that destroyed most of the business district, and rented a room in the boarding house where Bergette prepared the meals. A year later they married, then moved to her homestead to raise dairy cows and sheep. When the Solberg brothers joined the Alaska Gold Rush, they arranged for the Hjertooses to manage their dairy farm as well. Bergette and Andrew frequently made the difficult trek to Seattle, going first to Kirkland, then via steamer across Lake Washington to Madison, and then by streetcar to the Pike Place Market, where they sold fresh milk, cream and butter. Andrew continued to work in construction, often leaving her in sole charge of the livestock and their growing family.

In 1901 they purchased the farm at Tolt/Carnation and with their four children in tow, drove their herd of 100 cows, calves, sheep and horses over the hill across the Snoqualmie River ferry to their new home. The farm had several buildings including a boarding house which served as temporary shelter for immigrant families or harvest hands. There was a large orchard, extending down to the banks of both the Tolt and Snoqualmie Rivers. An impressive variety of trees produced apples, pears, peaches, plums, cherries and walnuts. In 1907 Andrew built the commodious farmhouse and later the barn that still stand. Actively involved in their community, the Hjertooses donated parcels of their land for the Odd Fellows Hall and the high school that was originally shared by the Tolt, Stillwater and Pleasant Hill communities.

Today their great grandson Roger Thorson, his wife Vivian and their children raise Christmas trees on the property, now called the Carnation Tree Farm. The Thorsons are restoring the old house and barn which are listed on the King County Register of Historic Places.

14.   Nan Fullerton Stuart Memorial Chapel
Tolt Congregational Church/United Church of Christ
Tolt Avenue, Carnation

Seventeen charter members met in 1895 to organize the Tolt Congregational Church and start a building fund. Three years later, the community turned out for the dedication of the new chapel. An early resident of the parsonage on the first floor was the Rev. Rosine Edwards, the church's only female pastor who served in 1899 and 1900. Her Sunday duties included weekly treks through the woods to the Healy Logging Camp at Stillwater where she ministered to loggers and their families.

An active organization in the church was the Ladies Aid which hosted memorable luncheons, dinners and receptions. Many a pupil, who went to the elementary school next door, remembers the 15¢ hot lunches served at the church each Wednesday. Giving strong support to the schools, the Aid invited teachers from Tolt, Stillwater, Pleasant Hill and Vincent to a festive annual reception.

When the wood-frame church burned down in 1936, Elbridge Hadley Stuart, founder of the renowned Carnation Milk Farms, offered to build a new structure out of stone. The beautiful Nan Fullerton Stuart Memorial Chapel, named in memory of his wife, was dedicated in 1938.

15.   Duvall Public Library
122 Main Street
Continue on State Road 203

Beside the front door of the Duvall Public Library is an ornate stained-glass window featuring a rose, and the meeting room in the new addition is called the Rose Room.   Both are in honor of Rose Norenburg who was hired by the King County Library System in 1957 when it took over management of the Duvall branch library. After her retirement in 1978, she continued to work as substitute librarian and janitor.

Rose is a member of the Duvall Women's Civic Club which purchased books in the 1920s and founded a lending library in the corner of a leaky building.   In the depths of the Great Depression, the club enlisted the help of the Works Progress Administration. Workers scrounged logs from the underpinnings of a deserted bridge and an old mill to erect the library's own building.

As librarian, Rose could always count on her clubsisters to raise funds for new acquisitions and read to preschoolers during the popular Friday story hour. A few charter members continue to attend the Civic Club's monthly meetings which are always held at the library.

16.   Dougherty Farmstead
NE Cherry Valley Road (NE 165th Street)
One-third mile east of the Duvall-Monroe Road (SR-203)

Kate and John Dougherty celebrated their wedding in the Seattle Catholic Church in 1882. While he was born in Iowa, she at age 24 had recently immigrated from Ireland where she had taught in a convent school. In their home on Camano Island, Kate gave birth to their first five children. In the recessionary `90s with a sixth baby on the way, John lost his job at the lumber mill. After a brief stay in Seattle, the Doughertys moved to Cherry Valley where they purchased their own two-story farmhouse for $2,500.

When John died in 1903, Kate took over management of the farm. She sold some of the heavily forested acreage but kept the five-acre fruit orchard with its 800 trees as their major source of income. As supplements, she ran the community post office in their front hall and took in loggers as boarders.

Kate's experience in Catholic schools stayed with her. When school was in session, she made sure that all of her eight children attended. The community's first Catholic Mass was held in her parlor and two of her children eventually chose religious vocations. Public-spirited citizens, Kate and six of her children joined the Cherry Valley Grange in 1909 as charter members. (Please see Chapter IV, Happy Valley Grange for information about the significance of this organization.)

Among the improvements that Kate made to the house was an indoor bathroom, complete with a huge claw-footed bathtub, toilet and sink that she purchased in 1917 for $5 from a passing riverboat merchant. An avid gardener, she grew roses and dahlias that were prized by later generations of Doughertys who lived in the house until 1982.

In 1984 the Duvall Historical Society began restoration of the farmhouse for a museum and community meeting place. It is slated to open in the near future, once negotiations between King County and the current owner, the Catholic Archdiocese of Seattle, are complete. The Dougherty House, built by James O'Leary in 1888, is listed on the State Register of Historic Places. The farm complex, which evokes a glimpse of rural life in the early 20th century, is a designated King County Landmark.

17. The Skykomish Hotel
Skykomish
From Duvall, take State Route 203 to Monroe, then go east on State Route 2

Located near Stevens Pass, "the Gateway to the American Alps," the town of Skykomish has a rich and varied past. It was founded as one of many small station towns linked to construction and maintenance of the Great Northern Railroad. As transportation opened up the area, lumber and mining companies began operations with laborers flocking to the Skykomish on their days off, their wages in hand. When the Skykomish Hotel opened its doors in 1904, tourists, sports fishermen, hikers and skiers were also booking rooms. During peak seasons, the town's saloons and hotels raked in profits, sometimes serving customers around the clock.

In the 1970s the Skykomish Hotel was renamed for a colorful woman who lived in the community to a ripe old age, regaling younger generations with bawdy tales of yesteryear. Molly Gibson managed the hotel when ladies of easy (but profitable) virtue plied their trade on the top floor. (Please see Chapter VIII, "Skid Road/the Tenderloin" for further information.) In keeping with the preservation of the town's historic district, the original name was recently restored.

Today, the hotel's major clientele is outdoor sports enthusiasts. The restaurant is a popular gathering place for old-timers who reminisce about the town's rich and colorful past, while keeping abreast of current developments.

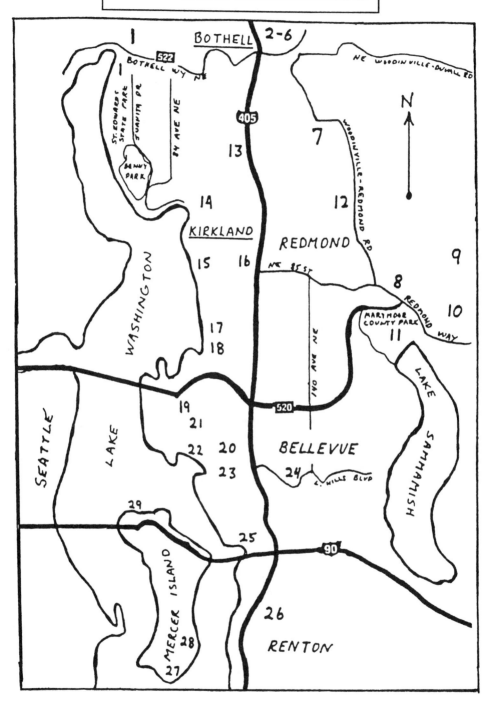

IV. THE EASTSIDE STORY

Kenmore to Mercer Island

Since World War II, the scenic area between Lake Washington and Lake Sammamish has sprouted like wildfire from predominantly berry and dairy farms into bustling cities and housing developments. Despite unprecedented growth, the Eastside has preserved its charm with an abundance of parks, recreational trails and historic sites. Your tour begins in Kenmore at the north end of Lake Washington and proceeds through Bothell, Woodinville and Redmond with visits to opulent estates, pastoral farmsteads, museums, and community centers.

Continue into Kirkland, a city with several historic buildings, which has the distinction of electing the first councilwoman in Washington state. Take a stroll at the site of the erstwhile shipyard for beautiful views of the lake and time to reflect on the women who worked there doing "men's jobs" during World War II. The wilderness preserve between the cities of Yarrow and Hunt's Point is one of several on the Eastside that owes its existence to women.

The route through Bellevue leads to sites that evoke a sense of continuity between women in the contemporary city and their rural and small-town forebears. The tour ends on the south end of Mercer Island with visits to a former Girl Scout Camp and a country schoolhouse, complete with a tiny cottage for the teacher.

1.   Wildcliffe Farm
7330 NE 170th Street, Kenmore
From State Route 522 turn south on 68th Avenue NE (Juanita Drive), then east on NE 170th Street

Charles and Elvera Anderson Thomsen built their lavish French Provincial country home in 1927 as a summer retreat. With an avid interest in gardening, Elvera supervised planning of the formal garden, a part of which remains intact. She also purchased 500 blueberry bushes to plant in the old Sammamish riverbed below the house.

Charles, whose father founded the Centennial Mill Company in Spokane, joined the family business, becoming manager of the Seattle plant and later president. Like heads of several other wealthy Seattle families, he retired early to move to the country, where he and Elvera made Wildcliffe their permanent home. Her gardening hobby was the catalyst for the couple's new business. From her original blueberry patch, they expanded to 27,000 bushes, built a cannery, and by 1954 were producing a 40-ton annual crop under the Wildcliffe Blueberry Farm label. Although no longer in operation, the farm is well remembered for hiring local labor during the harvest season. Since their children did not want the property, the Thomsens left it as a bequest for a non-profit charitable organization.

In the 1970s, the Easter Seal Society assumed ownership of the property, using the warm-water pool, grounds, and mansion for recreation and therapy. At the time, Ann Piggott Wycoff was a board member and a pioneering advocate for the differently abled. While studying social work at the University of Washington, she had worked at the Ryther Child Center and had recognized that some of the children, if given a chance, had the potential to become productive, contributing members of society. She approached the Seattle Junior League which voted to sponsor her proposed project, the state's first guidebook for the handicapped. On its publication in 1967, the Easter Seal board put the guidelines into practice, leading crusades for wheelchair accessible curb cuts on city streets and for new building codes to improve access for the differently abled.

Today, Wildcliffe Farm maintains a full weekday schedule of recreational therapy and support for people with crippling diseases, including polio and cerebral palsy. Income is generated on weekends when the facilities are rented out for weddings, corporate parties and other special events. The property is registered as a King County Landmark.

2.   Mary Murphy Memorial Park
18680 Bothell Way NE
Go east on State Route 522, Bothell Way NE

In 1971 the Bothell Beautification Committee dedicated a new city park in memory of one of its founding members, a civic-spirited community activist, best known for her work with the schools.

Since the 1920s, several of Washington's larger school districts had offered kindergarten and sometimes preschool programs.   In financially strained smaller districts, such as Bothell, they were frequently regarded as a frill. In the late 1940s and early 1950s, Mary Murphy led the Bothell Preschool PTA's vigorous and successful campaign for a special levy.   When the district established kindergartens in its elementary schools, she taught the first classes.

3.   Costie-Ruiz (Northshore) Swimming Pool
9815 NE 188th Street, Bothell
Across the street form Mary Murphy Memorial Park

When Candy Costie and Tracie Ruiz, both in their early twenties, brought home the gold from the 1984 Los Angeles Olympics, thousands of people turned out for their grand parade through downtown Bothell. To commemorate their victory, the city renamed the Northshore District Swimming Pool in their honor.

As children, Candy and Tracie took swimming lessons at Evans Pool at Greenlake and at the Redmond Athletic Club in Woodinville. Their coach of many years, Charlotte Davis of Lake Forest Park, trained them in the art of water ballet, choreographing their synchronized swimming routines. As students at Bothell High School, they were already entering international swimming competitions. In Los Angeles they fulfilled their dreams with a stunning synchronized performance that won them gold medals. Tracie capped the victory with a second one for her solo.

On their return home, both retired from competitive swimming, married, and changed their names to Candy Costie Burke and Tracie Ruiz-Conforto. But Tracie's competitive spirit was still unsatiated. At the 1988 Olympics she made a comeback, winning a silver medal for the United States.

4. Bothell's First Schoolhouse
Bothell Landing Historic Park
9919 NE 180th
From Bothell Way turn south on NE 180th Street

Following their father's death, Helen and Marmora DeVoe and their mother decided to move West. In 1885 Dr. Marmora DeVoe (later Moody) set up a practice in Seattle as the city's second female physician. Opting for country living, Helen bought 160 acres north of Bothell with the understanding that there was a cabin on it, but instead found a crude shack with broken door hinges. Exhausted but wary, she and her mother gathered fresh boughs for a bed, braced up the door as best they could, and slept with ax and shovel close at hand.

In 1886 when Helen heard that Bothell was starting a school, she applied for and got the first teaching job. Since no boarding place was available, Mary Ann Bothell agreed to have a ten-by-twelve-foot teacher's cabin erected next to the school in her yard. A graduate of Oberlin College in Ohio, Helen welcomed 23 pupils to their first four-month term at the new schoolhouse. To the disappointment of her pupils, she left her teaching post after just ten and one-half months, and to the disappointment of her many suitors, she never married.

For the next seven years, she worked to prove up her claim, then sold it to resume her career. She taught in the Seattle schools for 15 years, then in Alaska for two, and later in other country schools which she preferred to those in cities. She was a member of the Daughters of the American Revolution, the Washington Pioneers Association and a charter member of the First Unitarian Church of Seattle. She lived to the age of 97.

Bothell's pioneer schoolhouse was recently moved from its original site to Bothell Landing Historic Park.

In 1915 Alice Seaton took over Rural Route 1 in Bothell
She also cared for her husband, four children and two horses.
(Courtesy of Washington Women's Heritage Project Records,
University of Washington Libraries)

5.   Andrew and Augusta Nelson Beckstrom Cabin
Bothell Landing Historic Park

The Beckstroms, their two small children and Andrew's 70-year-old father were Swedish immigrants who made their first home in Kansas. From there they took the train to San Francisco, then a ship to Seattle, and then a rowboat to the forested banks of the Sammamish River, where they moved into the abandoned cabin on their homestead. One of their first visitors was Susan Woodin of Woodinville who acted as midwife, when Augusta gave birth to a son.

Andrew plied his trade as a painter. His father, a farmer, helped start a large garden among the stumps around their home and the dairy that became a lucrative family business. In 1884, the Beckstroms built their new cabin, where the family continued to grow to 16 children-- not unusual among the pioneers. Their friends and next door neighbors, Peter and Charlotte Quartman, who had been their travelling companions on the westward journey, also had 16 children.

In addition to managing their home and businesses, both Augusta and Andrew made time for community activities. Both served on the school board and were founding members of the Swedish Lutheran Church, which elected Augusta as its delegate to the national conference. According to the church's records, she "did not attend because she was disqualified as a voter; the reason -- she was a woman." As in other rural communities, lodges and churches were the hubs of social and community life. Augusta was a member of the Eastern Star, while Andrew was a Mason.

The old Beckstrom cabin is currently on loan to the Bothell Historical Museum by its owner Betty MacCleod.

6. Bothell Historical Society and Museum
Bothell Landing Historical Park
Phone: 486-1889

Organized in 1969, the Bothell Historical Society was grateful to Marian Caldwell, the city's longtime librarian who came as a teacher in the early 1900s, retired to marry and raise a family, then worked in the library until her retirement in 1956. Through the years, she maintained scrapbooks, clipping files and notes, documenting the community's early history and its growth and development. A charter member of the historical society, Gladys Hannan Worley donated the 1893 home where she was born for the city's museum. Volunteers moved it from Main Street to Bothell Landing, where Nancy Paris directed its restoration. An unsung hero, Sue Kienast, has been a driving force in the historical society and museum.

7.   Hollywood Farm/Chateau Ste. Michelle

14111 NE 145th Street
Phone: 488-1133 - the Winery. Grounds and tours available daily, 10:30 a.m.-4:30 p.m.
Go east on Bothell Way, State Route 522, to the Woodinville exit. Turn right at the stop sign to NE 175th Street and continue across the railroad tracks to stop sign. Turn left to State Route 202, drive two miles, then follow the signs

Frederick "Fred" Stimson and his wife Nellie Clarke Stimson moved from Michigan to Seattle where he founded the Stimson Timber Company. They built the extravagant country estate for a summer home, then made it their year-round residence, following his early retirement in 1918.

By then Nellie was an established businesswoman in her own right, having operated greenhouses at their former home on Queen Anne hill and a florist shop in downtown Seattle at Second Avenue and Stewart Street. Hollywood Gardens eventually became one of the largest and most complete floral establishments in the Northwest. At the Woodinville farm she installed several industrial-size greenhouses. Each day she shipped cut flowers by milk wagon and later by rail to her Seattle shop. From there floral arrangements were delivered by motorcycle or delivery van to destinations throughout the city. The shop also conducted a wholesale business, shipping flowers as far away as Honolulu and Nome. While Nellie concentrated on her floral business, Fred developed other parts of the farm into a massive agricultural demonstration project, establishing a dairyman's showplace with a large herd of prize-winning Holstein-Friesian cattle.

The Stimsons engaged in many philanthropic activities, including the founding of Hollywood Fresh Air Farm for undernourished Seattle children. Their mission was to give poor children an opportunity to experience delights of country living on summer days. Under the direction of the Anti-Tuberculosis League (now the American Lung Association), they provided a wholesome milk-product diet for groups of twenty children for two weeks at a time.

Influenced by the League and by the Seattle Mothers Congress (forerunner of the PTA), Fred took a lead in developing standards of sanitation and scientific procedures for producing pure milk. In 1913 the Mothers Congress held the first competitive milk contest of its kind in the United States, taking samples of milk from local dairies without previous notice and scoring them. By December, their tests showed a marked improvement in the city's milk supply which previously had been unregulated. At a time when bovine tuberculosis was a threat to children who drank raw milk, the local Mothers Congress acted to save lives, establishing a program that was quickly adopted throughout the nation. Products form the Stimson dairy always received top scores and were consequently in demand from Seattle consumers and their retail markets.

Nellie's interest in horticulture extended beyond her business to the landscaping of Hollywood Farm. When stumps were cleared form the logged-off land, she enlisted the help of neighbors to plant hundreds of holly trees. The grounds around the residence were rumored to have been the work of noted landscape architects, the Olmsted Brothers who designed Seattle's park system. Historians now concur that the credit was misplaced and that Nellie most likely designed the original grounds herself. While many elements of her landscaping remain, the grounds have been substantially altered by later owners.

Following her husband's death in 1921 at age 53, Nellie remained at the country estate until 1927, when she sold it to the Marlborough Investment Company. The property changed ownership several times and was purchased by St. Michelle Vintners, the present owner, in 1986. Most of Nellie's greenhouses were demolished the next year to make room for parking for outdoor summer concerts and other events. Hollywood Farm is listed on the King County and National Registers of Historic Places.

8. Nike Park

93rd Place and 172nd Avenue NE

Continue south on State Route 202; turn left on NE 92nd; turn right on 171st Avenue NE, then left at 93rd Place

During the Cold War of the 1950s and 1960s, community volunteers banded together to entertain servicemen stationed at Nike sites in Redmond Gardens and on Novelty Hill. Directing the program was Marguerite "Perky" Johnson Peterson, a civic-spirited eastside native who lived up to her nickname. She had financed her education at Wilson Business College in Seattle by doing housework and driving semi-trucks. When she and her husband Vonal moved to their wooded hillside lot in Redmond, he went to work in logging camps, often leaving her alone for a week at a time. Perky had babies, dug wells, shingled roofs, drove tractors, dug a root cellar, shot wild game, grew gardens and canned her produce.

In the 1950s she channeled her enormous energy into the United Service Organization "USO," heading the Redmond area program and attending county-wide meetings at the Women's University Club in Seattle. A major activity was the monthly dance held at the Odd Fellows Hall. Local women's organizations took their turn serving refreshments, young people loaned their records, and Perky recruited girls to serve as hostesses.

The girls, their mothers, county USO volunteers, and Army personnel held several meeting to plan dance programs. Some of the rules for hostesses were: "Be friendly and considerate of all races, creeds and religions. If you refuse a dance, do it graciously and BE SURE YOU ARE JUSTIFIED! Be a lady at all times. Stay in the hall or go directly home." A typical evening started with the Bunny Hop and the Hoky Poky as ice breakers, followed by popular dance tunes, some of which were Ladies' Choice. Redmond hostesses were bused to the Olympic Hotel in Seattle to help entertain servicemen at the annual Seafair Military Ball.

USO volunteers also organized programs for married servicemen and their wives, creating bonds between civilian and military communities. Many a Redmond family hosted service personnel, inviting them to their homes for barbecues, cards, or a day at the beach. Following her years with the USO, Perky Peterson was elected to the Redmond City Council.

9.   Farrel-McWhirter Park

Go south on 172nd Avenue NE; turn left at 172nd Place; turn left on Avondale Road NE, turn right onto Novelty Hill Road, then left on 196th Avenue NE to the park entrance

In the 1930s Earl J. and Elise Farrel McWhirter of north Seattle purchased this verdant 68-acre site for a summer place which eventually became their year-round residence. They built their home, planted an orchard, and raised farm animals in a clearing surrounded by second-growth forest. So that Elise could pursue her passion for horseback riding, they carved equestrian trails through the wooded grounds. Widowed in her later years, she lived a reclusive life, occasionally breaking her routine to give a lavish party for old friends.

On her death in 1971, she bequeathed her estate to the city of Redmond for a park which features horseback riding, day camping, picnicking, hiking and nature study. The barnyard was restored as a children's farm with animals and intriguing old farm implements. An early twentieth century portrait of Elise Farrel McWhirter by noted New England artist Benjamin Champney is displayed in the park's office/classroom building.

10.   Happy Valley Grange #322

19720 NE 50th Street
Continue southbound on Avondale Road; turn left on Redmond-Fall City Road (State Route 202); turn left on NE 50th

In 1909, 53 women and men met at the schoolhouse to organize the Happy Valley Grange, Chapter #322 of the Washington State Grange, which was chartered in 1889 as a part of the National Grange. Happy Valley is an unincorporated farming community three miles east of Redmond which boasts that it has never had a tavern or until recently, a store. Its pioneer residents were mostly Scandinavian immigrants, many of whom rarely left the valley. The Grange's motto, "the farm family is the backbone of America," struck a resounding chord.

During their first year, Happy Valley Grangers built their hall, where friends and neighbors gathered for box socials, potlucks, whist parties, dances and meetings. In keeping with the Grange's mission of promoting agriculture and the quality of rural life, the Happy Valley organization at first lobbied for local improvements. It was instrumental in introducing electricity and mail service. It also campaigned for road improvements on the Eastside and for more comfortable waiting rooms at ferry docks. The Grange was also a link to activities and issues that extended beyond the valley.

A charter member of the Happy Valley Grange was Agnes Johnson, a Swedish immigrant who had come with her family as a child. She later married Edwin Johnson (no relation to her family). For more than 20 years, she served as an officer of the Washington State Grange, where she rarely missed a meeting. She received the state's annual leadership award for designing the beautiful Rose Drill which is used by Granges across the nation. On two occasions the Johnsons' five singing daughters won the National Grange Talent Contest.

In the 1930s during Agnes's tenure, the organization created a Home Economics Department with an elected director who became the 17th officer. Traditionally, the Grange had been governed by 16 officers; the 17th was instituted nationally, following Washington's lead. Some of the department's projects were beautifying roadsides and working with school leaders to improve playgrounds and education programs. In the 1960s, the Home Economics Department changed its name to the Women's Activities Department.

From the start, the Grange was an egalitarian organization that admitted women as equal members who could vote and run for office and that also emphasized activities for families and children. Statewide and nationally, it has promoted crusades for woman suffrage, temperance, the equal rights amendment, comparable worth and other women's issues. In his 1989 book, WASHINGTON STATE GRANGERS CELEBRATE A CENTURY, historian Gus Norwood wrote, "About half of the officers of the Granges in Washington state are women. Probably in recent years there has been a shift from a slight preponderance of men to a majority of women. Hundreds of women have served as masters of their Granges....None as yet has served as state master." The Washington State Grange today has chapters in 401 communities with a membership of more than 60,000, making it one of the largest statewide associations in the nation.

Today's Happy Valley Grange still meets twice a month at the old hall. Even though it is not as strong as it once was, members still regard it as important. Many of the valley's current residents are not farmers, but escapees from city life. The Grange does its utmost to ensure

James W. and Anna Herr Clise Mansion. Now home of Marymoor Museum. (Courtesy of the King County Parks, Planning and Resources)

preservation of the community's rural character and to support local farmers. To earn revenue for upkeep, it leases its space to the Washington Dance Studio and other groups.

11.   Willowmoor Farm/Marymoor Park
Marymoor Museum
6046 Lake Sammamish Parkway NE, Redmond
Phone: 885-3684. Open Tuesday, Wednesday,
Thursday, 11 a.m.-4 p.m. and Sunday, 1-5 p.m.
Return to Avondale Road and follow signs into the park

James Clise, a 49-year-old Seattle banker, purchased the acreage along the Snohomish slough in 1904 and built an elegant summer hunting lodge. His wife Anna and their three children liked the countryside so much, that the family soon decided to make Willowmoor Farm a year-round home. They expanded the lodge into the two-story, 28-room, Tudor-style mansion that today houses Marymoor Museum. Following an early retirement, James devoted his efforts to developing a lucrative working farm. He raised prize-winning Morgan horses and imported a small herd of cattle from Scotland. As the famed Willowmoor Ayrshires, they became a source of both pride and profit.

For Anna the farm was a golden opportunity to pursue her interests in gardening and flowers. An English gardener designed the grounds in the style of an English manor estate, including unusual plants imported from Europe and the Orient. In her greenhouses, she cultivated roses for her gardens, along with the exotic orchids that she later donated to the Conservatory at Volunteer Park in Seattle, where visitors can still enjoy them.

Many of the gala parties that the Clises hosted at Willowmoor were benefits for Anna's most important legacy, Children's Orthopedic Hospital, which she founded with supportive women friends in 1907. (Please see COH, Chapter VI, #8.) When guests came from Seattle, the stylish four-horse tallyho met them at the Medina ferry dock and transported them along the winding road to the estate. In an interview with THE SEATTLE TIMES, the Clise's daughter Ruth Colwell recalled a typical party scene: "Gaily colored Japanese lanterns holding lighted candles were strung between the trees in the garden and down to the river, where their reflections created a romantic setting. The large rooms of the house and the spacious verandas provided ample room for dancing, the music drifting out over the garden."

Even as glaucoma gradually took away her eyesight, Anna continued her charitable activities. Her small dog Toby led her around the mansion and along the garden paths. With the help of a friend, she printed two books in Braille which were accepted by the National Library of the Blind in Washington, D.C. When James lost his health in 1920, the family reluctantly sold Willowmoor Farm and moved to California.

Faced with prospective residential or commercial development of the farm, King County voters came to the rescue in 1963, passing a bond issue to purchase Marymoor Farm (renamed by interim owners) for a park. The Five Corners Community Club of Kirkland and the Federated Eastside Women's Clubs presented the successful proposal for a museum to be housed in the north ten rooms of the mansion. Under the aegis of the Northeast King County Historical Association (later changed to the King County Historical Association), Marymoor Museum opened its doors to the public in 1968. Eastside women's history is a major emphasis in its rotating exhibits and archival collection. The Clise Mansion is listed on both the King County and National Registers of Historic Places.

12.   Lake Washington Technical College
11605 132nd Avenue NE, Kirkland
Take the Redmond-Kirkland Road (State Route 908) to 132nd Avenue NE; turn north

A native Montanan born in 1900, Ruth Brass divorced her husband during World War II and enlisted in the United States Army. Following the war, she moved to Kirkland where she met Morton

Johnson, the district's Superintendent of Schools. Recognizing her organizational genius, he hired her to direct the new adult education program. She recruited faculty and students for a wide array of subjects and personally taught classes in tailoring. The program mushroomed, occupying ever-changing temporary facilities.

When the school moved to its own campus as Lake Washington Vocational Technical Institute, it boasted 400 faculty members. In 1966 the state cancelled its support of adult education programs, posing a threat to the Institute's survival. When local community colleges tried to take over the program, students and faculty fought back and won. Ruth Brass, whom the students had sent on a Hawaiian vacation in appreciation of her leadership, remained on the job until the state granted the institute its vocational title. Reflecting its accreditation, it was recently renamed Lake Washington Technical College.

13.   Edith Moulton County Park

108 Avenue NE and NE 137th Place, Juanita
Continue north on 132nd Avenue NE, following the arterial onto NE Totem Lake Boulevard; turn west on NE 132nd Street, then north on 108th Avenue NE

Shortly after her birth in 1897, Edith Moulton's family moved to the sylvan tract north of Kirkland. As an adult, she worked as a school teacher in other parts of the state, then gave up her career to return home and care for her ailing grandmother and aunt. Unmarried and without heirs, she bequeathed her property to the community to preserve as a wilderness area.

14.   Shumway Mansion

11410 99th Place NE, Kirkland
Phone: 823-2303
Return to NE 132nd Street; turn west, then south on 100th Avenue NE; Follow the arterial onto 99th Avenue NE; the home is just south of 116th Street

In 1911 Kirkland voters elected Carrie Shumway to the City Council, the first woman in the state to hold the office. (Courtesy of the Seattle Public Schools Archives)

In 1881 the five Shumway sisters and their mother ventured West from Belchertown, Massachusetts to join their three brothers in the Puget Sound region. As teachers at Seattle's Central Grade School, Carrie, Emma and Mary were active in Plymouth Congregational Church and were founding members of bicycle and camera clubs. In 1910 eight adult Shumways pooled their money to purchase a seven-acre site in Kirkland and hire J. G. Bartsch, a highly regarded local contractor, to construct their seven-bedroom, eighteen-room mansion.

In 1911 after Washington women won the franchise, Kirkland voters elected Carrie to the City Council, the first women in the state to hold the office. A civic-spirited woman, she was a founding member of the Kirkland Women's Club and State Historian for the Daughters of the American Revolution.

In 1944 as the last surviving member of her family, Carrie sold her property. A series of different owners followed, most notably Dr. Ruth Heyer Hall, who converted the seven-bedroom second floor into a nursing home. Following its closure in 1970, she continued her chiropractic practice in two rooms on the main floor.

When new owners heard that developers wanted to demolish the four-story mansion and replace it with condos, they moved it to a safe location three miles up the road. It has been renovated as a gracious bed and breakfast that also has rental parlors available for weddings, receptions and other special events.

15.   Kirkland Congregational Church/Camp Fire Girls
106 5th Avenue
Continue south on the arterial to 5th Avenue, then turn left

Amelia Newberry, wife of the Reverend Charles E. Newberry of the Congregational Church, served on the city council and was called "Aunt Amelia" by local children. She is best remembered as the "Mother of Camp Fire" in King County.

In 1911 following the Sunday School picnic, 20 girls, ages 12 and older, met with "Aunt Amelia" to form the Es-Ke-Le-Da Camp Fire Girls group. Aside from churches, there were almost no organizations for girls at the time. Amelia coached the girls in plays which they presented each spring at the church, raising funds for summer camping trips. In her book OUR FOUNDERING FATHERS: THE STORY OF KIRKLAND, Arlene Ely describes the plays as "one of the social events of the year." In 1937 Amelia received Camp Fire's greatest tribute, the National Service Award. Her own girls planted a tree in her honor.

16.   Kirkland Public Library
On 1st Street across from the Congregational Church

In 1919 when the Kirkland Woman's Club began collecting books and raising funds for a library, one of its charter members, Councilwoman

Carrie Shumway, made arrangements for its temporary housing in the council chambers. Six years later, members of the club placed a "time capsule" containing dated materials beneath the cornerstone of their new public library building.

The building did double duty as a center for the club's other community service activities, including child welfare programs and a bi-monthly medical clinic for small children. The club continued to collect books, raise maintenance funds and provide volunteer librarians, most notably Brittania McKibbon who served faithfully for 46 years. Although the building is no longer used as a library, its preservation is assured. A source of community pride, it is listed on the National Register of Historic Places.

17.　Houghton Beach Park
Lake Washington at NE 60th Street
Continue south on the arterial which becomes Lake Washington Boulevard NE

Doris Cooper moved to Houghton in the 1940s and quickly became involved in civic life. She was one of a group of homemakers who raised federal funds to develop the public park. As a member of the Houghton Community Council, she was a founder of the annual Moss Bay celebration. Recognizing her outstanding leadership abilities, Kirkland's voters elected her to three successive terms from 1983 to 1989 as their mayor.

18.　Lake Washington Shipyards
Now the Seattle Seahawks training quarters and Carillon Center, a complex of restaurants, health club, hotel, marina, condos and shops
South of Houghton Beach Park

According to archival records at Marymoor Museum, Susie Gregg Parks returned to Kirkland in the 1920s as a national hero. She was also a widow with seven children whom she supported by working at the cafeteria on the Kirkland ferry dock from 1929-1941. The outbreak of World War II and mobilization of the shipyards suddenly transformed the peaceful, rural community into a boomtown that presented both a patriotic challenge and an economic windfall for Susie. As a sheet metal worker doing a "man's job," she was one of 6,000 employees who repaired 477 ships and built 33 tenders for the Navy during the war. The unprecedented salary of almost $1 an hour with overtime made Susie one of the new consumers that fueled urbanization of Kirkland and the Eastside. Following the armistice, demand for ships plummeted and the company decided to disband. Susie and most of her female co-workers once again faced limited job options in low status positions with diminutive paychecks.

After completing eighth grade in Kirkland, Susie Gregg had married and moved to New Mexico, where she worked with her husband, publishing a local newspaper. One night when he was away, she was caring for her baby and minding the office switchboard. At 2:00 a.m., she suddenly awoke to gunshots, galloping horses and shouts of "Viva Villa! Viva Villa!" From her window she saw friends being gunned down, buildings bursting into flame, uniformed mounted marauders and the signature plumed hat of Pancho Villa.

At first she huddled on the floor trying to protect her baby, but then decided that she had to act. When she lit a match to see the switchboard, a volley of gunfire shot through the window. With glass splinters and shrapnel tearing into her face and arms, she dialed Army headquarters in El Paso to sound the alarm. Within a few hours, the U.S. Calvary responded, chasing Pancho Villa and his army across the border. They were never again to be seen in the United States.

Susie Gregg Parks received national recognition for her heroism with presentations of the silver set, gold watch and silver cup that remain cherished family heirlooms. Her children, most of whom still live in the Pacific Northwest, remember her insistence that there is a way past any obstacle if you face it head on. Another of her lessons was not to neglect laughing, loving and having fun. Even in the depths of the Great Depression, she played her fiddle and kept music in the house in Kirkland.

19. Wetherill Nature Preserve
Cozy Cove between Yarrow and Hunts Point

The Jacob Furths, prominent Yarrow pioneers, kept this part of their summer place, "Barnabie," in its natural state. In 1989 their granddaughters, Marjorie Wetherill Baird and Sidonia Wetherill Foley, donated the land to the cities of Yarrow and Hunts Point to preserve as a haven for wildlife. Developers had been after the sisters for several years to sell their property which was privately appraised at four million dollars. Avid gardeners, they have been active participants in the Seattle and Yarrow Garden Clubs.

Thanks to their father's career as an Army officer, the sisters traveled around the world as children. Marjorie Baird combined her interests in travel and gardening as manager of the Northwest Horticultural Society's seed exchange. Her duties included caring for seed from all parts of the world and filling orders from an international membership. She has also been a mainstay of Marymoor Museum.

20. Rosalie Whyel Museum of Doll Art
1116 108th Avenue NE, Bellevue
Phone: 453-1137. Open Monday-Saturday 10 a.m.-5 p.m.; extended hours on Thursday to 8 p.m.; Sunday 1-5 p.m. Admission: $5 adults; $4.50 seniors; $4 children ages 5 through 17; younger children admitted free with an adult; family discounts available.
Take Lake Washington Boulevard south; turn east onto State Route 520; turn south on I-405; take the NE 12th Street exit and go west to 180th Avenue NE, then one block south

The magic begins with the first glance of the new salmon-colored building that resembles a Victorian dollhouse, complete with cupolas, dormers and an old-fashioned garden--a playful contrast to the neighboring Bellevue business district. At the urging of friends, Rosalie Whyel opened the museum in 1992 to share her world-class collection of some 2,000 antique and contemporary dolls with the public. Beginning with her first purchase of an antique doll nearly 30 years ago, her childhood hobby grew into an adult passion. Visitors to the museum enter a realm inhabited by dolls and related objects that is simultaneously historical, artistic, and fanciful.

Designed for children and adults alike, many of the exhibits are organized to explore themes and mores from women's history. An example is the Chinese "doctor's doll" once used by women too modest to tell the doctor where it hurt. Another display of clockwork dolls evokes the Victorian cult of "true womanhood" that espoused female virtues of piety, purity, domesticity, and submissiveness. Bustled and corseted mechanical dolls pour tea, powder their noses, or weep into a hanky over a broken toy. A museum highlight is the huge Victorian dollhouse with furniture and household goods all built to scale like the dolls inside, posed in their daily routines of housework and family life.

There are rare bisque dolls made by some of the world's most renowned doll artists. Some, such as the Marie Antoinette doll, are lavishly costumed and festooned with jewels. Others convey their own stories, such as the turn-of-the-century black doll, displayed as it was found with a mysterious suicide note in verse. A provocative display of multicultural dolls contrasts indigenous creations with European interpretations of foreign cultures. Contemporary Northwest doll artists are featured in a changing exhibits gallery.

21.   Overlake Service League Thriftshop
167 Bellevue Square
Go south on 108th Avenue NE, then turn west on NE 8th Street

The Overlake Service League traces its roots to 1911 when 15 Hunts Point women gathered at the home of Sally Bilger to form a chapter of the Seattle Ladies Fruit and Flower Mission--later renamed the Seattle Milk Fund. (Please see Chapter IX, Seattle Milk Fund.) The mission of Bellevue's first charity was to take fruit and flowers to the sick and provide food for the needy. During the Great Depression, the Eastside group voted to withdraw from the Seattle organization and adopt the new name, Overlake Service League. Members harvested and canned food to donate to needy Eastside families. To enable them to become more self-sufficient, they gave them seeds, fertilizers and cultivating tools, along with pigs, chickens and goats.

Rummage sales begun in 1939 proved so successful that the League decided to start a thrift shop, originally located on Main Street in Old Bellevue. One of the members was Bess Freeman, whose son, Kemper Freeman Sr., developed Bellevue Square in the early 1950s and contributed space for the shop. His son Kemper Jr. has continued the tradition in the new mall.

Today, the OSL continues to provide emergency aid to needy Eastside families. It also assists various youth programs and offers college scholarships. In recent years, the league has remained strong with more than 500 members in 15 neighborhood-based circles. Past president Jean Blakely said in an interview with the JOURNAL AMERICAN (8/26/86), "I don't think we'll run out of people to help and I don't think we'll run out of women interested in belonging to the organization because of its uniqueness and because we do a lot of good....It's local, and we've made our own rules. We can respond to the need of someone who calls today, instead of having to go through a lot of red tape."

22.   Bellevue Art Museum
Bellevue Square, Third Floor

The Bellevue Art Museum is rooted in the Pacific Northwest Arts and Crafts Fair, founded in 1947 by a local restauranteur and a board of directors. In an era that predated contemporary galleries and arts fairs, the innovative event captured public enthusiasm. Developer Miller Freeman, his son Kemper (founder of Bellevue Square), and grandson Kemper Jr. have always donated space for the annual fair and the museum. According to former fair chair Y'vonne Miller, "women volunteers have been the movers and shakers," planning and preparing year-round, then enlisting help from their families and friends. While exposing the public to high quality arts and crafts, the fair has been an important source of community building and bonding on the burgeoning Eastside, where families such as Y'vonne Miller's now boast three generations of dedicated volunteers.

Because of the board's commitment and because of volunteer support, artists receive 78-80% of the proceeds for their work. As the fair grew, juried competitions attracted some of the region's finest emerging talents, enabling struggling artists to advance their careers. Today, more than 1200 arts and crafts people compete for the 325 available booths.

LaMar Harrington, a volunteer in the 1950s and later paid director of the museum, recalls some of the artists for whom the fair was a godsend. Patti Warashina, now internationally recognized for her ceramic sculptures, had a booth with her husband Fred Bauer. At the end of the fair, as startled admirers looked on, they smashed everything that hadn't sold. Before he became famous, glass artist Dale Chihuly demonstrated his prowess, selling pieces that pleased him and giving away the ones he didn't like.

In 1971 the board established the Panaca Gallery as a year-round venue for artists and their Eastside customers. Named for the acronym of the Pacific Northwest Arts and Crafts Association, it continues to thrive in Bellevue Square, but for tax purposes in now a legally separate entity. In 1976 the fair association founded the Bellevue Art Museum with a long-term commitment to provide financial support. Opened to high critical acclaim, the museum, now located on the third floor of the Square, has become an important cornerstone of the Pacific Northwest arts scene. As LaMar Harrington notes, it has remained true to its origins with a broad definition of art that, like the fair, includes artistic crafts.

Although the museum has several paid staff members, all of whom are currently women, volunteers continue to be a mainstay. They sponsor fund-raising events, serve as docents, manage the gift shop, and present outreach programs in schools. With the exception of the paid coordinator and some contracted services, the Pacific Northwest Arts and Crafts Fair continues to rely on volunteers. As in the past, most women enlist the help of their families during the event that currently grosses more than a million dollars a year and that provides major support for the museum.

23. Lakeside Drug Store
102nd Avenue and Main Street, Bellevue
Go south on 105th Avenue NE, then west on Main Street

In 1934 Meta Jacobson Burrows graduated from the University of Washington with a degree in pharmacology. Her father bought her a partnership in the Lakeside Drug Store and by the end of the year, she bought out her partner. When she married Don Burrows, owner of a butcher shop, she continued to manage her own store. In her book BELLEVUE: ITS FIRST 100 YEARS, historian Lucile McDonald called her "a pioneer of women in management in Bellevue."

Meta was a charter member of the Chamber of Commerce and hosted informal sessions of the Business Men's Association in her store. McDonald wrote, "Meta's soda fountain was a gathering spot where many community projects germinated over coffee and cinnamon rolls. Her store was originally the bank building, and when she held the state liquor license from 1936 to 1942, the teller's cage served as the liquor store." When Meta closed her pharmacy in 1979, hers was the oldest continuously operating business in Bellevue.

24. Martina Villar Property
Kelsey Creek Park, Bellevue
Take I-405 south to Exit 12; go east on 6th Street

Born in 1903 in the Philippine Islands, Martina Villar with her daughter Anita emigrated to Seattle in the 1930s to join her husband in the predominantly bachelor Filipino community. At the outset of World War II, she purchased a grocery store at First and James at a bargain price. Its owners and most of their neighbors were being "relocated" from the area known as "Japantown." Martina worked ceaselessly from 7:00 a.m. to 10:00 p.m., seven days a week. She bought one store after another, built up the business, and then sold it to friends or relatives, helping to establish the Filipino community.

In 1949 she and her husband purchased 105 acres in Bellevue. Until the late 1960s, they cultivated their land as a truck farm. After selling part of the acreage to the city of Bellevue for Kelsey Creek Park, Martina bought two apartment buildings on Franklin Avenue which she managed until her death at age 80. Today, members of the family continue to reside in the Villar's house, which is next to the park.

25. Lucile Saunders McDonald House
3224 109th Avenue SE
Go west on SE 7th Place which becomes SE 8th Street; turn left on 112th Avenue SE which becomes Bellevue Way SE; turn right on 113th Avenue SE which becomes SE 34th Street; turn right on 109th Avenue SE

On March 9, 1991 Lucile Saunders McDonald, a sprightly and somewhat embarrassed nonagenarian, leapt onto the stage at Bellevue Community College to accept official proclamations and tributes, presented by Washington's First Lady Jean Gardner, King County Council Chair Audrey Gruger, and former Bellevue Mayor Nan Campbell. The occasion was the Heritage Resource Center's third biennial statewide women's history conference, where top state, county and city executives fittingly named Lucile McDonald Day in honor of one of the Northwest's most eminent historians.

Still a dynamo in her "retirement' years, the former SEATTLE TIMES and JOURNAL AMERICAN columnist spent several hours a day at her typewriter--an old friend that she steadfastly refused to replace with a computer. In more than half a century she had researched and written 100s of articles and some 40 published books, including ten juvenile fiction novels that she coauthored with the late Zola Helen Ross. Best known as an historian who enlightened and inspired her readers, her books focusing on King County include: THE LAKE WASHINGTON STORY, BELLEVUE: ITS FIRST 100 YEARS; SQUAK SLOUGH (co-authored with Amy Eunice Stickney); and

THE COALS OF NEWCASTLE (coauthored with her son Richard McDonald). Following her death in 1992 at age 93, Marymoor Museum published a commemorative selection of her JOURNAL AMERICAN features, entitled LUCILE MCDONALD'S EASTSIDE NOTEBOOK.

26. Borghild Ringdahl Middle School
Eastside Catholic High School
11650 SE 60th Street, Bellevue
Return to Bellevue Way SE; turn right and take the Freeway entrance eastbound onto I-90. Take exit #10 south onto I-405; take exit #9 onto 112th Avenue SE. Go south to SE 60th, then east

Borghild Knutsen Ringdahl is the only woman in Bellevue's history to have a school named after her. A Norwegian immigrant, she married in the 1920s and with her husband operated a strawberry farm in the Crossroads area. The Depression was the catalyst for her commitment to community service. In an oral history interview with Marymoor Museum, she said:

> We paid kids 25¢ a flat to pick our strawberries and took the berries to Seattle on the ferry. They rotted in the market because no one could afford them. That was when we started feeding people. I couldn't stand to see all the produce going to waste.

She called together like-minded friends, including several neighbors of Japanese ancestry, to fill bags with surplus produce which they distributed to some 13,000 people on welfare lines in Seattle and Bellevue. As a P.T.A. member, she organized a hot lunch program for local schools and was elected a founding member of the school board. When the district took over operation of the food service in 1947, she was hired as its first director, a position that she held until her retirement in 1968.

Shortly thereafter, the board voted to name the district's new middle school in her honor. She later wrote: "...Nowhere except for my beloved country, the USA, could such an act come about where a nobody like me, an ordinary individual citizen, would receive such great honor...." Governor Daniel Evans attended the dedication ceremony and presented her the Distinguished Washington Citizen Award; President Richard Nixon sent his congratulations; and the Washington Congress of Parents and Teachers presented her its Outstanding Service Award. During World War II, Borghild had protested against evacuation of her friends and neighbors to inland internment camps. In 1970 the city and the school district persuaded her to join a group visiting Bellevue's Sister City, Yao, Japan. A letter of introduction to Yao's mayor said:

> ....She has lived in Bellevue almost fifty years and has long considered the many Bellevue residents of Japanese ancestry to be among her closest friends. She is a most honored citizen of our community, state and nation with a heart as big as that of any person I have ever known.

Borghild Ringdahl Middle School was closed in 1989 and later reopened as the Eastside Catholic High School.

27.   Camp Tarywood, Girl Scouts (Site)
Southwest end of Mercer Island
Take I-405 north to I-90; go west to the 80th Avenue SE exit, then south, veering onto Island Crest Way

In 1932 in the depths of the Depression, Rosalind Clise, president of the King County Totem Girl Scouts Council, persuaded the Seattle Rotary Club to finance purchase of Camp Tarywood. Within a year, the forested waterfront site had a main lodge and several tent platforms and was ready for campers. At a bargain rate of $6 per week, hundreds of girls were able to enjoy swimming, hiking, boating, cookouts, crafts and camaraderie. In 1941 a new and expanded program made Tarywood the first residential camp in the nation to accommodate younger Brownies.

Faced with the pressure of urban sprawl and the lure of skyrocketing real estate prices, the Council voted to sell its valuable campsite in 1961. The lodge, purchased by the school district, is still in use as a meeting place for special classes and projects. The city purchased the shore-front which became part of Clarke Beach Park. Tarywood Park at the foot of Island Crest Way still bears the name.

The Totem Girl Scouts Council traces its roots to the late teens when girls and their mothers, who had experienced scouting in other parts of the United States, started King County's first troops. Nationally the organization was founded in 1912 in Savannah, Georgia, by Juliette Gordon Low (who had been a leader of Girl Guide troops in England), to promote good citizenship, sociability and outdoor life among girls, age seven to seventeen. In the 1920s normal schools in Bellingham and Ellensburg instituted leadership training courses, based on Low's guidelines, for Girl Scouts directors.

Today, members continue to win merit badges and promotions in rank for community service, for demonstrated proficiency in different skills, and for being "loyal, honorable, kind, and helpful in the home, in the school, in the field, on the playground, and in the Club Room." Their watchword is "Be prepared!" and their slogan, "Do a good turn daily." Through the years membership has ballooned, forcing changes in structure and revisions to keep apace with the needs of girls now in an expanded age range of five to eighteen.

The Totem Girl Scouts Council was reorganized in 1963 to form a central administrative unit to govern Clallem, East Jefferson, Kitsap, North Mason, King, Skagit, Snohomish and Whatcom Counties. Its headquarters are at 3611 Woodland Park Avenue N in Seattle's Fremont district.

28.   Lakeview School
Island Crest Way and SE 68th Street, Mercer Island
Go north on Island Crest Way

In 1888 Clarissa Coleman, daughter of King County Commissioner

James Colman and his wife Agnes, rang the bell to summon Mercer Island's first nine pupils to school. As in other rural schools, there was a high turnover of teachers, most of whom were single women, who would work long hours for considerably less pay than a man. In dimly-lit "shack" schools, the schoolmarm swept the floor, carried wood and water, built the fire, and taught grades one through eight with pupils ranging from age five to as old as 25. As part of her meager pay, the teacher received living expenses which often meant "boarding our"--lodging with different families and often sharing their daughter's bed.

In 1918 the school district replaced its original south Mercer Island structure that seated only nine pupils with the picturesque new Lakeview School. To attract and retain a dedicated teacher, a teacher's cottage was built next to the school. Such cottages, popularly called "teacherages," could once be found by the hundreds across the state, reflecting a progressive reform movement for rural schools.

The leading advocate was State Superintendent of Schools Josephine Corliss Preston who was elected to office in 1912, shortly after women won the franchise, and who served until 1928. An active clubwoman, Preston had the backing of her clubsisters. Women's clubs rallied to support her idea of the country school doubling as a "community center" to bring widely scattered neighbors together for meetings and recreation.

So successful were Preston's "teacherages" and "community centers," that with the backing of the General Federation of Women's Clubs, the concept rapidly swept rural America. Preston, who was also president of the National Education Association, gave women's organizations direction both locally and nationally, helping them to increase their effectiveness in the support of schools. In Washington state, her clubsisters got behind other progressive reforms that took shape during her administration including kindergartens, hot lunches, and school bus transportation. In 1923 Washington's public schools received a number one rating from the U.S. Bureau of Education.

Lakeview School served as a public grade school until the 1950s. From the beginning it doubled as a community center and for decades was the meeting place of the South End Improvement Club. When the school district no longer had use for the building, the club acquired it through a land swap. Since 1957 the Sunnybeam Nursery School has been the building's major tenant. Sharing the property is the Pioneer Park Youth Club which maintains a dance school and a riding club.

The handsome building with its columned portico and sunny classrooms has undergone few changes. The tiny two-room "teacherage" still stands on the northwest corner of the property, one of only a handful that remain in the state.

29.   Keewaydin Clubhouse/VFW Post #5760
1836 72nd SE, Mercer Island
Continue north on Island Crest Way; turn left on N Mercer Way

The seed for the Keewaydin Club was the McGilvra Improvement Club founded in 1914 by 21 women who wanted to improve the quality of island life and take necessary steps to protect the natural environment. Members lobbied for sidewalks and improvement of ferry docks. One of their chief concerns was the widespread practice of dumping sewage into Lake Washington. When men became interested in joining, the club changed its name and built the clubhouse in 1922. In addition to forming the community's social hub, the clubhouse did double duty as the center of island government. Today the building serves as the VFW hall.

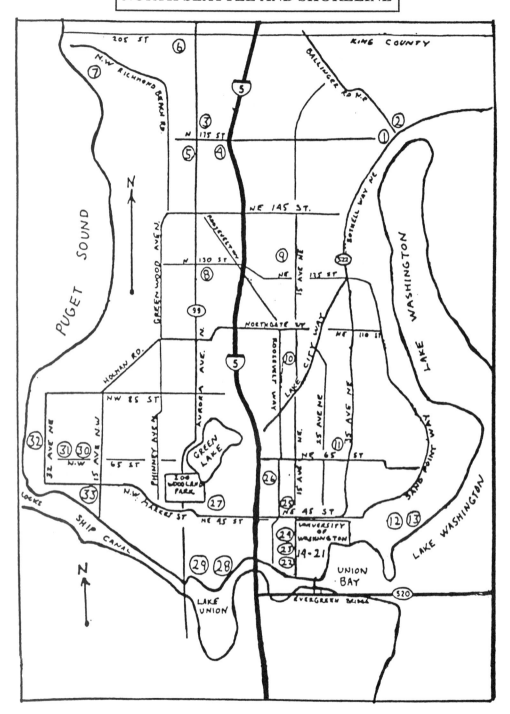

V. NORTH OF THE SHIP CANAL

Shoreline, Laurelhurst, North Seattle, Ballard

Your tour begins on the northeast shore of Lake Washington, then crosses the Shoreline district to Puget Sound. From there the route zigzags to Laurelhurst, then west to Ballard. Although it is predominantly a driving tour, you should plan to take comfortable shoes for walks through parks and park-like neighborhoods and visits to five different historical and art museums.

While you can drive past most of the designated sites at the University of Washington, it is best to park your car and tour the beautiful campus on foot. Ask for a map at an entrance booth (or pick one up in Room 320, Schmitz Hall at 15th Avenue and University Way), so that you can take alternate paths and identify additional points of interest. As you read this guidebook, you will find references to the 1909 Alaska-Yukon-Pacific Exhibition, Seattle's first world's fair which was held on the then-rural campus. Lasting legacies include several temporary buildings that were subsequently adapted to campus use and the spectacular landscaping, designed by the Olmsted brothers.

Before returning to your car, you may choose to walk past the sites listed on University Way. "The Ave." is a browser's mecca, abounding with an eclectic blend of bookstores, shops and ethnic restaurants. From the University District, your tour continues through Wallingford and ends with a Scandinavian flavor in Ballard. At this point if you want to visit additional women's history sites, take 15th Avenue NW south across the Ballard Bridge and turn to Chapter VI to continue with the next tour.

1.   Civic Clubhouse
17301 Beach Drive NE, Lake Forest Park
Take Bothell Way NE (State Route 522) to NE 170th, then to Beach Drive

The Civic Club is rooted in the earlier Women's Improvement Club "WIC," described by Barbara Bender in her book GROWING UP WITH LAKE FOREST PARK. In the late teens, this civic-minded group raised funds for a bathhouse, diving raft and picnic tables at the community beach. While men donated their labor, the women planted the silver maples that continue to provide shade.

During the Great Depression, the WIC took advantage of free Works Progress Administration labor to build an impressive clubhouse and the bridge across Lyon Creek. Using the $800 in the treasury as a down payment, members held chicken dinners, beach carnivals, and strawberry festivals to pay the remaining $2,000 debt. Park families joined in the 1936 celebration, when club president Estelle Lawson burned the mortgage.

The original clubhouse was destroyed by fire in the 1960s, but the Civic Club, composed of both women and men, soon erected another to take its place.

2. Wurdemann Mansion
17602 Bothell Way NE
Southwest corner of Bothell Way and 47th Avenue NE

In 1934 Audrey Wurdemann won the Pulitzer Prize in Poetry for her book BRIGHT AMBUSH. As a child she honed her writing skills with private tutors that her parents, Dr. Harry V. and May Audrey Wurdemann, brought to their lavish rural estate. In 1925 as a student at St. Nicholas School, she published her first book, HOUSE OF SILK. In the same year she was invited to join the Seattle branch of the prestigious National League of American Pen Women. She later married poet Joseph Auslander and moved to New York where league members elected her national president in 1939. Audrey Wurdemann's published works also include SEVEN SEAS, THE LEASE OF LUST, and POETRY BROADSIDES.

The mansion, which is listed on the National Register of Historic Places, was the Wurdemann home from 1914 to 1924, when the family moved to Seattle. Audrey is survived by her daughter Blossom who with her husband Arthur Morris is a long-term resident of Kenmore.

3. Virginia Smith's Family Home (Site)
17817 Wallingford Avenue N.
Her grandparents' home still stands at N 180th Street and Wallingford Avenue N
Go south on Bothell Way NE; turn right on NE 145th Street; go north on I-5 to the 175th Street exit; turn left, then right on Wallingford

In 1991 the University of Washington named Virginia Smith as Alumna Summa Laude Dignatus, the highest award that it can bestow on one of its graduates. Widely recognized for national leadership in higher education, she was president of Vassar College from 1977 to 1986 and was appointed the first director of the U.S. Department of Health Education and Welfare's Fund for the Improvement of Postsecondary Education.

In 1990 she stepped out of retirement to serve as interim president of Mills College. Yielding to fervent protests from students and alumni, the board had reversed its decision to admit male students as a means of bolstering flagging enrollments. Smith took over during the critical year when the alumni launched a major endowment drive to save the beleaguered school and preserve its traditional all-female student body. In a 1991 interview with COLUMNS: THE UNIVERSITY OF WASHINGTON ALUMNI MAGAZINE, she talked about the advantages of women's colleges:

> Anyone who has had any contact with women's education knows it's a different process. It would be great if, at some point, every woman could have some of this, sense the freedom of it.

Her parents fifth daughter, Virginia was born in 1923 shortly after her family, including maternal grandparents, moved from the Midwest to

Shoreline. Neither parent had completed high school and their father worked as a tool and die maker. According to Bessie Smith Francis, their mother and grandmother were in charge of almost everything in the predominantly female household. Unlike her older sisters, Virginia played football with neighborhood boys and was frequently caught with her nose in a book when she was supposed to be doing her chores.

During the Depression, Bessie had to forego her dream of going to the university to become a teacher. She married and made her home with her husband next door to her grandparents, where the closely-knit family took pride in Virginia's achievements. Bessie's two daughters graduated from the UW and charted education careers.

Virginia entered the University of Washington in 1941, working at a variety of jobs to pay for her education. She earned a BA in general studies in 1944, then went on for a law degree in 1946 and an MA in labor economics in 1950. Prior to becoming president of Vassar, she held academic and administrative posts at Seattle Pacific University, the University of Puget Sound and the University of California at Berkeley.

The Smith home was located at 17817 Wallingford Avenue N on property now occupied by four two-story homes. The grandparents lived next door in the house that still stands on the corner of Wallingford and N 180th Street. Today, Bessie is the only remaining member of her family in the neighborhood, where she lives with her husband on the property that her grandmother gave her.

4.   Ronald Bog Park
   N 175th Street and Meridian Avenue N
   Return to 175th Street; go west across Aurora Avenue N

When peat moss was mined from the bog, it grew into a small lake where the neighborhood children fished and explored the surrounding woods. One was Tora McCredy Baker who as a high school student entered the trenches of county politics to save the bog. Bordered by the new Freeway, it was imperiled by encroaching developers who were filling it in and applying for permits to convert the site to commercial use. Neighborhood and environmental groups voiced their protests.

A breakthrough came when Bob Barr, a reporter from the SEATTLE TIMES, rang Tora's doorbell and then wrote several articles to champion the cause. Since King County could only purchase larger sites for parks, it amended its regulations. Shoreline Community College and the Shoreline Public Schools pitched in to help restore the 15-acre wilderness tract, now a popular site for nature study, in the heart of this urbanized area.

5.   Shoreline Historical Museum/Ronald School
749 N 175th Street
Phone: 542-7111. Open Thursday-Sunday, 1-4 p.m.
Go west on N 175th Street

Stop by the Museum to explore a variety of interpretive exhibits that bring to light the area's heritage. Be sure to get a copy of the excellent brochure, "Shoreline Historic Sites Tour," which includes sites here indicated, as well as others with connections to local women. Founded in 1976, the Museum is housed in a Community Landmark, the historic Ronald School. The one-room schoolhouse that opened in 1906 was completed as it stands today in 1926.

Located next to the school was the original Richmond Highlands Recreation Center which doubled as a student cafeteria, gymnasium, auditorium and playfield. Built in 1918, the center was the brainchild of Anna Wright, a community activist who needled the county for a grant, then mustered her neighbors to raise funds for flowers, landscaping and picnic tables. In 1950 when the center moved to 16554 Fremont Avenue N, the Anna Wright Baseball Field was named in her honor.

6. Firland Tuberculosis Sanatorium (now Crista Ministries)

18303 Fremont Avenue N

Continue west on N 175th; turn right on Fremont Avenue N

In 1909 the newly organized Anti-Tuberculosis League of King County hired Bessie Davis, a visiting nurse who quickly convinced the commissioners that they faced a crisis. When the league set up tents on Queen Anne Hill for the city's first sanatorium, neighbors protested, including the broomstick brigade of irate ladies who met the ambulance wagons and turned them back.

Crawford Store, where Sadie Holloway (far left) served as postmistress. (Courtesy of Shoreline Historical Museum)

League president Horace Henry donated 34 acres of wilderness land north of the city where workers hastily erected several small cottages. In 1911 Firlands Sanatorium opened with Edna L. Robinson, RN as superintendent. So great was the need that she and her staff of one other registered nurse had to sleep on the floor of their office.

Henry contributed an additional $25,000 for the striking Tudor Revival style Administration Building, which along with several other buildings remains intact. In the late 1940s, King's Garden purchased the property and converted it into a private Christian K-12 school and senior center. The remaining TB patients were moved to the Naval Hospital in Seattle. (You may park your car and tour the grounds on foot.)

7. Holloway's Real Estate Office/Richmond Beach Post Office/Crawford Store
2411 NW 195th Place
Continue west on N 195th; turn left on 8th Avenue NW, then right on Richmond Beach Road, which becomes NW 195th

Transplanted Easterners, John and Sarah "Sadie" Holloway built their hotel on Main Street in 1889. While John worked at road building and in his real estate office next door, Sadie raised their five daughters and managed the hotel. She personally did the cooking and helped clean rooms for 50 to 60 regular boarders, along with other short-term guests. In her book SHORELINE OR STEAMERS, STUMPS AND STRAWBERRIES, LouAnn Bivens notes that Sadie enjoyed her dinner guests, especially on Sundays when she served her famous fried chicken. A "regular" from Seattle was Mr. Frederick of Frederick and Nelson Department Store.

When the Seattle Library donated 100 books to the community, Sadie set up a bookcase and for nine years served as librarian. She also took the post office into the hotel. In 1906 when she moved it next door into her husband's office, she continued as postmistress for three more years until her daughter Lena took her place. The old hotel burned down in 1924, but the post office building remains as Crawford Store, which is designated as a King County Landmark.

8. Helene Madison Pool
13401 Meridian Avenue N
*Return via Dayton Avenue N and N 175th Street to I-5. Go
south, then right from the 145th Street exit, then left on
Meridian Avenue N*

In 1932 Seattle held the biggest ticker tape parade in its history for
19-year-old Helene Madison. "Queen Helene," as the press dubbed
her, had returned home from the Los Angeles Olympic Games
sporting the three gold medals that she won for the United States.
Had there been more women's swimming events, most of her fans
agreed that she would have won them too.

Since the age of 15 when she made her debut in international
competitions, she had broken 117 United States and World Records.
She began swimming at age two in Seattle Park Department classes
at Green Lake, then learned competitive techniques from her coach
Ray Daughters at the Moore Hotel pool and at the Washington
Athletic Club.

Following her triumph at the Olympics and with no more records to
break, Madison turned professional. Two weeks after returning to
Seattle, she gave a performance for pay at the amusement park at
Bitter Lake. Lured by Hollywood, she then starred in a Mack Sennett
comedy, "The Human Fish," which turned into a box office flop.
Back in Seattle she bombed again in furtive efforts to make it as a
nightclub entertainer. In 1936 having lost her amateur standing, she
worked at a hot dog stand at Greenlake, while her former teammates
competed at the Berlin Olympics.

Her later years were filled with tragedy, including two marriages that
ended in divorce, indebtedness, and battles against diabetes and
cancer. In her final agonizing months, the SEATTLE POST
INTELLIGENCER, the Licensed Practical Nurses Association, and
many admirers came to her financial rescue. Her life ended in 1970 in

the basement apartment across from Green Lake that she shared with her Siamese cat and parakeet.

Today, Seattle has two Helene Madison pools, the one cited here near Ingraham High School, and the other at the Washington Athletic Club in downtown Seattle.

9. Nellie Goodhue School
Northend Administrative Annex
13720 Roosevelt Way NE
Go north on Meridian Avenue N, then left around the corner on Roosevelt Way N

Once called the Nellie Goodhue School, this building housed special education classes from 1954 to 1961. When the Seattle School District put it to different use, it was unimaginatively renamed the Northend Administrative Annex. Historically, the school is one of five that the district has named for women. The others commemorate Jane Addams, Sacajewea, Catherine Blaine, and Louisa Boren, none of whom were connected with local public schools. (Please see Louisa Boren Park in Chapter X and Catherine Blaine Junior High in Chapter VI.) Nellie Goodhue's name on the school kept her memory alive, but today she has faded into obscurity.

Goodhue's Child Study Laboratory was the forerunner of the Seattle Public Schools' guidance department and special education programs. Working in cooperation with the University of Washington, she and her staff interviewed and tested up to 4,000 pupils per year, studying each individual's problems and helping the child, his or her parents and teachers to understand each other.

Under Goodhue's tutelage, the school district's Cascade Special School developed individualized instruction programs. While children with severe limitations were still sent to Medical Lake, many others were able to remain in the public schools. For some the special classes treated reading disabilities or other handicaps, enabling the child to adjust to a normal classroom. Others who remained in the special school had an unprecedented opportunity to achieve their potential.

Nationally, Goodhue's work predated mental health care centers in the schools. On her retirement in 1929, the SEATTLE POST INTELLIGENCER quoted her as follows: "I can conceive of no greater thrill, no greater compensation for my years spent in teaching, then to know I have lightened the burdens of little children. Every child has been a new problem--a new individual with distinct needs and peculiarities and, because I have treated them just as I would grownups in trouble, there are men and women all over the United States who are now happy because I helped carry their burdens when they were children."

In the 1920s Nellie Goodhue deservedly received both national and local attention. Reinstatement of her name of the schoolhouse door would resurrect the memory of a pioneer educator who made a difference. Why not again rename the building the Nellie Goodhue Northend Administrative Annex?

10. Camp Fire Museum
9511 15th Avenue NE
Phone: 461-8550. Hours: weekdays by appointment
Go southward on Roosevelt Way NE, following the arterial; turn right on 15th Avenue NE

The Central Puget Sound Council of Camp Fire Boys and Girls has established a museum in its administrative headquarters. Included are interpretive exhibits of artifacts and photographs that showcase the organization's heritage and that trace its local origins back to the early teens. For further information please see: Chapter IV, Kirkland Congregational Church/Camp Fire Girls; and Chapter XI, Camp Sealth on Vashon Island.

11. Children's Home Society of Washington
3300 NE 65th Street
Go south on 15th Avenue NE, then left on NE 65th Street

The relatively new structure at the Seattle headquarters is a replacement of two stately three-story buildings with steep roofs and dormer windows, that old-timers regarded as neighborhood landmarks. Built respectively in 1906 and 1930, they doubled as the agency's administrative headquarters and an orphan home. The new building is better suited to the agency's revised mission of providing social services to troubled children and families.

The Children's Home Society of Washington traces its roots to the 1890s, when Libby Beach Brown canvassed the state to promote a then controversial alternative to institutional orphanages. Instead of regarding the orphanage as the child's new home, the society established temporary receiving homes, placing major emphasis on arranging suitable adoptions in families.

A trained social worker, Brown and her husband, the Rev. Harrison Brown, had been commissioned by national headquarters to found the statewide society. Due to financial pressures, he initially accepted a pastorate in Seattle while she carried forth their mission. In an unpublished memoir for the society, he later wrote, "Mrs. Brown was a fluent and interesting speaker and drew to the support of the society many people of intelligence and high standing in different parts of the state and her executive ability enabled her to organize and establish local advisory boards which became a network of activity covering the entire state....The contributions slowly increased and children multiplied in our hands."

Following Libby Brown's term, her husband and other men dominated the board of directors for decades. Women continued to serve as primary caregivers and caseworkers and as members of auxiliaries that have always been a mainstay of financial support. By the 1970s women were again assuming leadership roles. An outstanding example is Elizabeth Bannister who rose through the ranks to be selected as executive director in the late 1960s, a position that she held into the 1980s. (Please see Chapter I, Jeffs Home, now the society's South King County Center for further information.)

12. Children's Orthopedic Hospital
Children's Hospital and Medical Center
4800 Sandpoint Way NE
*Go south on 35th Avenue NE; turn right on NE 50th Street,
then right across Sandpoint Way into the parking area*

Please see Chapter VI, Children's Orthopedic Hospital/Queen Anne Manor for this institution's early history. By the late 1940s, the hospital on Queen Anne Hill was bursting at the seams with a postwar explosion of patients. Breakthroughs in medicine had given rise to several new departments that required space. COH was also beginning long and complicated negotiations that would eventually lead to its affiliation with the University of Washington Medical School.

Dorothy Stimson Bullitt, who was on the board and in the real estate business, chaired a committee that surveyed the city to select a building site. In Laurelhurst, one of the city's most desirable neighborhoods, she discovered the derelict Pacific Theological Seminary grounds that had stood vacant for 13 years. Bullitt entered quickly into negotiations, settling on a purchase price of $25,000 for the 25 acre site.

As president of the COH board, Frances Penrose Owen worked with another community leader, Paul Pigott, to steer a successful $3,500,000 campaign for the building fund. Owen recalls the tremendous outpour of community involvement that rendered the complicated move from Queen Anne cost free: "To move a hospital is not an easy job. The Far West Cab Company said they would transport all of the children and their nurses; the Teamsters Union offered to transport all of the equipment free." Volunteer workers gave up the previous weekend for a preliminary trial run, "so that they knew where all of the things were to go. We had every piece of equipment marked as to the floor and the location on the floor." Owen's conclusion is that "the City of Seattle has a heart!"

A recent name change to Children's Hospital and Medical Center reflects expanded objectives to treat all child ailments and to address all aspects of children's health care. Despite its growth and expansion, CHMC still gives the loving service that has always been its tradition. It remains a child-oriented facility with an all-female board of trustees and a supportive network of Orthopedic Guilds in communities throughout the Pacific Northwest. (Please see Chapter IX, Odessa Brown Clinic for further information.)

13. Sacred Heart Villa/Villa Academy
5001 NE 50th Street
Continue east on NE 50th

By 1910 there were more than 100,000 Catholics in the Seattle diocese, many from poor immigrant European families who had left their homelands in search of work and a better life. It was for the Italian contingent that the Reverend Mother Francesca Xaviera Cabrini, founder of the Missionary Sisters of the Sacred Heart, came to Seattle in 1903. Pope Leo XII had charged her with providing assistance to Italians who were pouring into the United States.

In the Italian working-class neighborhood on Beacon Hill, she established an orphanage and a church. When Seattle's regrading operations forced the sisters to abandon the site, she had to find a new facility. She spotted a summer vacation home, located on a spectacular 24-acre tract on Lake Washington, and persuaded its owner, Charles T. Connover, to sell it for a mere quarter of its appraised value. He also donated furniture and needed equipment, enabling the nuns and their orphans to move to their new home in Laurelhurst in 1918. To raise additional funds, pairs of nuns, including Mother Cabrini, walked for miles across rugged terrain in east King County, begging loggers and miners--many of whom were foreign born--for donations. Despite meager paychecks, they rarely refused.

The sisters constructed their main residential and school building in 1924, followed by the smaller St. Paul's Infant Home to the south which was completed in 1927. At age three, girls were moved from the Infant Home into the main building. Boys remained until they were seven years old when they were transferred to the Briscoe School in Kent. In the mid-1940s, the Sisters had 220 orphans in their care. After World War II changing philosophies that emphasized placements in foster homes gradually phased out this and most other orphan homes. In the early 1950s, the Sisters restructured their program, changing it to a private day school for education of Catholic youth in Seattle. (Please see Chapter X, Cabrini Hospital for further information.)

14. Thomas Burke Memorial Washington State Museum

University of Washington
Phone: 543-5590. Open Monday-Friday, 10:00 a.m.-5:30 p.m. and weekends, 9:00 a.m.-4:30 p.m. Free.
Go west on NE 45th Street; turn left on 17th Avenue NE into the campus. The museum is the first building on the right

The Thomas Burke Memorial Washington State Museum owes much of its heritage to women. On her death in 1925, Caroline McGilvra Burke left a substantial bequest to establish a monument to her late husband, Judge Thomas Burke. Her will directed that the funds be used for "...a building to advance the cause of a better mutual understanding between...the peoples of the Pacific shores." A pioneer member of Seattle's emerging establishment, she was a socialite, philanthropist, and world traveler, who had donated her own substantial collections--most notably northwest Native American artifacts--to the Washington State Museum.

That museum's precursor was the Society of Young Naturalists, founded in Seattle at the Territorial University in the 1880s. From the beginning women were involved, gleaning seashores and forests to gather specimens of insects, plants, etc. While such activity was popular at the time, the Young Naturalists pursued it with scientific zeal, carefully categorizing and preserving each new find. As the acquisitions grew, the museum expanded its focus so that under the long-term direction of anthropologist, Erna Gunther, it became a leading center for study of northwest Native American heritage.

When the aging building, located on the University of Washington campus, was condemned in the 1950s, the directors looked longingly at Caroline Burke's bequest. After considerable debate about expanding the museum's mission and changing its name, the state legislature yielded to financial considerations with the compromise moniker of "Thomas Burke Memorial Washington State Museum."

15.   McKee Hall, UW
Go east from NE 45th Street entrance on Stevens Way; turn left on Klickitat Lane

The southeast building of the venerable Hansee Hall women's dormitory complex is named for Ruth Karr McKee. Appointed to the University of Washington board of regents in 1917, she was elected president in 1923--the first woman at any major university to hold the position. McKee enjoyed strong support from the influential Washington State Federation of Women's Clubs, where she had gained valuable experience as a former president.

16.   Hutchinson Hall, UW
Return on Klickitat Lane to intersection at Stevens Way

In 1918 on her return from Red Cross duty in France, Mary Gross joined the University of Washington faculty to develop the women's physical education program. At the time there was a growing realization that physical education teachers needed a well-rounded education, including humanities, psychology, and health sciences.

Women's organizations throughout the state supported the program and lobbied for a new women's gym to replace make-shift facilities, then in use. When it was completed in 1927, the SEATTLE TIMES called the building a "monument to Miss Gross." She had collaborated closely with architect Carl Gould, paying attention to every detail, even the outer masonry that included bricks in hues of rose, blue and yellow.

In 1933 she married Arthur Hutchinson, a graduate of Yale Law School, then gave birth to a daughter at age 43. In her doctoral dissertation, A HISTORY OF WOMEN FACULTY AT THE UNIVERSITY OF WASHINGTON, Margaret Hall notes that Mary Hutchinson was one of few women faculty members to combine motherhood and career, and that she continued working until her death in 1947. As a lasting memorial, the university named the women's gym Hutchinson Hall. It was recently renovated as the new home of the School of Drama.

17.   McMahon Hall, UW
Continue southwest on Stevens Way; turn left at Whitman Court

Dedicated in 1963, this student dormitory is named for Edward and Theresa Schmid McMahon.   As a girl, Theresa Schmid rode horseback to the one-room country school on Mercer Island where she whetted her life-long appetite for education.   Since there was no local high school, she enrolled in the University of Washington's sub-freshman program in 1894 to earn her diploma, then went on for BA and MA degrees.   She married a fellow student, Ed McMahon and went with him to the University of Wisconsin where both completed PhDs--he in history and she in economics.   Recognizing her significance as one of the first women in the field, the university published her dissertation, WOMEN AND ECONOMIC EVOLUTION.

In 1911 both McMahons returned to Seattle to join the faculty at the University of Washington.   One of the first two women to rise to the rank of full professor, Theresa distinguished herself as a teacher, scholar and sought-after public speaker.   Despite the administration's objections, she was a social activist who lobbied for the eight-hour day, the minimum wage, and employer liability.

In 1937 at age 59, Theresa chose to retire and return to her girlhood home on Mercer Island, where she continued to write, propounding her belief that a time would come when sex-segregated work roles would be a thing of the past.

18. Women in Communications, Inc./Theta Sigma Phi Communications Building, UW
Return to Stevens Way; the building is past the intersection on your right

In April 1909, just before the opening of the Alaska-Yukon-Pacific Exposition, Georgina MacDougall (Davis) and her friend Helen Ross stayed up all night hatching plans to found an honorary society for women journalists. A few days later, the seven women in the newly instituted Department of Journalism appeared on campus wearing violet and green ribbons. They had adopted an official pin which was a reproduction of the matrix of the linotype machine and proclaimed themselves Alpha Chapter of Theta Sigma Phi. Junior and Senior women were invited to join if they demonstrated literary talent and if they intended to make journalism their life's work.

The seven founding members produced the first women's edition of the campus newspaper, the PACIFIC DAILY WAVE. They also began corresponding with other universities which were adding departments of journalism. The idea caught fire and within a short time, Alpha Chapter was issuing charters to new chapters across the nation.

At a later date the society changed its name to Women in Communications, Inc., emphasizing its revised objective to promote advancement of women in all fields of communication. According to Barbara Krohn, who recently retired as publisher of the UNIVERSITY OF WASHINGTON DAILY, WICI's greatest achievement was to establish women professionally in a field not traditionally regarded as "women's work."

19.   Raitt Hall/Department of Home Economics, UW
Walk east into the "Quad" to the northeast building

Look up at the cornices of this neo-Gothic building to see some of the university's most unique gargoyles. Designed by architect Carl Gould in 1916, they depict women performing a variety of domestic chores. The building is named for Effie Raitt who came to the university in 1912 to head the home economics department that at the time had only one other faculty member. While bringing scientific standards to the field, Raitt garnered staunch support from clubwomen throughout the state who lobbied the legislature for the new building. Under her leadership, the school grew and gained prestige. Thousands of former "co-eds" remember her saying, "Homemaking is the all important career for which we prepare our students."

Women's Building, University of Washington, during the Alaska-Yukon-Pacific Exposition.
(Courtesy of Special Collections Division, University of Washington Libraries, Neg. #1581)

In 1931 Raitt accepted President Herbert Hoover's appointment to chair a committee for the national conference of home building and ownership. In 1934 she was elected to a two-year term as president of the American Home Economics Association.

20. Cunningham Hall/Women's Information Center, UW

Phone: 685-1090
Continue on Stevens Way; the building is across from Architecture Hall

Every major American fair had its women's building and the Alaska-Yukon-Pacific Exposition (AYP) was no exception. As president of the Washington State Federation of Women's Clubs, Lena Erwin Allen presented a proposal to the State Fair Commissioners asking that the legislature fund a women's building which would celebrate women's accomplishments and which would later serve as a center for women students.

During the fair the two-story, wooden structure housed a student YWCA-sponsored restaurant that served 5¢ lunches, a nursery which cared for as many as 300 children a day, a juried exhibit of Washington women's arts, and a reception hall. Among the organizations that held conferences in conjunction with the AYP were the National American Woman Suffrage Association, the National Council of Women, and the Washington State Federation of Women's Clubs.

When the AYP closed in the fall of 1909, the building as planned became an activity center for campus women. It was home to the office of the dean of women, the campus Women's League, the Tolo Club (a senior honorary society which later affiliated with Mortar Board), the Sacajewea and Athena debating teams, Sororia Society for mature women students, and the student YWCA. Campus women lobbied for the letter "W" for women athletes in basketball, rowing, tennis, hockey, handball and baseball.

Women students, faculty and Seattle clubwomen came to the center which formed a bridge between the campus and the community. Student volunteers were recruited to work in hospitals and social service agencies. Campus and community women worked together to devise campaign strategies for suffrage, prohibition, and other women's issues.

Introduced to politics at the Woman's Building, a graduate student, Jeanette Rankin gave her first political speech at a suffrage rally in Ballard. On return to her native Montana, she was the first woman elected to Congress, where she had the distinction of being the only member to vote against America's entry into both World Wars.

In 1917 while Rankin cast her vote, the U.S. government commandeered the women's building to support the war effort. It was subsequently forgotten until the 1980s when women's organizations rediscovered it and pressured the university to restore it to its original purpose. Renamed Cunningham Hall, the building commemorates the pioneering artistic portrait photographer, Imogen Cunningham, who graduated from the UW in 1907 and who inspired generations with her work and spirit well into her nineties.

Today, Cunningham Hall houses the Women's Information Center which serves both campus and community women. It houses the Northwest Center for Research on Women, rotating juried exhibits by women artists, and a conference room for seminars, lectures and meetings. Once again, the Washington State Federation of Women's Clubs contributes its support, including books for the center's library. For further information, please see Karen J. Blair, "The Limits of Sisterhood: the Woman's Building in Seattle," FRONTIERS, VII, No. 1, 1984.

21. Henry Art Gallery, UW

Phone: 543-2280. Open Tuesday and Thursday, 11 a.m.-7 p.m.; Wednesday and Friday, 11 a.m.-8 p.m.; Saturday and Sunday, 11 a.m.-5 p.m.
Admission: $2

Continue on Stevens Way; if walking, turn right on George Washington Lane, if driving, turn right on NE 15th; the building is just past the pedestrian overpass

As you approach the building, you will see Loredo Taft's monumental statue of George Washington, a 1909 gift of the Rainier Chapter of the Daughters of the American Revolution. (Please see Chapter X, DAR, Rainier Chapter House for further information.)

Washington State's first public art gallery opened in 1927, the generous gift of Horace C. Henry who also contributed his art collection. While numerous women artists have held shows here and while others have contributed their support as board members and Friends of the Henry, one who deserves special mention is Zoe Dusanne.

With an eye for art, she began collecting in New York in the 1930s, then opened Seattle's first private fine arts gallery at 1303 Lakeview Place (now part of Interstate 5). From the start, she promoted works by local and visiting artists, helping several on their way to international recognition. The Seattle Art Museum honored her in 1978 with a special commemorative exhibit. On her death, arts patrons gave works to the Henry Gallery for the notable Zoe Dusanne memorial collection.

According to historian Esther Mumford, author of CALABASH, Dusanne's parents were black chiropodists, James and Letitia Graves. In 1915 she moved to Seattle with her young daughter Theodesia to live with them in their Beacon Hill home. Mumford says, "Because of her light skin, she was often mistaken for white, and apparently did not assert her racial origin."

22. Seattle Repertory Playhouse
4045 University Way NE
Go south on 15th Avenue NE, then west one block on NE 40th Street

In 1921 Florence Bean James and her husband Burton accepted Nellie Cornish's invitation to come to Seattle and teach drama at her new school. Within a short time the Jameses founded their own professional Seattle Repertory Playhouse, then in 1930 moved into the University District theater, designed for them by Arthur Loveless.

During the Great Depression when Florence became local director of the Works Progress Administration's (WPA) Federal Theater Project, she organized and directed Washington's first all-black acting company in Seattle. Sara Oliver Jackson, who starred in some of the Negro Repertory Theater's productions, considers it the best time she could have had as a young person. She recalls that some 50 black actors, employed by the company, were able to bring details of black culture into plays that attracted large multicultural audiences.

Florence James also created the WPA touring drama company that brought classic plays to high school students throughout the state. Supervised by the State Department of Education, the program received funding from the Rockefeller Foundation to become the first state theater in America. Scenery and costumes were transported by truck with a caravan of actors trailing in cars.

In rural communities, the troupe often played to standing-room-only audiences, made up of busloads of young people, transported by their school districts from miles around. In their first season, they performed before more than 70,000 students. After each show, the actors--still in their costumes--answered questions from the audience.

In the late 1930s as the Depression ebbed, both the Negro Theater and the young people's drama company lost their funding, but both left as their legacy a lasting impact on the region's cultural growth.

The Jameses continued to produce plays at the popular Seattle Repertory Playhouse until 1948 when they were called before the Legislative Fact-Finding Committee on Un-American Activities, headed by Albert Canwell of Spokane. Those subpoenaed were not allowed to call witnesses or defend themselves against charges that they were or had been Communists. Three professors were fired from the University. The Jameses were ejected from the hearings by armed guards when she tried to protest.

As public opinion turned against them, they had to close the Playhouse. Burton died shortly thereafter and Florence accepted a position with the Saskatchewan Arts Commission in Canada where she founded the acclaimed Globe Theater.

23. Sun Ning Chinese Tearoom
4207 14th Avenue NE--now University Way NE
Go north on University Way NE

In 1917 Dong Oy and her daughter Margaret "Maggie" Chin donned their native dress, bowed and smiled to customers, and served tea, homemade noodles, chop suey and traditional delicacies. Residents of Chinatown, they opened their Tearoom near the university where Maggie became the first female Chinese graduate.

Had Maggie been male, she would have inherited the fortune of her grandfather Chin Gee Hee, a pioneering Seattle Chinese labor contractor. On the family's return visit to China in 1905, he instructed his son to abandon Dong Oy and Maggie and find a new wife who could bear sons. The two women disguised themselves, pawned their jewelry and dodged Chin Gee Hee's spies for two months, until they could book passage to Seattle.

Dependent on her own resources, Dong Oy sewed and nursed for both Chinese and white families to attain her objective--a life of freedom and opportunity for her daughter. After her graduation with a degree in art, Maggie was the first Chinese woman to work at the prestigious Frederick and Nelson Department Store. Relinquishing any claim to Chin Gee Hee's substantial business holdings in Chinatown, Maggie and Dong Oy established themselves with many friends in both the Chinese and white communities. (Please see Chapter VII, Good Dip Building for related information).

24. University of Washington YWCA
4207 University Way NE (1970s)

In 1985 women students organized a campus YWCA which at first met for Bible study, facilitated by Ruth Chamberlain, chair of the English Department. Predating the university's first sorority by five years, it became the activity center for campus women. Its programs included women's employment services, English classes for immigrants, a loan fund for needy students, a lunchroom, and classes on topics such as leadership training, comparative religion and marriage. The association's first president was Ruth Karr McKee. (Please see McKee Hall, this chapter, #15).

Because of legal interpretations of the separation of church and state, the YWCA was evicted from the campus in 1926. In subsequent years, it has rented several different facilities in the University District, including Eagleson Hall which it shared with the YMCA from the 1940s to 1970. Unable to accept the YMCA's repeated proposals to merge into a Students' Christian Association, the YWCA moved into its own quarters up the stairway on the second floor of 4224 University Way NE.

During the 1970s, the association took its place at the forefront of feminist social services and advocacy. The Lesbian Resource Center, Seattle Rape Relief, and Aradia Women's Health Center (which provides supportive and accessible health care for all women, including safe, legal abortions) all began at the YWCA, then spun off as independent agencies. Today the University YWCA is housed at 4057 Roosevelt Way NE where it continues to provide a wide range of services and to advocate for social justice. In recent years it has worked to restore its erstwhile links with the campus.

25. Wilsonian Hotel (now Wilsonian Apartments)
Home of Mayor Bertha Knight Landes
4710 University Way NE

Bertha Knight Landes and her husband Henry Landes met in their student years at the University of Indiana. In 1895 they moved to Seattle where he was a professor of geology and later Dean of the College of Sciences at the University of Washington. A devoted wife and mother, she played leadership roles in some of the city's preeminent women's organizations, including the Women's University Club, the Women's Century Club, the League of Women Voters, and the Women's Auxiliary of University Congregational Church. In 1921, as president of the Seattle Federation of Women's Clubs, she orchestrated the week-long Women's Educational Exhibit for Washington Manufacturers. Staffed by more than 1000 clubwomen, it bolstered the spirits of the business community during a severe recessionary period.

Mrs. Landes made her decision to run for city council in 1922 with the staunch backing of her husband who said, "It's simply the natural enlargement of her sphere. Keeping house and raising a family are woman's logical tasks, and, in principle, there's no difference between running one home and a hundred thousand." In her article in the 1988 anthology, WOMEN IN PACIFIC NORTHWEST HISTORY, Doris Pieroth wrote, "Both Landeses saw her career as duty and service rather than an opportunity for fulfillment of her own ambition, and they both justified her political activities within the context of woman's proper place." To lighten her homemaking responsibilities, they moved from their family home to an apartment in the Wilsonian Hotel.

With her clubsisters managing her campaign, Bertha Landes won her election to the council by a landslide. As acting mayor, she attracted national attention when she fired the chief of police, a man who boasted publicly about corruption in his department. In 1926, running on a platform that stressed "municipal housekeeping," the 58-year-old Landes defeated incumbent, Edwin J. "Doc" Brown to become the first woman mayor of any major American city. She immediately set to work, calling on good citizens for help. She asked them to blow the whistle on suspected bootleggers and offered to pay $1 a year to those who pledged to report reckless drivers. She instructed the police force to see that regulations for dance halls and cabarets were enforced.

Although she had endorsements from Seattle's newspapers, the Central Labor Council, the Prohibition Party and women's organizations, she lost the 1928 election to Frank Edwards, a political unknown. Mrs. Landes attributed her defeat primarily to her opponent's lavish campaign budget and to "sex prejudice." Despite her widely acknowledged accomplishments, there was a popular sentiment that a city of stature should have a man at the helm. Ironically, Mayor Edwards was later recalled.

For Landes other leadership positions were in the offing. During the Great Depression she headed a job center for unemployed women; she was the first woman to serve as Moderator of Washington's Conference of Congregational and Christian Churches. A charter member of the Seattle Soroptimists in 1925, she was elected president of the national federation in the 1930s. She wrote extensively for national magazines, encouraging other women to get involved in politics which, she maintained, was their natural sphere.

26. Dr. Annie and Homer Russell Houses
5803 and 5727 8th Avenue NE
Go east on NE 50th Street; turn right on 11th Avenue NE; turn right on NE Ravenna Boulevard, then left on 8th Avenue NE

In 1904 Dr. Annie Russell commissioned F. A. Sexton to design these picturesque neighboring homes for herself and her son Homer. The two Craftsman-style chalets feature fireplace chimneys made of rounded river rock. Logs with knots left unplaned form porch posts and extend, crisscrossed from the corners, effectively blending the houses into their verdured landscapes.

Following her conscience, the pioneer woman doctor--one of only a handful in the city--provided safe, aseptic abortions. She found herself embrangled in a controversy that had surfaced in the Pacific Northwest as early as 1903 when Dr. Ernest Crutcher of Great Falls, Montana labeled abortion "the crowning sin of civilization." In 1915 a jury that included several female members handed down a verdict of guilty, convicting Dr. Russell as an abortionist. Her license to practice medicine was subsequently revoked.

27. Good Shepherd Home
Sunnyside and N 50th Street
Go south on 8th Avenue NE; turn right on N 50th, then left on Sunnyside into the parking lot

Contrary to popular lore, this imposing Italianate building on the walled, 11-acre site was not a home for unwed mothers. The myth may have evolved because of the walls that hide the grounds from public view. In an era when pregnant women did their best to conceal their condition and when middle-class ladies worried about prostitutes luring their husbands away, homes for unwed mothers typically kept inmates out of site.

Shortly after the turn of the century, the Sisters of the Good Shepherd built their home to care for orphans and troubled girls who were wards of the county court. Many of the girls came from what are now termed "dysfunctional" families; others had married in their early teens and were escaping from abusive husbands. To welcome and reassure a new girl, the Sisters placed her in the "guest room" for her first few nights. A SEATTLE TIMES reporter described it as "as pretty a room as you'd find in any nice home, all done in soft pink and rose shades." The room was decorated with "pictures of beautiful girls, happy families, young matrons and sweet-faced brides," suggesting new possibilities in the girl's future.

In his June 24, 1990 feature in THE SEATTLE TIMES, historian Paul Dorpat further described the girls' treatment. Once a girl began to gain confidence, she moved into the daily life of the home, which had its own accredited high school with a strong emphasis on arts education. In addition to studying classical ballet and music, the girls had their own orchestra and chorus--all of which contributed to their ability to express themselves and think creatively. Vocational programs in home economics prepared them to be wage earners as well as wives and mothers. In their free time, they could stroll through the beautifully landscaped grounds, or play volleyball or tennis on private courts. Inside they enjoyed ballroom dancing and listening to their favorite radio programs.

To support their home, the Sisters entered into a contract with the railroads to do laundry for passenger trains and with the Roman Catholic Archdiocese to prepare 50,000 sacramental hosts per week to be used in Sunday masses. Their labor force was the girls, each of whom was required to work three hours a day. Another important emphasis was recreation.

For her masters thesis from the University of Washington in 1957, Sister Mary, who worked in the home, did a follow-up study on 189 former residents. Only 15 had returned to delinquency; 117 were married and had families; after five years, 64% still kept in touch with the school and several maintained their ties as volunteers.

In the 1970s as social mores grew less restrictive, enrollment dropped, forcing the Sisters' decision to close the home. Now managed by Historic Seattle Preservation and Development Authority as a multipurpose community center, the site is listed on the Seattle and National Registers of Historic Places. Two of the current occupants are the Seattle Chapter of the National Organization for Women and the Pacific Northwest Needle Arts Guild.

28.   Lincoln High School
Interlake Avenue N and N 45th Street
Go south on Sunnyside; turn right on N 45th Street, then left on Interlake Avenue N

In 1973 when Roberta Byrd Barr became principal of Lincoln High School, she made history as the first woman and the first Black to hold the post in the Seattle Public Schools. By then she was well-known, as the moderator of "Face to Face," an acclaimed local TV discussion program where guests explored all sides of social and political issues. The program aired first on KING and from 1965 to 1973 on KCTS. While serving as vice principal of Franklin High

School, Barr emerged as a courageous and persuasive voice for civil rights and for the push for school desegregation, organizing parent and teacher groups to deal with racial tension. Because of shrinking enrollments, the school district closed Lincoln High School in 1981, at which time Barr retired to care for her ailing husband and mother.

29. Mother Ryther Home
4416 Stone Way N
Go one block west on N 44th Street

Ollie Ryther made a significant impact on Seattle's "orphan problem," as indicated in her 1934 obituary. "Thousands of men and women, who as children knew Mother Ryther as their only mother, will be grief stricken. Childhood has lost a real friend." THE KITSAP COUNTY HERALD article estimated that she and her staff had cared for more than 3,100 children during her 51 years of service.

The Rythers headed West from Iowa in 1881 and settled in a cabin on the outskirts of Seattle. When a neighbor died two years later, Ollie Ryther adopted the four children and from that time on continued to take in any orphaned child that came her way. Eventually she incorporated with a board of directors and staff of matrons to assist her. Mother Ryther Home sent all of its children to public schools, expecting the boys to learn a trade by age 16. After one year of high school, girls were sent to a business college so that they too could earn a living.

Mother Ryther had a talent for making do, even if her methods sometimes shocked a more orthodox business community and frustrated members of her board. With help from Emma Ray (Please see Chapter X, African-Methodist-Episcopal Church) and others, she worked the waterfront and the "red light" district, looking for orphans as well as donations. According to a June 16, 1946 article in THE SEATTLE TIMES, she kept no records or reports. When the rent was due or supplies ran low, she appealed to friends, neighbors and local businesses for help. Once when 25 of her charges needed shoes, she marched them into a shoe store and announced to the proprietor:

"These children are staying here until you fit them all with shoes--that'll be your contribution to the Ryther Home."

By 1920 the people of Seattle had come to appreciate Mother Ryther for her self sacrifice and devotion to children whom she had cared for in a series of rental homes. They build the large brick home for her and her "family" at 4416 Stone Way in Wallingford, where she remained until her death at age 85. In 1937 community women organized a network of Ryther Four and Twenty Clubs to raise funds to support the home and make mortgage payments.

In 1954 as traditional orphan homes fell out of vogue, the Ryther Child Center changed its name and moved to its ten-acre campus at NE 95th Street and 23rd Avenue NE where its revised mission is to care for moderately to severely disturbed children. The former orphan home on Stone Way is now operated by United Cerebral Palsy as a residential and program center.

30.   Trinity Methodist Church
6512 23rd Avenue NW
Go west on N 45th Street and follow the arterial which becomes N Market Street; turn right on 15th Avenue NW; left on NW 65th Street; and right on 23rd NW

As the first woman ordained by the Methodist Church, Gertrude Apel began her ministry in a Model T Ford, driving the snowy back roads of Montana and later through wheat fields in eastern Washington where she served isolated rural parishes. Her circuit riding days helped nurture a strong commitment to ecumenism (promoting Christian unity and cooperation), a movement that was locally in its infancy when she assumed the duties of associate pastor at Trinity Methodist Church in Seattle's Ballard district.

When it was organized in the 1930s, the Rev. Apel became first executive director of the Washington North Idaho Council of Churches and Christian Education. She facilitated sometimes impassioned discussions on issues such as censorship of movies and books, or national rearmament versus pacifism. During her tenure, the Council gained stature and stability, making endorsements and voicing opinions on public issues, When people of Japanese descent were interned during World War II, the Council spoke up on their behalf. It later protested the government's failure to grant amnesty to conscientious objectors and endorsed fluoridation of Seattle's water.

Apel was feted by Women in Communications, Inc. at the Matrix Table in Seattle and by the board of the National Council of Churches. After 29 years as head of the Washington North Idaho Council, she retired, whereupon the organization split into today's Greater Seattle Council of Churches and the Washington Association of Churches.

On parade with American and Swedish flags.
(Courtesy of the Everett Public Library)

31. Nordic Heritage Museum
3014 NW 67th Street

Phone: 789-5707. Open Tuesday-Saturday, 10 a.m.-4 p.m.;
Thursday, 10 a.m.-9 p.m.; Sunday, noon-4 p.m.
Admission: $2.50 adults; $1.50 seniors; children 6-16 $1;
under 6 free
*Go west on NW 65th Street; turn right on 30th Avenue NW
and left on NW 67th to the parking lot*

Founded in 1979, the Nordic Heritage Museum is located in the old
Webster Elementary School building in the heart of Ballard, a
community that was settled predominantly by Scandinavian
immigrants. Under the direction of Marianne Forsblad, the museum
has always taken an inclusive approach to history, treating men's and
women's legacies as equally valuable. Its primary purpose is to
document, preserve and interpret the heritage of Nordic people and
their descendants who made their home in the Pacific Northwest.

The unforgettable Dream of America exhibit and its sequel the
Promise of the Northwest are permanent installations that accompany
emigrants from their homeland, across the Atlantic ocean, through
Ellis Island and onto the new shore. Their struggles and conquests in
an often heartless land are poignantly documented, as they work their
way westward to their new home. On the museum's top floor,
Finnish, Norwegian, Swedish, Danish, and Icelandic groups each have
a room of their own with exhibits that interpret their heritage in the
Pacific Northwest. Other exhibits feature Estonians, Latvians and
Lithuanians. (Please see Chapter I, Danish Hall, Enumclaw, for
further information about Scandinavian women who came to the
Northwest) The museum hosts numerous events for the public
including traditional festivals, dinners featuring Scandinavian cuisine,
lectures and Scandinavian language classes.

32. Sunset Hill Park
34th Avenue NW near NW 75th Street
Go north on 30th Avenue NW; turn left on NW 75th Street

On this spectacular viewpoint overlooking the Shilshole Bay Marina,
the Halibut Fishermen's Wives' Association erected a 11,900 lb.

commemorative stone monument to honor fishermen lost at sea in September 1959. The inscription reads: "Dedicated to the men of the sea fishing fleet who reaped their living from the sea and found their final resting place beneath its waves."

The mini-park with its diminutive rose garden has benches and picnic tables. If possible, plan an evening picnic to view a breath-taking sunset with the craggy Olympic Mountains providing a dramatic backdrop.

33.   Ballard Public Library
2026 NW Market Street
Return via 30th Avenue NW to NW Market Street and turn left

Located in the Ballard Historic District across from the Firehouse, the classic Carnegie Library was built in 1904, three years before the city of Ballard's annexation to Seattle. The library traces its beginnings to the Dewey Women's Christian Temperance Union which in 1890 raised funds through basket socials and fairs to finance a free reading room on Ballard Avenue. (Please see Chapter I, the Auburn Public Library for a description of the WCTU's mission and its connection with the founding of public libraries.)

The library was a great source of pride to the community which matched the Carnegie Foundation's $15,000 building grant with the requisite donated site in the heart of town and maintenance costs. In addition to reading materials, the library included a spacious community service center on its main floor and a large auditorium on the upper floor that for many years functioned as a performance and meeting hall.

By 1910 librarians were already complaining about cramped quarters, attesting to the success of school and community clubs that raised funds to contribute new books. After several abortive attempts, voters finally passed a bond issue in 1962 to fund a new library building at 5711 24th Avenue NW. The former Carnegie Library is now an antique store with law offices on the upper floor.

QUEEN ANNE AREA

NORTH SEATTLE

PUGET SOUND

GREEN LAKE

BALLARD

④

LOCKS

I-5

DISCOVERY PARK

GOVERNMENT

GILMAN AVE W.

BALLARD BRIDGE

③

②

SHIP CANAL

44

EMERSON

⑥

34 AVE W.

THORNDYKE W.

15 AVE W.

①

⑨

⑩

⑪

⑫

QUEEN ANNE AVE

AURORA AVE

AURORA BRIDGE

LAKE UNION

⑬

⑭

MAGNOLIA BLVD

⑤

W. GARFIELD

⑦

⑧

ELLIOTT BAY

⑲

ELLIOTT AVE W.

MERCER ST

SEATTLE CENTER

W. DENNY WY

20-23

N

15-18

ALASKA WAY

DOWNTOWN SEATTLE

VI. ON AND AROUND QUEEN ANNE HILL

Magnolia to Eastlake to Bell Town

One of the most varied tours in this guidebook begins nautically on the south side of the ship canal, introducing you to women in the Northwest's marine and fishing businesses. Continue west along the canal to Discovery Park, formerly Fort Lawton. Hikers can enjoy a vast network of trails through grassy meadows and wooded ravines to salt-water beaches. Designated sites in the park are the home of the Northwest's first Filipina and Daybreak Star Indian Cultural Center, located at one of Seattle's most spell-binding viewpoints.

Your scenic route continues onto Queen Anne Hill passing the homes of affluent, middle-class women who founded and supported some of the region's most enduring institutions. Two that are located on the hill are the former Children's Orthopedic Hospital building and Seattle Children's Home.

At the bottom of the hill near the south end of Lake Union you will see King Broadcasting Corporation, a media empire that was founded and developed by Dorothy Stimson Bullitt. From there continue on to the east side of the lake for a visit to magnificent St. Spiridon's Russian Orthodox Church, where immigrant women have preserved and shared their cultural traditions.

Retrace your route via Denny Way to Seattle Center, then park your car for visits to the Pacific Science Center, the Seattle Opera House and the Phelps Center for the Pacific Northwest Ballet. These three jewels in Seattle's crown owe much of their sparkle to the talented and creative women noted in this guide.

From Seattle Center, go west on Denny Way to Myrtle Edwards Park, a one-and-a-half-mile stretch along the shore of Elliott Bay, complete with jogging trail and spectacular views. Your tour concludes in Bell

Town, located between Seattle Center and downtown, with designated sites where women have made significant contributions in the arts and in business.

1. Seattle Pacific College (now University)
3rd Avenue W and W Nickerson Street
South of the Ship Canal between the Fremont and Ballard Bridges

The beautiful Weter Memorial Library is named for Dr. Winnifred Weter's father, a prominent Seattle attorney who left a substantial bequest for the new building on the campus where his daughter chaired the Department of Classics. After graduating from Garfield High School, Winnifred earned university degrees in Eugene, Oregon and in Chicago, then returned to Seattle in the depths of the Depression when universities across the nation were tightening their belts. At her mother's suggestion, she applied at Seattle Pacific College (SPC) whose student body numbered only 300. In 1934 the school hired her to teach Greek and Latin and also head the women's physical education program--a temporary assignment that she held for the next 13 years. For 40 years, her courses in Latin and in classical and modern Greek were in demand.

Dr. Weter's extra-curricular activities included memberships in Prospect Congregational Church, the Audubon Society, the Women's International League for Peace and Freedom, and the American Association of University Women. As members of AAUW, she and her mother--who joined in 1905, a year after the Seattle chapter was chartered--worked to raise scholarship funds for women and to promote the status of women students and faculty in higher education. (Please see Chapter VII, Women's University Club for further information about AAUW.)

On her retirement in 1975, SPC established the Winnifred Weter Faculty Lectureship. Each year, the endowment fund gives selected faculty members paid time off plus an honorarium to prepare a public lecture, relating their field to Christian philosophy.

2.   Foss Maritime Company
660 W Ewing Street
Go north to W Ewing, then west

The headquarters of one of the Northwest's largest vessel and container operations provides services linking Alaska and Puget Sound. Foss Launch and Tug, which began in Tacoma and expanded its services to Seattle in the teens, owes its beginnings to a Norwegian immigrant named Thea Christiansen Foss.

In 1890 Andrew and Thea Foss and their three sons moved into a one-room floating home on the shore of Tacoma's Commencement Bay. A construction worker, Andrew was away when Thea purchased a rowboat for $5 from a disgruntled fisherman, sold it for $15, then bought two more which she cleaned up and painted green and white. Since boating was a popular form of recreation, she began renting her skiffs for 50¢ a day, saying, "People like to know they can hire boats right here at the float....No matter at what time of day or night they come, I am always ready." As the company grew, "Always Ready," like the green and white, became its indelible trademark.

When Andrew returned home, he found that Thea had made more money in two weeks than he had in two months. Thereupon he switched to building rowboats. An innately astute businesswoman, Thea recognized the needs of freighters in the bay and of logging firms that then relied on costly railroads to transport logs. The Fosses began to build bigger, more powerful boats to launch their successful tugboat operations.

Combining her business and domestic roles, Thea took the work crews into their home. As many as 30 men slept in the dormitory room upstairs and joined the family for meals that she prepared herself. A deeply religious woman and a generous benefactor of the Norwegian Church, she was also a founding member of the local chapter of the Daughters of Norway. The older Fosses eventually passed their multi-million dollar family business on to their sons, one of whom headed operations in Seattle.

Although Thea was nothing like the feisty heroine of Norman Reilly Raine's "Tugboat Annie," a reporter linked the two, creating a confusion of mixed identities that still exists. Raine had invented his story while in Seattle. When Metro-Goldwyn-Mayer's movie version premiered at the Fifth Avenue Theater in 1933, audiences took "Annie" to their hearts, as starring actress Marie Dressler piloted her tug about the familiar waters of Puget Sound. Heralding the premiere, ships and tugs sounded their whistles at noon; thousands of balloons rose from the waterfront accompanied by blank-loaded cannon blasts; and as the star-studded throng emerged from the theater, fireworks lit up the sky. It would have been a fitting tribute to Thea Foss.

3. **Seattle Fishermen's Memorial**
    Fisherman's Terminal
    Salmon Bay
    West of Ballard Bridge on the south side of the Ship Canal

In 1985 twelve women active in the fishing industry formed the Seattle Fishermen's Memorial Committee. They raised $100,000 to erect a monument, engraved with names of men and women of the Seattle fishing fleet who lost their lives at sea. The memorial, created by Seattle sculptor Ron Petty, is the centerpiece of the newly renovated Fisherman's Terminal. Topped by a bronze fisherman bringing in a catch, the 28-foot stone pillar rises from a cast bronze bas-relief depicting 32 different forms of marine life.

A prime mover on the committee was Katherine "Tink" Mosness, a member of a fishing family who has been around boats all of her life. The editors of WINDS OF CHANGE: WOMEN IN NORTHWEST COMMERCIAL FISHING interviewed Tink regarding her research of records dating back to the turn of the century. She said, "The immense job of compiling names to be memorialized has given us a deep appreciation of the immense size of the industry and the interlocking nature of families and the feeling of community among members of this industry." A political activist for the commercial fishing industry, Tink is active in the Women's Fisheries Network which began locally in 1983 as a resource for anyone interested in meeting other women working in the industry. It is currently located at 2442 NW Market Street, Room 199 (742-2810).

Although often unrecognized, women have always been part of the Pacific Northwest's fishing industry. Native American women dried and stored fish to feed their people in the winter months. In commercial fishing industries, women have worked in processing plants since the 1880s and have also provided shoreside support for family businesses. In the 1970s, they began making inroads into jobs that were previously restricted to men. In small but growing numbers, women now own and operate their own vessels. Today they are engaged in all phases of the industry from skippering to owning their own seafood businesses, and they have been accepted as equals by Northwest fishermen.

Fisherman's Terminal is home to one of the world's largest fleets of halibut and salmon trollers. Its wharves teem with all kinds of working boats, net drying areas, and chandleries that sell mariners' supplies. Restaurants cater to people in the fishing business and visitors alike, and you can purchase the daily catch at the Wild Salmon fish market.

4. Discovery Park

Phone: 386-4236; Open daily from dawn to dusk
Daybreak Star Indian Cultural Center--Phone: 285-4425;
Open Wednesday to Sunday, 10 a.m.-5 p.m.
Go west on Commodore Way along the Ship Canal into the park, then follow signs to Daybreak Star

The former military base with breathtaking vistas of the Olympic Mountains and Puget Sound encompasses 400 acres of beaches, open meadows, ravines and woodlands--a welcome escape from the bustling city. You may want to plan a picnic or a hike, since much of the park is accessible only by trail.

Your first stop is at Daybreak Star Indian Cultural Center which displays Indian art and which frequently hosts Native American gatherings and cultural events. In 1970 when the Defense Department declared Fort Lawton surplus, the United Indians of All Tribes Foundation, a Washington State non-profit organization with both male and female leadership, held a successful sit-in demonstration at the site, winning a 99-year renewable lease.

Follow signs to the Main Gate and Visitors Center at W Government Way and 36th W, where maps and guided tours are available. One of the few remaining houses on historic Officers' Row is a wood-frame duplex that was home to the state's first Filipina, Rufina Clemente Jenkins. She married a black U.S. Army sergeant, Francis Jenkins, who was stationed in the Philippines during the Spanish American War. In 1909 she and their five children immigrated to the United States to join him at Fort Lawton. In his book FILIPINOS: FORGOTTEN ASIAN AMERICANS, Fred Cordova quotes their daughter, Francisca Jenkins Robinson, who recalled a happy childhood at the fort: "We lived there two years....below the hill, they had what they call non-com, non-commissioned officers....There were duplexes. We lived in the first one...."

Like Rufina, many other women called Fort Lawton home. Some volunteered to serve as nurses and in communications. In 1942 when Congress opened up the military to women, making them eligible for rank, pay, and benefits, members of the Women's Army Corps (WACs) joined the fort's population. Throughout the fort's history, officers wives formed social, cultural and service clubs. And during wartime, community volunteers provided services through the Red Cross, the Minute Women, and the United Service Organization (USO).

Before leaving the park, follow the road to the West Point Lighthouse, where Lynn Larson's Anthropological/Archeological Services have excavated sites revealing centuries of Native American heritage. Here as in other King County archeology projects, women have played major roles.

Daughters of U.S. War Veterans drill team, named for officers from Fort Lawton who lost their lives in the Philippines in the Spanish-American War. 1930s. (Courtesy of the Everett Public Library)

5. Lady Willie Forbus House (a private residence)
2580 Magnolia Boulevard W
Go south then west around the park; turn south on Magnolia Boulevard W

From 1924 until shortly before her death in 1993 at age 100, Lady Willie Forbus mowed her own lawn and enjoyed gardening. The picture is a sharp contrast to much of her life. Born in rural Mississippi, she was named after her father, a plantation supervisor, and in the southern tradition was christened Lady Willie. She had to struggle to get an education, putting herself through the University of Mississippi and then the University of Michigan Law School. As the only female in her graduating class, the dean gave her a stinging send-off that she never forget: "Goodbye, Lady Willie. You will make a good stenographer for some lawyer someday." She moved to Seattle in 1918, passed the state bar exam, and became one of the city's pioneering female lawyers. A staunch advocate for equal rights, she resisted the term "woman lawyer," maintaining that there was no reason for women to set themselves apart. As a sole practitioner, she defended her clients' personal rights and won the respect of her male colleagues.

In the 1930s she made two unsuccessful bids for King County Superior Count Judge. Politically, her breakthrough came during World War II, an era when women had to take over men's jobs and when some of the age-old barriers began to erode. In 1942 she won her election to the state Senate where she served until 1946, chairing the Judiciary committee.

A divorced mother who single-handedly raised two daughters, Lady Willie was actively involved in community affairs. She served as president of the Magnolia Community Club, the Financial District Women's Business Club, and the Florence Crittenton Home for Unwed Mothers, and on the boards of Friends of Discovery Park and the American Civil Liberties Union of Washington. She continued to practice law on a limited basis until 1991.

6. Catherine Blaine Junior High School
2550 34th Avenue W
Continue south; turn left on Montevista, then left on W McGraw, then left on 34th Avenue W

Prior to marrying the Reverend David Blaine and venturing West, Catherine Paine attended the nation's first women's rights convention, held in 1848 at Seneca Falls, New York. Her signature appears with those of Elizabeth Cady Stanton, Lucretia Mott, Frederick Douglass and others on the Declaration of the Rights of Sentiment, the document that launched more than a century of struggle.

While her husband pastored Seattle's first church, Catherine opened the city's first school in the spring of 1854. It was housed in Bachelor's Hall on what is now First Avenue between Columbia and Cherry Streets. Parents paid tuition costs for thirteen girls and one boy who attended school five days a week, from Tuesday through Saturday. Sunday was the Lord's day and as every good woman knew, Monday was washday. following the Indian War of 1855-56, the Blaines were transferred to Oregon and the school closed.

When their junior high school opened in 1952, the students honored Catherine Blaine by publishing a weekly newspaper appropriately called "The Pioneer." They also began their annual "Pioneer Day" celebration, where students and faculty dress in period costumes, performing skits and plays throughout the day and entertaining parents in a gala evening pageant.

7.   Betty Bowen/Marshall Viewpoint
7th Avenue W and W Highland Drive
Go north on 34th Avenue W, then east on W Barrett Street, veering north on 30th Avenue W, then east following the arterial which turns south to W McGraw; Go east to 7th Avenue W, then south

This spectacular vista overlooking Magnolia bluff and Puget Sound is appropriately named for one of Seattle's foremost patrons of the arts and historic preservation. Born in Kent and a graduate of the University of Washington, Betty Bowen began her career as a reporter for the SEATTLE TIMES, then worked as Assistant Director of the Seattle Art Museum under founding Director Richard Fuller until his retirement in 1973.

Often called "the mother of the city's arts," she was an original member of the Seattle Arts Commission and a founder of the Pacific Northwest Arts and Crafts Center. She also served on the city's first Allied Arts Historic Conservation Committee and was a prime mover in the successful crusade to preserve the historic Pike Place Market. A member of the Audubon Society, she joined in campaigns for bird sanctuaries and other programs to conserve the region's natural environment. Two days before her death in 1977 at age 58, Mayor Wes Uhlman named her Seattle's First Citizen and proclaimed Valentine's Day in her honor.

8. Kerry Viewpoint
W Highland Drive and 2nd Avenue W
Go east on W Highland Drive

This beautiful viewpoint was donated to the city by Albert S. and Katherine Glen Kerry who made their home in the nearby mansion at 421 W Highland Drive. While he made his fortune in lumber, his wife and daughter left lasting legacies of service to the community.

Katherine Glen Kerry was a composer and a leader in Seattle's musical circles. In the 1920s when financial pressures almost forced Nellie Cornish to close her school and move to Los Angeles, a group of well-to-do women founded the Seattle Music and Arts Foundation with Katherine, as first president. It raised funds to assist the school, along with other struggling cultural activities in the city. Later in the 1950s, the foundation assumed ownership of Cornish Institute and put it on an even financial keel.

The Kerry's daughter Olive shared her mother's artistic interests, participating as an actress in amateur theater. In 1929 Olive was elected first president of Seattle Visiting Nurses, now a part of the Seattle/King County Department of Health. Once called the most untiring worker in the city, she also served on the boards of the Washington State Society for Mental Health, Children's Orthopedic Hospital, Cornish School, the Sunset Club, and Ruth School for Girls.

9. Seattle Children's Home
10th Avenue W and W McGraw Street
Continue east on W Highland Drive; turn north on Queen

Impoverished families, especially abandoned mothers and their children, were victims of neglect in pioneer Seattle. In the spring of 1884, a group of the city's leading ladies--among them Sarah Yesler, Babette Gatzert, Caroline Sanderson, and Mary Leary--organized a Ladies' Relief Society with the object of "aiding and assisting the poor and destitute, regardless of creed, nationality, or color." At first board members opened their own homes to provide immediate and temporary assistance to indigent people.

In 1885 the trustees narrowed their focus and determined to build a home especially for orphans. They successfully persuaded county commissioners to allocate $15 per month for each child and raised $3,600 in donations for "The Orphan Home." The box-like structure which initially housed 30 children was erected on a site donated by David and Louisa Boren Denny at what is now Seattle Center's Fun Forest. Meals were simple but nutritious with meat supplied once a day and pies and cakes "utterly forbidden."

Businesses and private citizens alike made generous donations including cash, property, supplies and recreational outings for the children. Drs. C. A. Smith and Caspar Sharples contributed free medical care. The society expended nothing for salaries with board and committee members volunteering their services. In the words of one writer, "No grass grew under the high-laced boots of these women." By the early 1890s the home was accepting abandoned mothers with their children and was also doing general relief work, providing groceries, clothing and room rent to Seattle's most needy.

Relief funds left over from Seattle's great fire of 1889 were eventually allocated to the Ladies' Relief Society so that it could expand its facilities and build the Seattle Children's Home on the 29-lot site atop Queen Anne Hill. Today the stately pillared building that was designed by Elizabeth Ayer has been replaced by a complex of newer structures, tailored to the agency's revised mission. Through the years the century-old orphanage has evolved into Washington State's first comprehensive mental health center for psychiatrically impaired children. It has the distinction of being the city's oldest existing charity.

10. Children's Orthopedic Hospital now Queen Anne Manor
100 Crockett Street
Go east on W McGraw; turn south on 1st Avenue N, then east on Crockett

Seattle's turn-of-the-century hospitals had no special facilities for children and generally placed child patients in wards with adults. the state maintained services for blind, deaf and mentally ill children, but offered nothing for those with other afflictions. Recognizing this need and having lost a child of her own, Anna Herr Clise consulted with children's hospitals back East, then called together 23 of her affluent women friends each of whom contributed $20 to establish a similar facility in Seattle.

Beginning with a temporary seven-bed ward at Seattle General Hospital, the all-female board handled administrative and financial matters, but left medical treatment to professional staff. One of the first children to be admitted was four-year-old Julia B. who suffered from tuberculosis of the hips. Eight months later, she was able to walk again. There was indeed hope for children suffering from such maladies as osteomyelitis, tuberculosis and emaciation, if sufficient rest and treatment were provided.

In its first year, the board was approached by black women from the Dorcas Society who asked if they would admit a 14-year-old black girl with tuberculosis of the knee. Members voted to establish the lasting policy of accepting any child, regardless of race, religion, or parents' ability to pay with the poor given first preference. To recruit young patients and make their services known, they walked the streets, looking for malnourished and crippled children, then urging their parents to send them to the hospital.

The energy and spirit of Anna Clise and her friends quickly spread into the community. A men's advisory committee, composed of business and community leaders, was organized to support the board. Women throughout the city formed Orthopedic Guilds which held effective and imaginative fund-raising functions: at pound parties guests brought a pound of food for the hospital; Kirmess, a carnival with extravagant stage shows by board and guild members, became a major community social event; and on "Hospital Sunday" guild members collected contributions made by area churches.

In 1908 the association financed and built a 12-bed cottage at Warren and Crockett designed by trustee Maude Parsons, a former architectural student, and Bess Wilson. Three years later, the 54-bed hospital was built next door at 100 Crockett. Children could recuperate in a cheerful environment with doctors, nurses, and volunteers working together to make them more comfortable. To accommodate young patients who frequently stayed for several months or even years, the Seattle School District supplied a teacher.

Due to long-term recovery periods, nursing was a vital component of the children's treatment and COH was particularly responsive to the advancement of the nursing profession. On recommendations from the medical staff, the board appointed Lillian Carter, a health care professional, as Superintendent of the Hospital. She was instrumental in establishing a pioneer student nursing program and a visiting nurses' service for convalescent children.

In the 1950s the then-crowded hospital moved to new facilities in Laurelhurst. (Please see Chapter V, Children's Orthopedic Hospital.) The old building has been converted into Queen Anne Manor, a retirement home.

*Orthopedic Guild members on fund-raising campaign.
(Courtesy of Children's Orthopedic Hospital and Medical
Center Records, University of Washington Libraries)*

11.   Anna Louise Strong House (a private residence)
508 N Garfield Street
Go south on Queen Anne Avenue N, then left on N Garfield

In her mid-20s with a PhD in philosophy, Anna Louise Strong worked for the United States Education Office as an advocate for child welfare. She organized an exhibit which she toured extensively throughout the United States and abroad, bringing it to Seattle in May 1914, where it attracted more then 6,000 people per day.

An avowed socialist, she recognized Seattle as one of the most politically liberal communities in the nation and came to live with her father, the Rev. Sydney Strong, progressive pastor of Queen Anne

Congregational Church. When she ran for the Seattle School Board in 1916, she won easily, thanks to her reputation as an expert on child welfare. As the only female member, she maintained that the public schools should offer social service programs to ameliorate inequities for underprivileged children and that they should also serve as community centers.

Her endorsement of controversial liberal causes set her apart from her colleagues, most of whom were business and professional men. A pacifist, she spoke out against the draft and against American involvement in the war in Europe. While the PTA and women's clubs joined her in opposing military training in the schools, she was branded unpatriotic by Seattle Minute Men, many of whom were veterans of the Spanish-American War. As a reporter for the UNION RECORD, she covered the bloody conflict between the International Workers of the World (Wobblies) and armed guards, hired by Everett mill owners to keep them out. At first an impartial observer, she soon became an articulate spokesperson for workers' rights.

The pacifist stance of the IWW led to mass arrests at the Seattle office where Louise Olivereau, a typist, was mailing mimeographed circulars to draftees, urging them to consider becoming conscientious objectors. In 1918 at her trial for sedition, Strong stood by her side. When Olivereau was found guilty and sent to prison, Strong's fellow school board members jumped on the bandwagon to launch a recall campaign which she lost by a narrow margin.

Making an appearance at the next meeting, she appealed for a woman to be appointed as her successor. Although her former colleagues acceded to her request, they made it clear that they wanted a more mainstream representative. In the words of one speaker quoted in the board minutes, "the woman should be a mother, and preferably one with children in the schools, whose patriotism is absolutely unquestioned." The board subsequently appointed Evangeline C. Harper, a prominent clubwomen.

Strong became more openly associated with the liberal press, writing forceful pro-labor articles and promoting the new Soviet government. In 1919 when union workers organized the Seattle General Strike, she proclaimed in her famous editorial for the UNION RECORD: "We are undertaking the most tremendous move ever made by LABOR in this country, a move which will lead--NO ONE KNOWS WHERE!" After four days the strike that shut down the city ended as it began-- peacefully and with its goals still undefined. Disillusioned, Strong became a correspondent in the Soviet Union and later in China for radical American newspapers. She made periodic visits to Seattle where she was always in demand as a lecturer.

12. Ida Culver House
1004 Queen Anne Avenue N
Go south on Queen Anne Avenue N

In his book GOOD SCHOOLS, historian Bryce Nelson notes that between 1900 and 1911, only a small percentage of Seattle teachers were products of local high schools and colleges. About two-thirds came from the Midwest and one-sixth were from the East Coast. The board instructed Superintendent Frank Cooper to hire only the best candidates with "high personal character, liberal education, and strong bodily health."

The school district's high standards attracted an exceptional pool of applicants. Although salaries were equal to better than those in other areas, hours were long and evening preparation for classes was a requirement. Married women could not teach, since it was thought that divided priorities between professional and domestic responsibilities would weaken their commitment to the job.

An exemplary elementary schoolteacher was Ida Culver, a graduate of Iowa State Teachers College who taught in the Midwest before coming to Seattle in 1910. Her local career spanned 23 years at John B. Allen School and two years at Hawthorne School where she was serving at the time of her death. To improve herself professionally, she continued her education during the summers, taking courses at several prestigious American universities.

In addition to her classroom responsibilities, Culver was active in the Seattle Teachers Association, the Seattle Grade Teachers Club, Business and Professional Women, and American Association of University Women. Unlike most other dedicated teachers, her name is remembered as a charter member of the Seattle Educational Auxiliary, a group of women teachers that purchased their residence and convalescent home at 1004 Queen Anne Avenue. She bequeathed much of her estate to the SEA whose major purpose was to purchase additional homes where teachers could live and retire. In 1949 the Retired Teachers Association opened the 43-unit Ida Culver House in Ravenna, which it later enlarged with new additions. The expansive new Ida Culver House and Nursing Care Center in Broadview is managed by the University of Washington School of Nursing.

13. KING Broadcasting Corporation
333 Dexter Avenue North
Go south on Queen Anne Avenue; turn left on N Mercer Street, then right on Dexter Avenue N

In 1932 at age 40, Dorothy Stimson Bullitt's traditional lifestyle took a dramatic turn with the deaths of her husband, father, and only brother. A widow with three children, she was suddenly the head of one of Seattle's most prominent families. In the centennial biographical portrait, WASHINGTONIANS, John S. Robinson wrote:

> Mrs. Bullitt entered a man's world at a time when women were neither present nor welcome. Needless to say, wolves waited in the offing; the new widow no doubt appeared easy prey. "I didn't know the difference between a lease and a permit to go swimming," (she said). "I didn't even have a lawyer. Can you imagine?"

In the depths of the Great Depression, she found a lawyer and went to work, personally shepherding the family's floundering downtown properties back to financial health. She had a B.A. in music from

Julliard. Years later when she reflected on her education, she said that women in her circle "learned music, singing and how to prune roses." While entering the male-dominated world of business and politics, she maintained her life-long commitment to the arts and remained actively involved in organizations such as the Seattle Junior League and Children's Orthopedic Hospital.

In 1947 Mrs. Bullitt embarked on a new venture when she purchased a failing radio station and negotiated a swap for the call letters KING, thus matching her station with the name of King County. From the start her programming emphasized classical music, a gift to the listening public that continues today as "Classic" KING-FM.

In 1949 she made what many considered an extremely risky move, purchasing Seattle's only television station for the price of $375,000. There were only 6,000 television sets in the city and her station for a time was the only one north of San Francisco and west of Minneapolis. She renamed it KING-TV and quickly affiliated with the National Broadcasting Company. In her application to the Federal Communications Commission, she promised to provide at least 100 minutes per week of public service announcements. Almost immediately, television sets began cropping up in homes all over the city. Within a few years, her company acquired stations in Portland, Spokane and Boise and later in Honolulu and San Francisco. At the same time Mrs. Bullitt heavily underwrote the local education/non-profit station KCTS, Channel 9.

As president of KING, she set high standards for regional television, giving her staff the support and editorial license to deal with controversial topics. She had a firm policy against selling air time to religious organizations, but donated such time, most notably to her own St. Mark's Cathedral for the Christmas Eve midnight service and the weekly Sunday evening service.

In 1961 Dorothy Bullitt stepped down as president, replaced by her son, Stimson. She continued to chair the board until 1977 when her daughter Priscilla "Patsy" Collins took her place. Her other daughter

Harriet Bullitt also served on the board. Until 1989 a few weeks before her death at age 97, Mrs. Bullitt came to her office four days out of five, continuing to exert a strong influence on the company.

Sharp, witty, and involved in the Pacific Northwest that she loved and nurtured, she enjoyed canoe adventures on Puget Sound, white river rafting, and outings in the Cascade Mountains until well into her nineties. Following their mothers' death, Harriet and Patsy, KING's major shareholders and both in their sixties, launched their own new venture. They sold the corporation so that they could pledge the proceeds to preservation and rebirth of the Northwest environment. They carefully screened prospective buyers to ensure preservation of their mother's commitment to community service and they retained ever-popular "Classic" KING FM Radio. It was a move that their mother had approved. (Please see Chapter X, Stimson/Green Mansion for further information.)

14.   St. Spiridon Cathedral Russian Orthodox Church
400 Yale Avenue N
Go east on Mercer to Yale Avenue N

In the early twentieth century, White Russians fled from the Bolsheviks, often taking with them little more than their clothes, their faith and their memories. In Seattle newly-arrived immigrants joined St. Spiridon Cathedral, the state's first Russian Orthodox parish. Founded in 1892, it moved into its magnificent, onion-towered cathedral in the 1930s.

Female members helped preserve age-old religious rites and symbols. In the 1930s, they revived and shared their colorful tradition of children's theater. Maria Rychkoff served as director, while Galena Gorohoff designed and painted the elaborate stage sets. Other women pitched in to sew children's costumes which typically included a fanciful headgear. Performances were staged at St. Spiridon's, the Masonic Temple and the Women's Century Club.

15.   Pacific Science Center

200 2nd Avenue N
Seattle Center
Phone: 443-2001. Open 10 a.m.-5 p.m. daily in the winter
and 10 a.m.-6 p.m. in the summer. Admission: $5 adults 15-
64; $4 children 5-14 and seniors; $3 children 3-5.
*Go south on Yale to Denny Way, then west to Seattle Center;
park and follow signs to the next four sites. A second option
is to drive around the Center's periphery to the street
addresses*

The architecturally stunning Pacific Science Center was originally the
federally-funded Science Pavilion which opened in 1962 as a
cornerstone of Century 21, Seattle's World's Fair. Its purpose was to
make science understandable and appealing to the general public. A
member of the advisory committee was Margaret Mead, curator of
anthropology at the American Museum of Natural History and the
nation's most famous anthropologist.

The other female member was Dixy Lee Ray, Associate Professor of
Marine Biology at the University of Washington, where from 1945
until the 1960s she was one of only three women faculty members in
the departments of mathematics and sciences. The daughter of
working-class parents, she graduated from Stadium High School in
Tacoma, won a scholarship to Mills College, then worked as a
teacher, lab assistant and janitor to put herself through Stanford
University.

In 1963 two years after the fair, Ray accepted the position of director
of the Science Center, which was in desperate need of funding and
strong leadership. She is widely credited with its survival. In an
interview with Jennifer James-Wilson and Brenda Owings-Klimek,
authors of MAKING A DIFFERENCE: A CENTENNIAL
CELEBRATION OF WASHINGTON WOMEN, she described her
approach to her new job:

I began to realize that the way we teach science is just

calculated to kill that interest in most kids except those that have a natural bent for it and are able to do well. By the time people reach their adult life, the tendency is to think, 'Well, I know science is important but it's beyond me.'...There ought to be a place where ordinary human beings who chose to do other kinds of things could come and find out things they always wanted to know in a setting that they could get their questions answered.

Over the protestations of some members of the scientific community who objected to the idea of popularizing science, Ray produced fascinating exhibits ranging from the Moon landing to earthquakes that engaged visitors of all ages. In the early days of public television, she invited KCTS, Channel 9 to the Center where she gave lessons on seashore life before the cameras. She later broadened her focus, calling the weekly program "Doorways to Science." The popular series was produced for National Education Television and ran for several years.

After nine years at the Science Center, Ray resigned in 1972 to accept President Richard M. Nixon's appointment to the Atomic Energy Commission, which she later chaired. When the AEC was absorbed into the State Department, President Gerald Ford appointed her Assistant Secretary for the Bureau of Oceans, International Environmental and Scientific Affairs. After a brief six months, she resigned and permanently burnt her bridges, stating publicly that it was impossible to get things done under Secretary of State Henry Kissinger unless you were a member of his little "palace guard."

As Washington State's first woman governor from 1977 to 1981, she raised the hackles of many who had voted for her, when she abolished the State Women's Commission and took unpopular stands on environmental issues, such as minimizing the risk of oil spills in Puget Sound and the dangers of nuclear waste. As her longtime friend Lou Guzzo explained, she was a scientist who did not compromise what she thought to be the truth and was unwilling to play political ball. Warm, witty and loved by her admirers for her candor, her nemesis was media people for whom she named the pigs on her Fox Island farm. On the plus side, her administration balanced the budget and ushered in the state's full funding of basic education.

Until her death in January 1994, she continued to write, lecture and enjoy a new hobby of woodcarving. She was the recipient of numerous awards including 21 honorary doctoral degrees and the Peace Medal of the United Nations (1973).

Mayor Bertha Knight Landes breaks ground for the Civic Auditorium, now the Seattle Opera House. (Courtesy of Special Collections Div., University of Washington Libraries, Neg. #343)

16. Seattle Opera House/Seattle Symphony
321 Mercer Street, Seattle Center

In 1928 Mayor Bertha Knight Landes broke ground for Seattle's Civic Auditorium which 34 years later underwent extensive renovation to become the Seattle Opera House. The original structure housed conventions, fairs, basketball games, and concerts. It also became the part-time home of the Seattle Symphony, the legacy of a coterie of determined women.

A prime mover was Harriet Overton Stimson who in 1903 planned a program and recruited a conductor from New York, then pulled together an orchestra of local male musicians for the 1903 premier concert in the Arcade Building. Stimson's daughter, Dorothy Bullitt later related an anecdote about the event. Determined that things would be proper, her mother and other ladies raided their husbands' closets to borrow formal attire for the musicians. On opening night, several of Seattle's prominent men sat in the audience in rented tuxedos, looking at their own coats and tails on the stage.

As publicity spread, the infant symphony attracted increasingly larger crowds. In 1907 Stimson and other music-minded women incorporated as the Seattle Symphony Orchestra Society. As it gained prestige drawing packed houses to performances, the SSOS changed to an all-male board with only the program committee remaining in women's hands. The symphony floundered during World War I, but revitalized with a successful fund-raising drive in the late teens, only to collapse under increasing financial pressures in late 1920.

Stepping in to fill the void was Madame Mary Devenport Engberg. Born in a covered wagon near Spokane, she had gone to Denmark as a young woman to study music. A violin virtuoso and composer, she is said to have been the first woman in the world to conduct a symphony, having made her debut with the Bellingham orchestra in 1914. In Seattle she conducted the new Civic Symphony of 90 musicians, along with an amateur orchestra of gifted students. At a time when most orchestras were restricted to men, she offered equal opportunity to women. The skeptical critic who reviewed her first concert at the Metropolitan Theater noted "a surprisingly high level of excellence." Following the orchestra's last performance in late 1923, Mme. Engberg took up the baton of the new Seattle Civic Opera.

In 1926 Stimson, Katherine Glen Kerry and others renewed their efforts, this time recruiting the dynamic Karl Krueger who was conducting in Europe, to revitalize the Seattle Symphony. He was reportedly amazed at the quality of local musicians, many of whom had been Cornish students and/or members of Mme. Engberg's orchestras. A budding impresario, Cecelia Augsburg Schultz took charge of ticket sales. Musical enthusiasm burgeoned with the symphony's move into the new Civic Auditorium where in 1928, it played to a record audience of 6,500.

With Schultz as its manager, the Symphony met the Great Depression head on, hiring a new conductor for a scaled-down orchestra that continued to draw unprecedented audiences to the auditorium. In addition to her position with the Symphony, Schultz entered into contract with the Moore Theater. She booked Sergei Rachmaninoff, Chaliapin, Lawrence Tibbett and other world-class artists to perform with the symphony, then give a recital at the Moore. Reportedly the first woman symphony manager in the United States, she made her mark. In his book SEATTLE 1921-1940, historian Richard C. Berner says, "It is doubtful that the Symphony would have been sustained..., if Cecelia Schultz had not been bringing artists, opera and dancing groups to the city, and drawing upon the symphony to provide the necessary accompaniment."

Despite large audiences, the drafty Civic Auditorium had its drawbacks, most notably poor acoustics. The canvas sheeting under the folding chairs did little to muffle the noise of scuffling feet. After playing there the great violinist Jascha Heifetz told conductor Milton Katims, "I'll never come back to Seattle to play if I have to play in that damn barn." As the Seattle World's Fair dawned, Schultz--by then popularly known as "Mrs. Music"--took a lead in the successful campaign to renovate the old auditorium and convert it into the contemporary Seattle Opera House. She contributed the three elegant chandeliers that grace the lobby, along with furnished practice rooms. The building's Cecelia Augsburg Schultz Music Room and Cecelia Schultz Library were later named in her honor.

As today's Seattle Symphony strives for a home of its own, it continues to rehearse and perform before enthusiastic audiences in the acoustically sound Opera House. Some of its staunchest supporters are the Women's Symphony Association and the younger Women's Symphony League.

17.   Pacific Northwest Ballet--Phelps Center
301 Mercer Street, Seattle Center
Phone: 441-9411.   Call to schedule a tour and watch rehearsals.

As passers-by look up into the windows of newly renovated Phelps Center, they see ballet dancers practicing for performances, staged next door at the Opera House. The former Exhibition Hall, built for the 1962 World's Fair, has been transformed into Pacific Northwest Ballet's long-awaited permanent home, with space for the ballet school (400 children and 500 adults), rehearsal studios for the 45 professional dancers and orchestra, and extensive costume and set design departments. PNB owes much of its success to its school director, Francia Russell, who doubles as the company's co-artistic director--a position that she shares with her husband, Kent Stowell.

Russell is one of only a handful of women to serve as artistic director of a ballet company. Most are men who, like Stowell, are choreographers. As a dance student in the legendary George Balanchine's school, Russell caught the master's eye and began her professional career as a soloist with the New York City Ballet. When she later taught in the school, she learned Balanchine's teaching techniques. Within a short time he promoted her to ballet mistress, then made her one of the first ballet masters to produce his works with other companies throughout the world.

That Balanchine ballets have become a mainstay of PNB's repertoire is no surprise. Along with Russell, company pianist Dianne Chilgren was chosen by Balanchine to play for the New York City Ballet and later, the Zurich Ballet where she learned his musical intentions first hand. In addition to playing the complex scores for rehearsals,

Chilgren is known to PNB audiences as a vistuoso piano soloist.

As co-directors of the Frankfurt Ballet, then PNB, Russell and Stowell have expanded their repertoire beyond Balanchine to include a wide range of choreography and music. Best known of the ballets choreographed by Stowell is Tchaikovsky's NUTCRACKER with captivating set designs by Maurice Sendak. Since its debut in 1983, it has become a popular movie and a Christmas tradition for Northwest audiences who pack the house for a holiday season of 40 performances.

While PNB has had several beautiful dancers, one deserves particular mention historically. Deborah Hadley came to the company at age 27--five years after retiring from professional dance and by then with two children in tow. She credits "the excitement of dancing" for motivating her to get back into shape. With Hadley as Odette/Odile, the company gained its first national acclaim for its production of SWAN LAKE in the early 1980s. Following performances with PNB in Taiwan, Honolulu, New York, and the Kennedy Center in Washington D.C., she appeared on the cover of DANCE magazine. Hadley retired from PNB in 1991 and is once again redirecting her energy and experience, as founding director of the Washington Academy for the Performing Arts in Redmond. Other principal ballerinas who have graced PNB's stage in the early 1990s include Colleen Neary, Patricia Barker, Sylvie Guillaumin, Lucinda Hughey, Louise Nadeau, and Julie Tobiason.

PNB's new home at Seattle Center is named the Phelps Center in honor of Patricia Phelps, who died in 1990, and her husband Sheffield, both founding members of the board. Two years earlier Francia Russell wrote: "Patty bears credit for what we are today, and what we are in the future. The exuberance of the ballet and of the dancers performing in it are offered as a fitting tribute to the boundless energy and unfailing devotion of Sheffield and Patty, without whom there would be no Pacific Northwest Ballet."

18.   Women in Trades Fair
Center House and Flag Pavilion, Seattle Center

Each year on the third weekend of May, the throng gets larger, as women in the skilled trades convene to celebrate and share their stories with each other and the public. Beginning in 1979, the fair was conceived to create greater public awareness and support of women in nontraditional careers. In addition to programs that explore job-related issues, it features hundreds of booths and displays.

The Women in Trades Fair traces its roots to the early 1970s when the federal government established Region X, headquartered in Seattle. Lazelle Johnson, an Afro-American woman, was appointed regional director of the Department of Labor's Women's Bureau. Her initial challenge was educational, trying to change deeply entrenched attitudes about women's limitations and what they were capable of doing. Known for her poise and composure, she readily admits that it was often difficult.

At a time when women were excluded from many apprenticeship and journeyman programs, she pulled together a committee interested in expanding their access to lucrative skilled trades. Included were representatives from the Seattle Office for Women's Rights, the King County Women's Program, women's programs at area community colleges and vocational-technical institutes (all of which were founded in the early 1970s), and the YWCA.

While planning the first fair, the committee also worked with Renton Vocational Technical Institute (now Renton Technical College) to establish the Apprenticeship and Nontraditional Employment for Women (ANEW) program. Since its inception in 1980, the pathbreaking program has enrolled more than 1,000 women in its Job Skills for Trade and Industry program.

The Women's Bureau provided seed money for both the fair and ANEW with additional support coming from Employment Security and the Bureau of Apprenticeship and Training. On her retirement in

1992, Johnson reflected on changes she had witnessed, saying, "In Seattle we're spoiled with women in so many non-traditional jobs." (Please see Chapter VII, Seattle City Light for related information.)

19.   Myrtle Edwards Park
On the waterfront north of Pier 70
Go west on Denny Way

Joggers, beachcombers, picnickers, and sunbathers can escape the bustle of downtown within minutes. Awaiting them is an expansive park that offers intimate connections with the marine life on Elliot Bay and stunning views of water, ships and the distant Olympic Mountains.

The nautical park is appropriately named in memory of one of Seattle's leading citizens. Myrtle Edwards accepted her appointment to the city council in 1955 and was elected the following year. She continued to serve until 1969 when her peers chose her as president. In August of that year, a stunned city mourned her death, caused by an automobile accident.

The park's intriguing sculpture "Adjacent, Against, Upon" was given to the city by the Virginia Wright Fund, established by her father in her honor. One of the Northwest's and the nation's foremost collectors of contemporary art, Virginia Wright personally manages the fund which has generously contributed additional artworks to the city.

20.   Olive, Virginia and Lenora Streets
Go east on Denny Way, then south on Fifth Avenue, which intersects the three streets, located between Seattle Center and the downtown business district

While many of Seattle's streets bear the names of prominent men, only a few are named for women. These three were named for some of the youngest members of the Denny Party that came ashore on Alki Beach in 1851. Olive and Virginia were the daughters of William and Sarah Ann Bell who staked their claim in this part of Seattle, known as Bell

Town. Lenora was the daughter of Arthur and Mary Ann Boren Denny. (Please see Chapter XI, Birth of Seattle Monument for further information.)

21. Dimitrious Jazz Alley
Sixth Avenue and Lenora Street
Turn left on Lenora

On return engagements at the club, jazz great Ernestine Anderson continues to dazzle local audiences, including fans who have been with her from the start. Her family moved to Seattle during World War II where she became part of the flourishing after-hours jazz scene on Jackson Street, described by Paul de Barros in his recent book, JACKSON STREET AFTER HOURS.

After 1956 when the former Black Musicians Union merged with Musicians Local 76, jazz moved into venues throughout the city with ensembles, audiences and clubs becoming racially integrated. Anderson won the hearts of Seattle jazz fans, then rose to international fame. If you visit Jazz Alley, look for her portrait by Dean Williams in the club's permanent exhibit. She is also one of the subjects of I DREAM A WORLD: PORTRAITS OF BLACK WOMEN WHO CHANGED AMERICA, a stunning book by Oregon photographer Brian Lauker.

22. The Westin Hotel
Fifth Avenue and Stewart Street
Go southwest to Stewart

Gretchen Mather's three decades in the restaurant business have been trailblazers. In 1992 she became first female president of Washington State's 63-year-old Restaurant Association which with 2,400 members is the largest in America. Armed with a degree in hotel and restaurant administration from Washington State University, Mather began her career as an administrative dietician for Stouffer Foods in New York. In 1966 Western International Hotels (now Westin) made her its first female executive at Seattle's new Washington Plaza. In 1979 she opened her first Gretchen's of Course restaurant in the Pike Street Market which quickly expanded into a successful catering business. She recently joined forces with Schwartz Brothers Restaurants and is an operating partner of Seattle's Gretchen's of Schwartz.

When Gretchen started her career, women were usually relegated to the ranks of waitresses and kitchen helpers. In the 1990s Washington women hold more than half of the owner, management and chef positions in an industry that has 7,000 food and beverage establishments and that employs 160,000 people.

23. Moore Theater
1932 Second Avenue
Go west on Stewart

When real estate developer James A. Moore opened his opulent theater in 1907, it became one of the Ladies' Musical Club's favorite halls for the annual four-concert Musical Artists Series. Guest artists extolled the Moore for its outstanding acoustics, domed ceiling and lavish mosaics. For 40 years, Rose Morgenstern Gottstein, the club's concert manager, made her annual trip to New York City where, with a purse of at least $20,000, she negotiated with agents to bring some of the world's foremost musical talents to Seattle. Local audiences flocked to performances by luminaries such as Fritz Kreisler, John McCormack, Madame Ernestine Schumann-Heink, Alma Gluck, Jascha Heifitz, and Marian Anderson.

In addition to sponsoring guest artists, the Seattle LMC, which was founded in 1981, established another tradition--presenting concerts by members, all of whom were required to pass a club audition to join. While inviting a high percentage of women to perform in its Guest Artist Series, the Seattle LMC also supported the professional aspirations of its members. Madame Mary Davenport Engberg (described under Seattle Opera House/Seattle Symphony) was a member of the Bellingham and Seattle LMC's which promoted her as a conductor, violin virtuoso and composer. Another member of the Seattle club was Mary Carr Moore, the first American woman to compose and conduct a grand opera. Her NARCISSA dramatized the Whitman massacre. Soloists came from New York's Metropolitan Opera Company with a support cast of 70 local singers, including several of Moore's clubsisters. The gala premiere, held in 1912 at the Moore Theater (James Moore was not related to the composer), received high critical acclaim in the local press.

In 1935 Cecelia Augsburg Schultz became the only woman impresario west of Chicago when she leased the Moore Theater, hoping to make it known as the "Home of Music." for the next 14 years she staged morning musicales, matinees, evening concerts and ballets at the Moore, now registered as a City of Seattle Landmark. (Please see this chapter, Seattle Opera House/Seattle Symphony for further details.)

DOWNTOWN SEATTLE

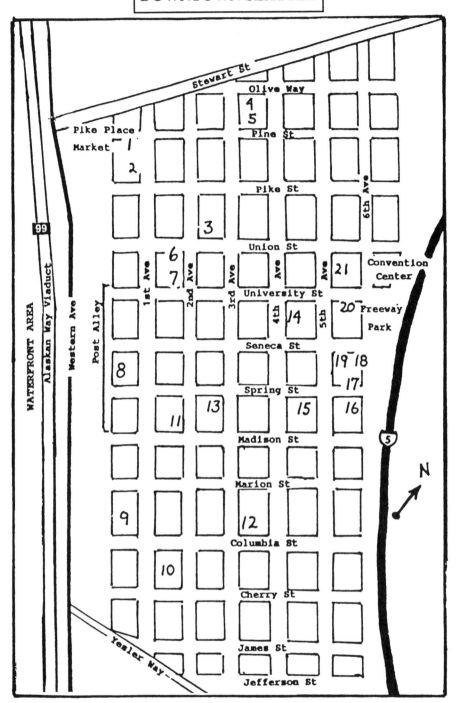

VII. DOWNTOWN SEATTLE

To get the most out of this tour, wear comfortable shoes and plan to walk. If you get tired, you can board any Metro bus and ride for free in the downtown area. Your first destination is the historic Pike Place Market, the oldest continuously active farmers' market in the United States. Thanks to preservationists and citizen support, the Market was spared from developers who in the 1970s hatched plans to demolish it. Stop by the Information Booth on the corner of Pike Place and First Avenue for a map, then proceed through sumptuous displays of fresh produce and seafood. Built on pilings against the bluff overlooking Elliott Bay, the Market includes several stories of arts and crafts booths, a variety of shops, restaurants and take-out food stands, social service centers, and great views.

Your next sites in the downtown business district underscore women's historic influence on the city's economic, cultural, social and political life. Today's business district has spread east into the four-block area that since the late 19th century has constituted one of the city's major centers of women's enterprise. Included are the Seattle Public Library, bronze plaques commemorating the site of Seattle's First Providence Hospital, the elegant Women's University Club, the eight-story flagship headquarters of the Seattle/King County YWCA, the site of the Salvation Army's Evangeline Home, and Plymouth Congregational Church. These sites brought women of diverse backgrounds together in sometimes tenuous alliances, where they consolidated their power to meet the needs of women and children and to improve the quality of life in the city. Several of the buildings are living landmarks, where contemporary generations of women perpetuate the legacies of their forebears.

1.   Pike Place Market
First Avenue and Pike Street and Vicinity

The Pike Place Market, one of Seattle's most cherished institutions, was born in 1907 to accommodate small truck farmers from outlying farmsteads (who wanted to sell their produce for more than the price-gouging middlemen would pay) and also "housewives" (who were tired of paying exorbitant prices to the merchants). Despite the efforts of merchants to block the market, it was an overwhelming success from the beginning. While women were in the majority as consumers, they also had a strong presence as retailers.

When the market was just three months old, 120 farm families were making the sometimes difficult trek to Seattle to sell their produce. Almost 80% of the stalls were operated by Japanese with Italians as the second major ethnic group. In the mid-1920s when a new law restricted Japanese immigration, Italians gained the upper hand with several families remaining for generations.

In his LITTLE HISTORY OF THE PIKE PLACE MARKET, Jack Evans tells the story of Angelina Genzale, a market personality who for almost 50 years sold produce and flowers raised on the family farm in Sunnydale near what is now Sea-Tac. After working for eight years to purchase ten acres, Frank "Cheech" Genzale returned to southern Italy in 1929 for his wife and their son Tony.

Even before she spoke English, Angelina sold home-grown vegetables at the market. With the exception of Sunday afternoons, a time for family and friends, the Genzales planted, harvested, cleaned and crated their vegetables. Mornings began at four o'clock, when they left for the market to get one of the best stalls. Later, Angelina grew flowers and herbs to add to the inventory. During her 50 years at the market, she enlisted the help of her son and grandsons. Today, her grandson Frank Genzale, who began working with Angelina at age five, his wife Sue, and their four children live on his grandparents' farm, where the family continues to grow vegetables and flowers with everyone pitching in at Frank's Quality Produce in the Corner Market Building.

Evans also writes about Millie Padua, today's Market Master who comes to work at 5:00 a.m. each day to assign some 200 table spaces to farmers, artists and craftspeople and to give permits to street musicians. She does her best to maintain market traditions, giving priority spots on the basis of seniority, and deciding which newcomers to accommodate. In 1948 Millie and her husband Andy, an immigrant from the Philippines, purchased a farm near Kent, then began selling vegetables at the market where she faithfully staffed their stall. Thirty years later when Andy was killed in an accident, Executive Director George Rolfe offered Millie the job of Market Master.

As in the past, the market is a place of continuity and change. While some families have made it their working home for generations, it continues to welcome newcomers such as Hmong and Mien refugees from the Vietnam War who have encountered enormous cultural and linguistic barriers in American society. Southeast Asian Design began at the market as a retail outlet for the women's intricate traditional embroidery. It has contributed to the economic stability of their community, while stimulating public interest in their culture.

2.   Trudy and Lenora's Barbershop
Pike Place Market
In the back part of the Stewart House building

Viola Brown is a third generation barber who inherited her business and trade from her mother and grandmother. In the early 1900s when the local chapter of Journeymen Barbers International refused membership to women, the Seattle Central Labor Council granted them their own charter for a Lady Barbers Union. According to the Pacific Northwest Labor History Association, "Ladies' barber shops were fairly common at this time. They were respectable businesses where the ladies gave excellent shaves and haircuts, nothing more and nothing less." Viola's grandmother, Hilde Sullivan, was born in Friday Harbor, a member of "Captain Cook's blue-eyed Indian tribe of Orcas Island" and a relative of Angeline, the daughter of Chief Seattle. She worked long hours in a fish cannery to put herself through Mohler's Barber School in Pioneer Square and establish her business. Her daughter Lenora and granddaughter Viola followed in her footsteps, going to the barber school and then working in the shop. When she made her friend Trudy a partner, Lenora changed the name.

Lenora's career spanned some 50 years with some customers relying on her from boyhood until they were grandfathers. Following her retirement in the 1960s, Viola continued the business, maintaining her mother's and grandmother's traditions of friendship and caring for long-term customers. Now a grandmother herself, Viola is a treasure trove of market history, as reflected by the photographs and memorabilia that decorate her shop. The yellow plum tree on the little patio behind it is said to have belonged to Angeline who made her home in a nearby shack.

Labor Day Parade, Seattle, 1903
(Courtesy of Ross Rieder)

3. Waitresses Hall (site)
1420 Second Avenue

The Seattle Waitresses Union (now Dining Employees Local #3) moved into its own hall in 1902, which had a large meeting room, an office and a comfortable reading room, enjoyed by members in their leisure time. A key organizer was Alice Lord, a waitress who in 1900 sparked formation of the pioneering women's union, one of the first to be chartered by the American Federation of Labor. Lord had no illusions about the desperate need to improve conditions for women who often worked 14-hour days, seven days a week for wages of $3 to $6 per week.

Waitresses Local 240 had a triple agenda: to improve the status of working women, to promote the rights of the working class as a whole, and to win suffrage for women. Beginning with a study of union issues, the waitresses learned tactics of strikes, negotiations, and lobbying. In the early 1900s when the new Labor Temple was under construction, the Western Central Labor Council and some of the men's unions held their meetings at Waitresses' Hall. In a show of support for the new women's union, the Council elected Lord and others to office.

When Lord led her union to Olympia to lobby the legislature for protective wage and hour laws, she had strong support from the Washington State Federation of Women's Clubs, the Ministerial Alliance, and the State Federation of Labor. The "Waitresses' Bill" for the eight-hour day, first proposed in 1904, gained passage in 1911 on the heels of the woman suffrage amendment. Two years later, the legislature enacted a landmark minimum wage of $10 per week (excluding agricultural and domestic workers).

Recognizing strength in numbers, the waitresses helped unionize other groups of working women, among them garment workers, hotel and domestic maids, "hello girls," (telephone operators) and lady barbers. Lord also worked with wives and female relatives of union men to organize the Seattle Union Card and Label League, which supported the unions while also forging a bridge between working- and middle-class women.

As members of the National Consumer League and supporters of the National Women's Trade Union League, clubwomen advocated for protective labor legislation, so that working women would have the means and the time for educational and cultural enrichment. Echoing their sentiment, Lord described activities in the Waitresses' Hall in the January 6, 1906 issue of the SEATTLE UNION RECORD:

....a very pleasant sight it is to see some practicing music, others sewing and a few studious ones with their books endeavoring to obtain knowledge and train their mental talents so they may prove themselves worthy to be called American women.

4.   Chinese Embroidery Shop
Third Avenue storefront between Pine and Stewart Streets, now the Bon Marche block

Cheng Hiang, the Rev. Joseck S. Hwang and their two daughters immigrated from China to Seattle in 1909, when there were only a few Chinese families in the state. Following the births of four more daughters, the Rev. Hwang abandoned the family, leaving his non-English speaking wife to fend for herself. Cheng Hiang enlisted the help of relatives in China to begin importing embroidery, then with the help of her English-speaking daughters opened the Chinese Embroidery Shop in 1920. To save money on taxes, she occasionally moved her shop to Yakima and Spokane, and for 52 years, she sold embroidery from her booth at the Puyallup Fair. Eventually, all six daughters went to the University of Washington, becoming respectively an M.D., a librarian, a dietician, a pharmacist, a teacher and an artist. If they had had to depend on a Baptist minister's meager salary, it would not have been possible.

5.   The Bon Marche
Between Pine and Stewart Streets and Third and Fourth Avenues

From its modest beginnings in 1890 in Belltown, Josephine Nordhoff worked with her husband Edward from 7 a.m. to 9 p.m. daily to run the store. As a young mother, not yet 20, she stocked shelves, kept the books, cleaned and mopped, and waited on customers, often with a baby in tow. So that she could better serve Native American customers, she learned to speak Chinook. In 1897 during the Alaska Gold Rush, the Nordhoffs moved their store to Second and Pike, close to the heart of downtown where their business boomed. Two years later following Edward's untimely death, Josephine became president of the corporation. Joining her as business partners were her brother-in-law R. G. H. Nordhoff, who moved to Seattle from Buffalo, New York, and in 1901 her second husband, a respected local merchant, Frank M. McDermott.

By 1916 the store had 400 employees and 25 different retail departments. In his book SEATTLE AND KING COUNTY, Clarence Bagley commented: "Absolute courtesy to all patrons is demanded from their employees [sic],...Each Saturday night they give concerts to which the customers are welcome, and the generosity and liberality with which they conduct the business has brought them hosts of friends." He sites Josephine as "the efficient president of...one of the largest and most popular department stores in the northwest," and notes that she "....has an individual interest in those who are in her service, and all know that fidelity will lead to promotion as opportunity offers."

Like many other employers, the Bon hired union workers and readily responded in the mid-teens when the legislature enacted some of the nation's most liberal minimum wage and hour laws for working women. The successful lobbying campaign had been a cooperative venture on the part of middle-class clubwomen, Union Card and Label Leagues (made up of non-working wives of union men), and union women. In 1919 members of Seattle's labor unions supported shipyard workers in what became the nation's first general strike. For five days the highly unionized city was virtually shut down with only emergency services and soup kitchens in operation. When the non-violent strike ended, labor had proved that it could temporarily cripple the city, but little else.

A cautious middle class began to link labor's demands with calls for revolution by the Bolsheviks in Russia and the Wobblies at home. The result was an "open shop" movement among many employers, including the Bon. When the Card and Label Leagues attempted to organize a consumer boycott against the Bon for what the unions considered to be unfair practices, clubwomen no longer supported their cause. The Retail Clerks Union with a large female membership lost its clout, but the Bon continued to flourish.

In 1929 Josephine and her business partners welcomed a throng of 135,000 people to the gala grand opening celebration of the beautiful art-deco building that continues to serve as the Bon's flagship store and corporate headquarters. It is designated as a City of Seattle Landmark.

6.   Arcade Building
Between First and Second and Union and University
Go south to Union; turn left

Today the new Seattle Art Museum has replaced the south half of what was formerly the full-block Arcade Building, where sales at Rhodes Department Store were just one of many magnets that lured women through the brick arches. Shortly after the turn of the century, the building became a hub of Washington women's political and altruistic activities. The western Washington division of the Women's Christian Temperance Union was headquartered there. In addition to organizing effective grassroots crusades for social and political issues, the WCTU established a Women's Exchange where house-bound women could market their needlework, jams, and baked goods.

Under the leadership of Esther Levy and her daughter Lizzie Cooper, the Ladies Hebrew Benevolent Society (now Jewish Family Service) established a free dispensary in the Arcade, complete with a clinical laboratory that offered both medical service and aid to the "deserving poor."

Feminist physician and avid mountain climber, Dr. Cora Smith Eaton, had her office there. When Emma Smith DeVoe, a seasoned organizer for the National American Women's Suffrage Association, was elected president of the newly revitalized Washington Equal Suffrage Association in 1906, Dr. Eaton contributed part of her office for headquarters. On November 8, 1910, Washington's male voters passed the suffrage amendment by a majority of almost two to one. Breaking a 14-year period of doldrums, Washington became the fifth state in the nation to enfranchise women.

In 1911 from their headquarters in the Arcade Building, leaders of the WCTU and the WESA joined forces with Seattle clubwomen to launch a recall campaign against Mayor Hiram Gill. Gill had broken his pre-election promise to confine sin to the Skid Road area and instead had granted sanction to his cronies to build the world's largest brothel--250 rooms--on 10th Avenue South. With the campaign slogan, "Ladies: Get Out and Hustle!," Seattle's newly enfranchised voters ensured Gill's defeat, when they hustled him out of office. The intended brothel, which never opened, was converted into a legitimate rooming house.

Buoyed by the riding tide of reform, WCTU President Emma Wallingford Wood was a leader in the carefully-orchestrated grassroots crusade for dry laws. In 1914 the state's voters ratified the prohibition initiative with Seattleites favoring it by a 61 percent margin. The law was enacted in 1916, followed three years later by the Volstead Act that prohibited manufacture or sale of liquor throughout the nation, except for druggists.

During World War II, the Arcade Building became headquarters for the King County USO (United Service Organization), a consortium composed of the YWCA, the YMCA, Catholic Community Services, the Salvation Army, the Jewish Welfare Association and Travelers Aid. The organization's purpose was to provide religious, social, and recreational activities for members of the armed forces and defense workers. Junior and senior hostesses volunteered for dances, recreational outings, at home dinners and other activities designed to entertain troops and restore normal conditions for both women and men. Some member organizations, such as the YWCA, scheduled activities 24 hours a day to accommodate defense workers on swing and graveyard shifts.

7. Seattle Art Museum

Second Avenue and Union Street
Phone: 654-3100. Open Tuesday-Sunday, 10 a.m.-5 p.m.;
Thursday, 10 a.m.-9 p.m.; and on some holiday Mondays.
Admission: Adults, $6; seniors and students, $4; children
under 12 are free with an adult. Free admission on the first
Tuesday of each month with extended hours, 10 a.m.-7 p.m.

Please see the original building at Volunteer Park (Chapter X) for the
Museum's early history. Now as then, women are among its strongest
supporters. One who has made a decisive difference is Virginia
Bloedel Wright, a noted connoisseur and collector of contemporary
art, and a leader in the fund-raising drive for the new building. The
founder of the initially controversial modern art department in the old
building, she has contributed a wealth of important pieces to the
museum and to communities throughout the region as public art. One
of them is Jonathan Borofsky's "Hammering Man" who labors
tirelessly near the entrance.

Another important influence on the new Museum is the Junior League
of Seattle which made a substantial contribution to the capital
campaign for construction of the children's educational area. JLS
volunteers worked with museum staff to develop the space, resource
materials, and the extensive children's arts education programs.

8. Holyoke Building

107 Spring Street
Go south to Spring, then west

Named for lumber baron Richard Holyoke, the handsome building was
one of the first to rise from the ashes of the Great Seattle Fire of 1889.
While the lower floors were commercial, the fourth floor housed the
new Conservatory for the Arts founded by Mrs. Celeste Langley
Slausson and Mrs. Frederick Jewell Laird. With the economic
depression of the 1890s, artists took over most of the upper floors

with combination apartments and studios.

A January 2, 1904 article in the SEATTLE MAIL AND HERALD says: "Many world famous musicians have paused...in their wanderings over the earth and found shelter within these musical walls." The reporter canvassed the building, studio by studio, describing the artists. "Nellie Cornish shared studio space with Miss Harla M. Sloan....very successful teachers of the piano, mandolin and guitar." A graduate of Smith College, Harriet Colburn Saunderson headed the Saunderson School of Expression. Violinists Rose and Frank Egan got their start at the Holyoke and later moved to Los Angeles to found the Egan School.

In 1927 the nostalgic local press referred to the building in its heyday as "a temple of music and art which Seattle has not been able to duplicate since." The Holyoke is listed on the National Register of Historic Places and is a designated City of Seattle Landmark.

9. American Red Cross Society of Seattle/Elks Hall
34 Colman Building
811 First Avenue
Continue south on First Avenue

"Remember the Maine" was the rallying cry of 100 women who met at Elks Hall in the Colman Building in June 1898 to organize civilian support for American troops going to war against Spain. The women responded enthusiastically when Mary B. Brainerd, a close friend of Clara Barton, suggested forming a Red Cross Society. Members sewed comfort bags, knit bandages, and collected truckloads of food to ship to soldiers stationed in Cuba and the Philippines. According to Brainerd's report in the Red Cross archives, "There was much to do as the nine transports which sailed from Puget Sound received their last American cheers from us."

Having witnessed the work of the International Red Cross during the Franco-Prussian War, Barton had founded the American agency in 1881. By a later Congressional mandate, it was charged with providing relief to disaster victims and with serving as a vehicle of communication between United States civilians and their Army and Navy. In times of war, it was to care for the wounded and perform other duties in accord with the Geneva Convention. Following the Spanish-American War, the Seattle Red Cross turned its attention to disaster relief, sending aid to victims of the San Francisco earthquake in 1906 and to famine sufferers in China in 1907.

The United States' entry into World War I galvanized unprecedented activity among male and female volunteers, then headquartered in the Cobb Building at 1305 4th Avenue. Church- and clubwomen considered it their patriotic duty to join the Red Cross, mustering at a furious pace to organize sewing circles, canteens, Liberty Loan campaigns, nursing departments and more. Clad in spiffy uniforms, members of the women's motor corps drove their own cars to taxi soldiers and sailors, wartime visitors, and goods made by sewing circles from one end of town to the other.

In an era when well-to-do people hired private duty nurses, rather than go to a hospital, Red Cross recruiters trumpeted the new patriotic slogan, "Luxury Nurses Must Be Given Up!" At the beginning of the war, there were only 400 active duty nurses in the Army and 160 in the Navy. When peace was restored in 1918, an estimated 24,000 nurses had served, caring for troops, veterans and their families both at home and abroad.

Celebration of the armistice was tempered by the virulent flu epidemic that swept the nation, claiming half a million lives. Locally, Red Cross nurses ministered to flu patients in private homes and hospitals, frequently contracting the disease themselves. Assisting them was the sewing department that made flu masks for people to wear in public, while members of the canteen department prepared and delivered meals to the sick.

As normalcy was restored, the Red Cross revitalized programs that had lapsed, including water safety, first aid, and home nursing classes. In the depths of the Great Depression, courses in nutrition and food preservation were in demand. Presaging the "victory gardens" of World War II, the agency gave away packages of garden seed, urging homemakers to grow and share their produce.

Today the Seattle/King County Chapter of the American Red Cross is housed at 1900 25th Avenue S., where it keeps apace, adjusting its programs to address needs of a changing society and world. It continues to promote public health and safety and to provide disaster assistance in times of both war and peace.

10. Traditions and Beyond: Indian Art Then and Now
American Indian Women's Service League
113 Cherry Street
Continue south; turn left on Cherry

This one of a kind retail shop has a threefold mission: to showcase Indian art and artists; to generate scholarship funds for Indian people; and to heighten public awareness of Indian art and culture. It is one of many legacies of the American Indian Women's Service League (AIWSL), chartered in Seattle in 1957. The next year, the league established the Seattle Indian Center in a converted church at 1900 Boren. Like many of the other programs that the league founded, it later spun off as an independent agency.

A member of the Makah tribe, Pearl Warren served as the Center's first director. In an April 1967 interview with SEATTLE MAGAZINE, she said that the state inter-tribal council had conceived the idea of the AIWSL, whose mission was "to make Indians part of the community they live in and to get non-Indians to recognize us as an Indian group." With a bare bones $15,000 budget from United Good Neighbors, the league founded a network of related organizations, including United Indians of All Tribes, the Seattle Indian Health Board, the American Indian Youth Activity Club, and the Indian arts and crafts shop. The Indian Center provided a preschool program, tutoring for high school students, emergency food and clothing, education and employment counseling, scholarships, and a gathering place for the city's estimated 5,000 Indians.

From the start the center welcomed non-Indian visitors. To raise funds and publicize their cultural traditions, the league published a cookbook and designed calendars featuring the work of local Indian artists. In 1958 it began publication of a monthly newsletter that grew into a tabloid, THE NORTHWEST INDIAN NEWS, and later became an independent Indian-owned company. Charter league member Ella Aquino, served as editor and wrote the popular column "Teepee Talk" which led to her taped radio programs, broadcast on station KRAB. In cooperation with the University of Washington's Communications Department, the newspaper helped train and place Indian journalists.

The league was at the forefront of the decades-long lobbying effort for the permanent Seattle Indian Center, now established at 611 12th Avenue S. In 1970 when Fort Lawton was returned to the city, league members participated in the successful sit-in to win the site for Daybreak Star Indian Cultural Center. (Please see Chapter VI, Discovery Park for further information.)

In the 1970s the league and the Seattle Indian Services Commission, a spin-off organization that took over management of the Indian Center, purchased the old Henry Broderick Building at 113 Cherry. While volunteering in the center on the upper floors, league members opened their non-profit arts and crafts shop on the ground floor. A popular attraction was the display case of artifacts including intricate traditional baskets and beadwork--family treasures contributed by each of the 100 charter members. (A member who is studying anthropology is currently documenting the origins of each piece.) In 1982 when they sold the building, its new owners agreed to let the shop remain. It continues to serve as headquarters for the AIWSL.

In recent years, the league has established a special annual award of one to two large scholarships to a deserving Native American women who lives in King County. A requirement is that she maintain above a "B" average in college. President Lillian Chappell says: "We want to get the message across to young people that they should try to excel in their schoolwork and go on to get a graduate degree, so that they can succeed and contribute to the community in their chosen profession." A major source of funding is the league's annual salmon bake at Alki Beach.

11.   Methodist Protestant Church (site)
NW corner of Second and Madison
Go one block east to 2nd; turn left

Popularly known as the "Brown Church," Seattle's first church was founded in 1862 with the Reverend Daniel Bagley as Pastor. In 1871 Susan B. Anthony and Oregon suffragist Abigail Scott Duniway made a 10-week, 2,000 mile-lecture tour of the Northwest to plant the seeds for the crusade. At the Brown Church, they inspired the formation of a city suffrage association with Sarah Yesler as president. A Seattle delegation joined Anthony and Duniway to participate in the first territorial suffrage convention in Olympia. (For further information about Washington's suffrage crusade, please see Chapter I, Joseph and Martha Jane Steele Foster Home; this chapter, the Arcade Building; and Chapter VIII, Skid Road.)

12.   Adams and Brooks; Adams and Reynolds, U.S. Patent Attorneys
500 Central Building
310 Third Avenue
Go south one block to Marion, then one block east

Admitted to the bar as a patent attorney in 1901, E. Arlita Hewitt Adams was the first woman in the United States to practice patent law. After graduating from the University of Washington, she married Frank E. Adams, a registered patent attorney. They opened their office in the new Central Building, which at the time was Seattle's largest office building. Following Frank's death in 1914, she formed a new partnership called Adams and Reynolds with Henry L. Reynolds.

The only woman accepted as a member of the prestigious Commercial Club, she was also a member of the Chamber of Commerce and active in the Republican Party and the Episcopal Church. She and her daughter lived in the Washington Hotel and had a summer home on Mercer Island.

Seattle First National Bank, 1905
(Courtesy of Special Collections Division, University of
Washington Libraries, Neg. #2084)

13. Seattle City Light Building
1015 Third Avenue
Go north on Third Avenue

Built in 1935 as a two-story structure and expanded in 1959, the building's notable feature is Jean Cory Beall's Venetian colored-glass mosaic that interprets the wonder of electric power. For decades human power in the utility's work force was a white male domain. Women such as Janet Shockey, who began as a clerk in 1954, were relegated to low status, low paid clerical positions.

In 1972 Shockey made headlines when Mayor Wes Uhlman appointed her director of City Light's administrative services. As the highest ranking woman in city government, she supervised 115 employees in six subdivisions. She was past president of Totem Chapter of Business and Professional Women and was a past board member of the National Management Association which awarded her its 1973 Certificate of Achievement.

After a year in her high post, Shockey surprised city officials and the media by resigning, citing "harassment" from her boss, Gordon Vickery, as the reason. In an interview with the SEATTLE TIMES, she said, "I was the token woman and he came to City Light from a paramilitary organization, the Seattle Fire Department." When a reporter checked back with her in 1979, she said, "He didn't understand that women had been brought up with a clerk typist mentality and it was impossible for them to move right into a supervisory position without extensive training." He in turn acknowledged her as a catalyst for the utility's Affirmative Action program.

During her brief management tenure, Shockey had worked to establish leadership training programs for other women. In 1979 she reflected, "....now there are women all over in supervisory positions. So I guess we had some success. We made a start." Working in concert with her in the early 1970s were newly established entities in City government, created to promote equity for women, ethnic minorities, and sexual minorities. They included the 15-member Seattle Women's Commission, the Office for Women's Rights, and the Human Rights Department.

As some women began to climb the white collar ladder, others struggled to gain a toehold in lucrative blue collar trades. In 1974 City Light hired ten women for an electrical trades program that was soon dismantled. When the women protested, all but two were fired. They took the issue to court and won, opening the doors to the utility's apprenticeship programs and journey-level status.

Pioneering women and ethnic minorities in the skilled trades suffered injuries twice as often as white males, sometimes because of hostile co-workers. In their zeal to excel, women often overextended themselves, performing tasks for which they were not adequately prepared. Heidi Durham, who walks with a cane since falling from a pole and breaking her back in 1977, recalls that when she gained consciousness, she apologized for holding up the work. Teri Bach, the first woman to graduate from the apprenticeship program, fell and broke her neck. Now working as a cable splicer, she recalls trying to prove herself to people who had no intention of regarding her as their equal. When another woman charged a male lineworker with unhooking her safety harness and trying to pull her off a 30-foot pole, supervisors were slow to respond.

Slapped repeatedly with harassment and discrimination lawsuits, the utility's bosses grappled to learn and enforce a new set of rules. They hired Melinda Nichols, who had struggled through a carpentry apprenticeship program as a lone woman, to revamp the training and recruitment programs. Although Durham, Bach, and some of their co-crusaders feel that City Light should be much further along, it has clearly learned from past mistakes and is making progress. It is now recognized as a national equity leader among utilities with 70% of its apprentices and 60% of new hires since 1985 being women and minorities.

In 1992 when Superintendent Roberta Palm Bradley became the first female and the first Black to take the helm, her goal was to create a work force that would be prepared for the year 2000 when according to census figures only 15% of new workers will be white males.

14. The University of Washington (site)
Now the Four Seasons Olympic Hotel
Between Fourth and Fifth and Seneca and University
See commemorative plaque near entrance on University
Go west to Fourth, then north to University

In 1861 the new Territorial University building, crowned with a fluted cupola, emerged regally atop Denny's knoll overlooking the city and Elliott Bay. Since few scholars in the territory were eligible for admission, the city used part of the building for its first public school, taught by Lucy Whipple Carr. Several of the Territorial University's faculty members were women, including Ellen J. Chamberlin, the influential chair of the English Department. In 1876 Clara McCarty (later Wilt) made history as the first graduate. Her career advanced from teacher to Pierce County Superintendent of Schools.

The University's first president was Asa Shinn Mercer, an idealistic 22-year-old who hatched a plan to alleviate the local "bachelor problem." In King County men outnumbered women three to one, and most of the women were married. Mercer embarked on a journey to economically depressed New England, where women were in the majority due to loss of lives in the Civil War. If a woman wanted to consider marriage, he could guarantee her a choice of suitors in Washington Territory; if she wanted a career, there was ample opportunity; and in addition there was the Homestead Act of 1862 which granted 160 acres free to a settler if she or he would live on and improve the land continuously for five years.

When Mercer returned home with eleven adventuresome women (later immortalized in the TV series "Here Come the Brides"), Seattle's bachelors, primed for courtship, awaited them at the dock. The entire community turned out for a welcoming reception, held at the University.

Buoyed by his success, Mercer announced that he would go East again and enlist the help of President Abraham Lincoln, a friend of his family, to bring back a shipload of hundreds of unmarried women. To finance the journey, he asked local bachelors to contribute $300 in advance, but from there on his luck turned sour. When he arrived in New York, he was shocked to hear that the president had been assassinated the previous night. Bent on his quest, he travelled about, recruiting young women with assurances of the wealth of opportunities that awaited them. A New York newspaper changed most of their minds when it reported that he was nothing but a pimp, whose "real" intent was to place them in brothels.

Despite his protestations, only a few stuck with him, and since he had totally depleted his capital, he had to ask them to pay their own passage. His party of 95 eventually included some married men and families, along with widows and their children. After journeying around the Horn with visits to several South American ports, some of the women opted to disembark in San Francisco; still others accepted marriage proposals from members of the crew. In his own interest, Mercer courted Annie Stephens whom he later married.

Those who made it to Seattle received warm welcomes from men and women alike. All but one of the "Mercer Girls" eventually married. The exception was Lizzie Ordway, a well-educated member of the first expedition, who rejected several suitors, declaring, "Never shall I give up the life of single blessedness!" She rang the bell to welcome the first pupils to Seattle's new Central School, later served as Superintendent of Schools in Kitsap County, and was a leader in the suffrage crusade.

With their hopes of marriage diminished, lonesome bachelors who had financed Mercer's second voyage criticized him for squandering their money and not making good on his promise to import "hundreds of women." After their wedding at the Brown Church, Mercer and his bride packed their belongings and moved to Wyoming.

15. Seattle Public Library
Between Fourth and Fifth and Spring and Madison
Go one block south

Seattle's City Charter, ratified by citizens in 1890, included a provision for a public library department to be governed by five commissioners, at least two of whom should be women. When men lost interest in the early pioneer library association, women reorganized in 1888 as the Ladies Library Association to preserve some 1500 volumes and to sustain the library's popularity. Sarah Yesler was the first librarian, while Catherine Maynard provided a reading room in her home.

Initially, the library was a low priority, as the city worked to rebuild its business district in the wake of the Great Fire. During the recessionary 1890s, library supporters weathered hard times, moving their collection through a series of temporary quarters until 1898 when Henry Yesler donated the elegant 40-room Yesler mansion in memory of his deceased wife. Located at the present site of the King County Courthouse, the building inspired an outpour of public support, enabling the library to add its first children's department.

But good times were short-lived. On New Years Day 1901, fire consumed the mansion, while volunteers salvaged what they could of the contents. Five days later, the POST INTELLIGENCER announced a substantial gift from the Andrew Carnegie Foundation which financed construction of the stately Carnegie Library at Fourth and Madison, the site of today's modern downtown library.

As proof of its continued allegiance to women's groups, one librarian's job was to maintain records of club programs and to help members prepare papers to present to their organizations. The female-dominated "temple of culture," oriented many of its services to women and children. With the dawning of prohibition, it had to pay more attention to the needs of men. In their recently published history of the Seattle Public Library, Judy Anderson, Gail Lee Dubrow and John Koval wrote:

> Male smokers anticipated female resistance to their proposal for a smoking room, but women's clubs defied expectation when they supported the idea of building a portable room at the rear of the main library building as a 'smokers' paradise.' No doubt the clubwomen's position was shaped by optimism about the civilizing influences of literature, a continuing belief in the propriety of separate spheres for men and women, and an urgent search for substitutes for the saloon.

The book also cites an article in the October 10, 1915 SEATTLE

TIMES, showing that the Seattle Waitresses Union supported a men's smoking room, but for an interesting price. The Union proposed that in exchange, the library should:

> recognize the rights of women by installing also a refreshment room where fair patrons of the library may enjoy ice cream sodas, sundaes, chocolates and other concoctions dear to the feminine heart.

The authors were unable to determine whether an ice cream parlor or smoking room ever came into being. In any case prohibition nearly doubled the library's patronage.

Like teaching and nursing, librarianship was a female-dominated profession, requiring educated employees who would work for low wages. The situation persisted until the 1980s when Seattle's young library union and women activists in public employee unions made the issue of pay equity a top priority. The result was a settlement that brought library workers' salaries in line with those of comparable positions in city government.

16. Providence Hospital (site)
Now occupied by the Federal Courthouse
Between Fifth and Sixth and Spring and Madison
Across Fifth Avenue from the library

Both the Seattle Historical Society (now the Historical Society of Seattle and King County) and the Washington State Advisory Council on Historic Preservation have installed bronze plaques beside the Courthouse steps to commemorate the site of Seattle's first hospital. Founded by the Sisters of Charity of Providence, it opened on April 25, 1878 and continued operation until September 24, 1911, when its founders moved to their larger new facility on First hill.

In the 1870s, Seattle was a wide-open town where loggers and miners worked at hazardous jobs, then often squandered their paychecks in the city's red-light district at equally hazardous play. From laborers to prostitutes to townsfolk, people were in desperate need of health care. The city's lone hospital facility consisted of two small rooms in Doc Maynard's home where his wife Catherine provided nursing care.

Community leaders longingly eyed successful hospitals in Vancouver and Portland which were built and managed by Mother Joseph of the Sisters of Providence. A self-trained architect, she had learned carpentry skills from her father prior to entering the convent. Accompanied by four other nuns, she left the order's headquarters in Montreal, Quebec in 1856 to make the arduous journey to Fort Vancouver, Washington, where the sisters embarked on their mission to build schools and hospitals throughout the Pacific Northwest.

Three of the sisters ventured north to Seattle, when Father Kauten contracted with King County Commissioners to care for the indigent sick and poor at "the Work House," commonly called the Poor House, on the Duwamish River. Wearing long black habits, the French-speaking nuns encountered a strong anti-Catholic sentiment in the community, made up predominantly of Protestants and the unchurched. Sister Chronicler wrote, "At our arrival the people were so prejudiced that they prevented the sick from coming to us...The Poor Farm prevented some from coming, as they considered it a disgrace."

Despite obstacles, charity cases and paying patients alike began to rely on the sisters. With support from community women, they held bazaars and went on "begging tours" to solicit donations for their work and for a new hospital building. In 1878 Mother Joseph came from Vancouver to draft plans for the four-story, wood-frame hospital that eventually covered the entire block. Clad in her habit with hammer and saw dangling from her belt, she personally supervised the construction, sometimes ripping out faulty work and redoing it herself.

Until 1907 the nuns provided most of the care themselves, assisted only by a few non-professional staff members and "several old people who help where they can." In response to increasing needs, they established Providence School of Nursing, modeled after their school in Portland. Admission requirements were non-sectarian, based only on a girl's moral character and ability to learn.

In 1910 the sisters needed larger and modernized facilities. Since Mother Joseph had died in 1902, they hired an architect to design their new hospital at Seventeenth and Jefferson. Today the Sisters of Providence of Washington State are headquartered in Seattle, where they continue to expand their facilities and services.

Popularly known as "the Builder," Mother Joseph designed 28 schools and hospitals in the Pacific Northwest. She was posthumously recognized by the American Institute of Architects as the Northwest's first architect. In 1980 her statue was erected in Statuary Hall in the nation's capitol, joining that of Marcus Whitman as Washington State's two most distinguished citizens. She is one of only six women nationwide to be so honored.

17.   The Women's University Club
1105 Sixth Avenue
Diagonally across the intersection from the Federal Courthouse

Founded in 1914, the Women's University Club occupied a temporary building until 1922 when it celebrated the grand opening of its own elegant clubhouse. The original aim of the club, composed of college graduates, was to cultivate interest in the sciences and liberal arts, stimulate and advance general education and educational opportunities for women, and encourage social and cultural activities among members and guests. Most of the charter members also belonged to the Association of Collegiate Alumnae (now American Association of University Women).

The ACA was chartered in New England in 1882 and locally in 1904, when educational opportunities for women were few and openings for trained women even fewer. Frustrated by their circumstances a group of college alumnae banded together to advocate for more equitable standards. The ACA restricted its membership to graduates of institutions--such as prestigious women's colleges Back East and Mills College in Oakland--that met its own strict standards. While the University of Washington made the grade in 1915, most of the state's colleges and universities consistently failed. Renamed American Association of University Women in 1921, the organization did not relax its criteria until the 1930s at which time female graduates of any accredited four-year college were welcome to join. The ACA's national charter discouraged building clubhouses and instead encouraged members to meet in private homes, so that funds that they raised could provide graduate fellowships for qualified women.

A major purpose of the Women's University Club was to establish a clubhouse. Laura Carr, one of the founders, is quoted in the club's HISTORICAL HIGHLIGHTS:

> In those early years there were few attractive places in downtown Seattle for women to lunch and dine; automobiles were very scarce, and two car families virtually non-existent. Friends in West Seattle and Laurelhurst seemed as far away as if they were in Tacoma. When eastern dignitaries came to town, there was no appropriate place to entertain them, and the college and university women began to feel that they must have a downtown meeting place of their own....

At first the club emphasized cultural activities such as Carr's book reviews, performances by the Drama League, and an impressive array of classes. During World War I, it offered Red Cross training and adopted a ward in the hospital at Camp Lewis (now Fort Lewis). A member, Dr. Mabel Seagrave, was decorated by the French government for her work in a French relief hospital.

The clubhouse has rooms for out-of-town visitors and residents, a theatre, dining and meeting areas--all elegantly appointed and a source of pride for its members. During the 1920s, the club's agenda was primarily social and cultural. In accord with changing opportunities for women, it has expanded its focus with study groups and programs to promote equity and education for women and girls. With more than 1,000 members, it remains an important cornerstone of a city block with a legacy as a center for women.

18. Evangeline Young Women's Residence
(Now the Holiday Inn Crowne Plaza Hotel)
Sixth Avenue and Seneca Street
Next door to the Women's University Club

In 1927 the Salvation Army reopened the old Piedmont Hotel as the Evangeline Young Women's Residence. The home for single business women had rooms for some 80 permanent residents and 45 hotel guests who convened for breakfast and dinner in the attractive dining room. A succession of Salvation Army officers and their wives managed the home, organizing vesper services, classes and activities, and making sure that gentlemen callers did not go beyond the dignified lobby floor. Torn down in 1981, the building was replaced by the elegant new hotel.

19. YWCA of Seattle/King County
Fifth and Seneca
Next door to the Holiday Inn Crowne Plaza Hotel

A third cornerstone of this significant block is the Young Women's Christian Association, founded in 1894 by 28 public-spirited women to help the "working girl" toward self support. During the recessionary period, girls--sometimes as young as 12--came to the city alone in search of work, only to fall prey to unscrupulous "white slavers," who forced many of them into prostitution.

In the commodious downtown storeroom, donated by Mary Shorey, board members created a comfortable lounge and the city's first cafeteria, serving 10¢ lunches for working girls. They then hired a trained secretary from the national association to provide administrative and counseling services. Support came from Union Pacific Railroad Company with funding for a depot matron who met trains and steamers "to guard and guide young women traveling alone."

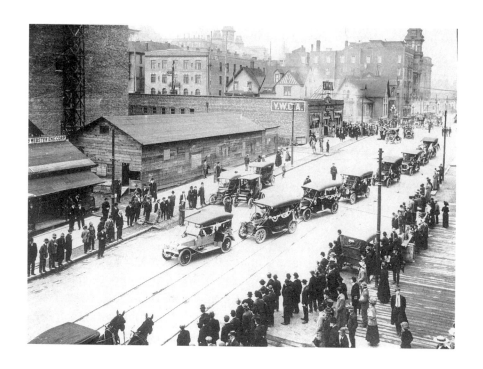

*Riding in style, members of the YWCA paraded down Fourth
Avenue in 1913 to raise funds for their new building
(Courtesy of YWCA of Seattle King County Records, University of
Washington Libraries)*

Clubs for Girls and Women

From its early history the Seattle YWCA organized a variety of clubs
to keep young women and girls "interested in the best things and
thereby prevent their being attracted by questionable amusements."
There were clubs for young married women, domestic workers,
factory workers, and women who worked in offices (the forerunner
of the local chapter of Business and Professional Women). The
Cosmopolitan Club drew local women into world fellowship activities.
Black women joined the Culture Club, and Japanese, Chinese, and
Russian women had their own respective clubs. High school girls
donned middies and blue skirts to become Girl Reserves, while
younger girls joined Bluebird or Rainbow Clubs.

A Class-A Building of Its Own

In the early teens, the board and the clubs launched a whirlwind fund-raising drive for a YWCA building that would be "the best of its kind in the country." Prior to canvassing businessmen, working women throughout the city contributed what they could. Designed by E. Frere Champney, the eight-story brick building opened in 1914. Its amenities included a tearoom "overlooking the city front and the harbor," a cafeteria, Turkish Baths, a swimming pool, a hotel, clubrooms, and a vocational school. A jubilant President Emma Wallingford Wood announced that the association had paid the total $400,000 cost and was debt free.

A friend of the Working "Girl"

In 1914 when the legislature enacted the landmark $10 per week minimum wage for working women, the YWCA declared its chief aim to be "the training and fitting of girls to enable them to earn at least minimum wage." A full two stories of the new building housed the Vocational Training Department with classes in millinery, dressmaking, general sewing, cafeteria work, tearoom management, practical nursing, manicuring, and salesmanship. In response to homemakers' needs, a home economics program prepared girls for marriage or for work as cooks, household assistants, or nursemaids. There was also a course for matrons that taught them reasonable expectations and regard for their maid's rights.

The association developed strong relations with the business community, arranging job placements for clients, while promoting better conditions for women in the workplace. Cooperative companies sponsored athletic teams and welcomed YWCA teachers who offered informal lunch-hour classes. (Please see Bemis Brothers Bag Factory in Chapter VIII for an example.)

Commitment to Racial Justice

In 1919 the Culture Club established its own branch in the heart of the black community. Despite the YWCA's commitment to racial justice, social mores of the day prevailed in the downtown building where black women could not rent a room and where they could swim in the pool only on Saturday afternoons--before it was drained and cleaned. From the start the branch sent a non-voting representative downtown to board meetings.

As the new representative in the 1930s, Bertha Pitts Campbell protested, saying that if she was expected to attend meetings, she wanted to vote. The board requested a change in policy from the national association which granted its approval, making the Seattle association the first racially integrated board in the nation. In a later interview, Campbell said that despite difficulties, she felt that the city's racial climate might have benefited, because "the 'Y' always listened." (Please see chapter IX, Phillis Wheatley Branch of the YWCA for further information.)

<u>Today's YWCA of Seattle/King County</u>
Today the YWCA maintains facilities throughout King County, fulfilling its mission to advance the quality of life for women, children and families of all races and faiths. As in the past, it is governed by an all-female board of trustees.

The exterior of the flagship downtown building remains substantially unaltered. The interior has undergone two major renovations that often make it difficult to visualize the original design, especially in the lobby that was once elegantly appointed, complete with balustraded balconies and decorative plaster cornices.

20. Plymouth Congregational Church
Sixth Avenue between Seneca and University
On the east half block across Seneca from the YWCA

In the early 1920s, the YWCA de-emphasized social and cultural clubs, opting to channel its energies into welfare work. Knowing how cold and austere the city could be, General Secretary Florence Oren turned to Plymouth Congregational Church in the next block to propose a nondenominational organization for working women. The venerable, ivy-covered church (replaced by the contemporary building in 1967) became home to the 900-member Plymouth Girls Club.

On Monday evenings, single working "girls" from age 18 to nearly 40 came to the church for dinner, singing, and entertainment. Talented men and women throughout the city volunteered to teach classes in literature, nature study, parliamentary law, personal budgets, arts and crafts, eurhythmics, glee club, millinery, "charm," and more.

A memorable instructor was Lois Beil Sandall who directed a theater group called the Plymouth Players and who organized one of the city's pioneer children's theaters. To earn income, the Girls Club sponsored dramatic performances, concerts and guest speakers. In 1928 when Mayor Bertha Landes introduced Will Durant to lecture on the "History of Philosophy," response was so great that hundreds of people had to be turned away.

Because of the Monday evening club's success, the Plymouth Women's Association and Oren instituted similar programs on Tuesday evenings for mature married women, on Wednesday evenings for women who worked in factories, and on Thursday evenings for young married women.

In 1926 the congregation purchased a three-story brick building at the corner of Sixth Avenue and Seneca Street (now part of the church site). The Women's Association transformed the former Engineers Clubhouse into Plymouth House, a boarding home for young women and a meeting place for city women's organizations. During the Great Depression, the building became a financial albatross, forcing the church to tear it down and replace it with a more lucrative parking lot. Because of declining membership and a tight budget, Plymouth also decided to disband the Girls Club in 1935. By that time other churches and organizations throughout the city had formed similar clubs, creating programs for girls in their neighborhoods.

One of the final highlights of the Plymouth Girls Club era was the first of many recitals in the city by the great American contralto Marion Anderson. In 1931 a standing-room-only audience packed the church to hear her sing to the accompaniment of a racially mixed local orchestra. Because of rampant racism at home, Anderson had established her career in Europe. When impresario Sol Hurok heard her in Paris in 1930, he tried to book her in Constitution Hall, the national headquarters of the Daughters of the American Revolution, who turned her down. Responding decisively, First Lady Eleanor Roosevelt dropped her membership in the DAR and invited the diva to sing at the Lincoln Memorial. A throng of 75,000 turned out for the concert that was broadcast nationwide, making Anderson's name a household word.

In 1979 Plymouth Congregational Church leased space to the Seattle Infant Development Center for a pilot project with a mission to fulfill child-care needs of working parents. CBS Television featured the project as the first downtown center in any major American city to provide professional care and early childhood education for infants. The YWCA quickly followed suit, instituting similar programs in its building across the street. Early mornings and late afternoons are lively times when parents who work downtown flock to the neighborhood to deliver and pick up babies and toddlers. The programs allow parents to spend time with their children during work breaks and during the commute to and from home.

21. Fifth Avenue Theater/Skinner Building
1326 Fifth Avenue
Go west one block to the northeast corner of Fifth and University

The most opulent feature of the 1926 block-long building is the interior of the Fifth Avenue Theater, designed by Gustav Liljistrom, a Norwegian painter who studied in China. Modeled after the Forbidden City in Peking, the exotic theater is Seattle's best-preserved example of the vaudeville and movie palace era that reigned from the teens into the thirties.

A national pacesetter was Alexander Pantages, the Northwest's premier theater developer, whose empire grew into the country's largest chain of vaudeville houses. As a young Greek immigrant, Pantages went to Alaska in search of gold, which he found in the heart of "Klondike Kate, Queen of the Yukon." From her parents' home in Spokane, Kathleen Eloisa Rockwell had joined the Savoy Theatrical Company to perform in Yukon dance halls at the height of the Gold Rush. Dancing the night away with rowdy miners, she became both famous and rich. She bankrolled Pantages, enabling him to build his first Seattle theater in 1902.

One of the stars of the vaudeville circuit was a West Seattle native with the stage name, Gypsy Rose Lee. Born in 1916, Rose Louise Hairek began acting lessons at age three, making her debut two years later with her sister at the Knights of Pythias Lodge in Ballard. As a popular kiddy act, the sisters toured the nation on the vaudeville circuit.

In her teens, Gypsy turned to striptease, stealing the show in the Ziegfield Follies and capturing the attention of the press. She once said, "I never try to stir up the animal in 'em. Did you ever hold a toy in front of a baby, just out of his reach? Notice how he laughs. That's your strip audience." Although she no longer called Seattle home, she remained a star attraction for local fans. She later hosted a nationally syndicated TV talk show and wrote the best-selling G-STRING MURDERS, where a stripper was strangled with her own scanty costume. A year before her death in 1969, she visited troops in Vietnam.

Still regarded as Seattle's most exotic theater, the Fifth Avenue has been carefully restored. While continuing to host nationally prominent shows and artists, it serves as a reminder of a colorful period in the city's past. The Skinner Building (Fifth Avenue Theater) is listed on the National Register of Historic Places.

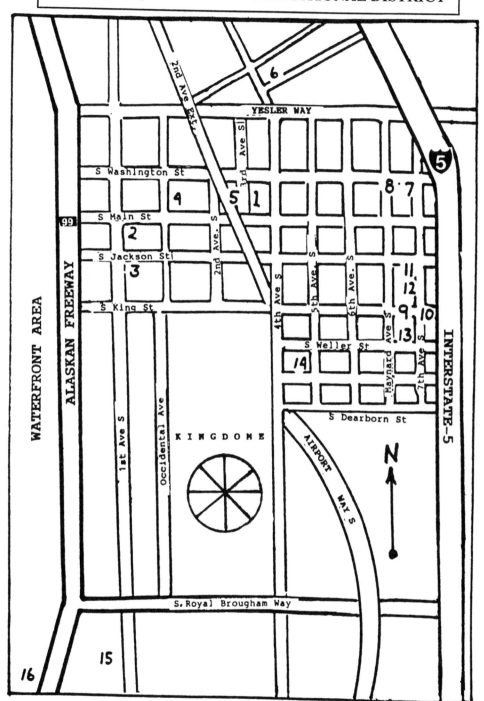

VIII. PIONEER SQUARE AND THE INTERNATIONAL DISTRICT

Ideally, this is a walking tour, so wear comfortable shoes. If you get tired, you can always board a Metro bus and ride for free along the tour route which begins at the south end of downtown in historic Pioneer Square.

In the 1850s, lumbermen skidded logs from wooded hills down Mill Street (now Yesler Way) to Henry Yesler's sawmill and wharf. While Seattle's business district extended north, working men's hotels and pleasure palaces dominated to the south in the district known as the Skid road, or the Tenderloin. Pioneer Square--resplendent with Richardsonian Romanesque buildings--emerged from the ashes of the Great Seattle Fire of 1889, but by the late teens, the business district resumed its northward press and the area fell into decline. Until the 1970s when it was designated as Seattle's first Historic District and targeted for restoration, Pioneer Square was rife with deteriorating warehouses, flophouses and taverns.

Your tour begins with a stroll through the district and observations about some of its historic female residents, including stalwart pioneers, philanthropists, successful businesswomen, and "soiled doves." On the edge of Pioneer Square is the King County Courthouse, where women lawyers and judges waged prolonged struggles to break the ranks of the judiciary. Continue on to the heart of the city's diverse and cohesive Asian community. Until recently, it was popularly called Chinatown and has been added to the Seattle Landmarks Register and the National Register of Historic Places. The district sprang to life in the early 20th century when people of Japanese and Chinese descent made it their home and commercial center. They were followed by Filipinos and later by Koreans, Vietnamese, Indochinese and other Asian groups. Several sites on your tour are connected with women who have made a difference here and in the greater Seattle community. Don't miss the Wing Luke Asian Museum and, if you can, take in a performance at the Nippon

Kan Theater or the Theater Off Jackson, all of which are discussed in this chapter.

From the International District, go down the hill past Union Pacific Railroad Station, the original home of the Travelers Aid Society. The final two sites are located south of the Kingdome. One is a factory whose owners were among the first to respond to the needs of women employees. The other is the Coast Guard Museum with exhibits that offer insights into the history of women in the military.

1. Skid Road/ the Tenderloin
South of Yesler Way between First and Fourth Avenue South
"White Chapel District" Plaque
East side of Third Avenue South between Washington and Main

One of the characteristics of Seattle in the late 19th and early 20th centuries was the demographic imbalance between men and women. That explains why there were so many transient and bachelor hotels in Pioneer Square, Downtown and Belltown. It also gives grounds for the enormity of the vice trade. The plaque that designates the area as the "White Chapel District" names it for the infamous district in London, England.

As you walk down broad, tree-lined boulevards, browsing through art galleries, antique shops, bookstores and restaurants, picture an earlier time when many of the same buildings housed rollicking brothels and saloons with "women of easy virtue" catering to the baser instincts of men. A look beyond the popular western stereotype of the colorful prostitute reveals a grim reality. While an occasional madam made it rich running a parlor house, most women in the trade struggled to survive, spending their hard-earned money on basic needs and payoffs to the police. At the bottom rank were unwilling victims of all races, abducted and sold to work out a contract or to remain enslaved. Still others--some of whom were married--worked shifts in infamous cribhouses (complexes of tiny sparsely furnished rooms) without even a brothel to call home.

While the Florence Crittenden Home and the Women's Christian Temperance Union managed to rescue some women from the trade, most found themselves in a downward spiral from which they could not escape. If they had children, their daughters often followed them into the trade. Their marital prospects were usually limited to men who thought little of abusing them. With increasing age, disillusionment, and illness, prostitutes frequently opted for suicide as a means of retirement.

In Seattle as in other communities, proper ladies did their best to confine or eliminate the trade. From 1883 to 1887 when Washington women won and lost the right to vote, Protestant churchwomen donned white ribbons of temperance, waging a strenuous campaign to ban vice from the city. Charles J. Woodbury, a correspondent for New York's EVENING POST, wrote of Seattle, "Even the bars of the hotels were closed; and this was the worst town in the territory when I first saw it. Now its uproarious theaters, dance-houses, squaw brothels [which employed Native American women] and Sunday fights are things of the past. Not a gambling house exists." Seattle weathered its purity for only a year. As loggers and miners squandered their paychecks in more liberal communities, city coffers diminished. At the next election voters threw law and order proponents out of office; they repealed anti-vice laws and welcomed back the madams, pimps, and saloon keepers. As in the past, sin taxes became the city's major source of revenue. In 1910 when Washington women finally regained the franchise, they again gave reform coalitions a decisive edge. (Please see Chapter I, Joseph and Martha Jane Steele Foster home, and Chapter VII, the Arcade Building for further information about the suffrage crusade.)

At first glance the drama that has been replayed repeatedly in Seattle history appears to be an example of the good versus evil theme of western mythology. In reality it is much more complex, as noted by historian Patricia Nelson Limerick in her recent book THE LEGACY OF CONQUEST. She observes that a look at the history of prostitution restores "a gritty, physical reality" to western history that moves beyond the domain of stereotypical do-gooders and neer-do-wells to a fully human cast of characters--"males and females whose urges, needs, failings and conflicts we can recognize and even share."

While discussing the stratified trade that included women of diverse races and incomes, she notes that respectable women elevated themselves by downgrading the disreputable. She says, "Prostitutes offered men an outlet that enabled wives to hold on to the role of pure creatures set above human biological compulsions. Most of all, prostitution was an unending reminder of the advantages of conventional female domestic roles. The benefits of marriage never appeared more attractive than in contrast to the grim and unprotected struggle for subsistence of the prostitute." In Seattle the Skid Road District provided a catalyst for solidarity among respectable women who launched repeated crusades for social reform.

Limerick noted that the history of prostitution also brings to light complexities in a stratified society. "The economic elite...often owned the real estate in which prostitution took place; vice districts were among the more rewarding Western investment opportunities. And the official representatives of the law took their cut of the enterprise, in regular payoffs to prevent arbitrary arrests."

Few personal records remain from women who plied their trade in Seattle's Tenderloin. One who might have worked there is Abbie Widner who moved from town to town throughout the Northwest. The Eastern Washington State Historical Society has a few of her letters, written in March 1905 to "Dear Little Sweetheart," "Johnie," whom she longed to join in Tacoma. The following excerpts from her letters (with her own spelling, grammar and underlines) reveal the danger and degradation of her work, her sense of entrapment in the business, and her mistrust of other prostitutes.

On March 11, she wrote about two men, fighting over her in her room: "I told the dam fools to go out and fight it out and the one that won I would go with him. I hate them both like snakes but I get good money out of them both. I am so tirred of this damed life I could die but I see no other way before me but to live in disgrace and shame...."She tells of coming home at 2:00 a.m., "ofell tirred," of "my headake so bad from taking quinine [sometimes used for birth control]," and of leaving her roommate Kitty because she was afraid "the little thief...would steal twenty more from me."

Unlike some in the trade, she had a family that cared about her. She wrote, "I rec'd a letter from my sister today such a nice letter that I am a shamed that I live this way....She felt so bad to think I would not let her know where I was living....I ought to treat my folks better but I cant, but Kid you are all I care for in the world..." It appears that Johnie is all that keeps her going. She reminisces about going dancing with him and "what a nice time we had." She says, "Johnie...bee a good boy you little Triffler. I mean that and wont take it back. with all your falts I love you still....you are dearer to me that any." Accepting the fact that he frequents brothels, she cautions him, "Don't get the C [clap--slang for gonorrhea]."

In another letter she says, "I have made this week $39.50, so I am not doing bad if I dont have it stolen from me but ever time a man tuches me it I had a dager in my hand I would stab him to the heart, but I wont always bee a sport, no so help me God I wont if I haft to wash for a living..." She continues, "...but sweetheart some day wee are going to be happy, if wasnt for the plesent thoughts of you I would bee crazzed."

That she saw herself as breadwinner and caregiver is clear. She wrote, "Johnie how would you like me to go up into the gold fields for a while untill I mak a stake and then come to my boy. dont you think that a wise plan?" She abandoned the idea, writing a few days later,"....I am comming close to you Kid in about a week I am coming to Tacoma...and set me up when I come for if you are the way you drowed the picture I feare for you."

2.   Globe Hotel
300-310 First Avenue South

The turn-of-the-century building that houses Elliott Bay Book Store is located on the site of Seattle's first hospital, where Catherine Maynard nursed her husband's patients in their two spare bedrooms. It was also the site of Conklin House, built in 1859 and named for its proprietor, Mary Ann Conklin. Nicknamed Madam Damnable, she was known up and down the coast for her salty language, deadeye aim with a rock, and good cooking. Prior to moving to her own hotel in 1859, she had operated nearby Felker House, Seattle's first hostelry, where many a pioneer family found a temporary home, along with itinerant loggers, sailors, and the city's first "soiled doves."

3.   Seagrave Company
814 Security Building
512½ First Avenue South

From her position as stenographer, Helen Courtney advanced to branch manager of the Seagrave Company, responsible for selling $10,000 fire engines. An August 1920 article about her in SUNSET MAGAZINE reports, "Miss Courtney...looks like an attractive ingenue in the latest musical comedy success...and to associate her with a big, shiny, nickel-plated motor fire-engine is quite incongruous." Of her business philosophy, the 25-year-old said, "I never talk fire-engines to a man if he isn't ready to listen. I let him talk about what he is interested in, until the chance comes to tell him what I am interested in."

Comfortable with feminine tact, she sometimes persuaded all-male city councils to buy her company's engine because it would make their community happy. But if anyone asked mechanical questions, she had the answers. In preparation for her job, she donned overalls and took apart greasy engines in truck repair classes. Her office was filled with truck parts and books about fire engines which she diligently studied at night.

4.   Waterfall Garden
NE corner of Second Avenue South and South Main Street
Go one block east, then north

Built in 1978 by Sasaki Associates, the enticing, enclosed garden with its cascading waterfall commemorates the site where United Parcel Service was founded in 1907. Members of the Casey family delivered their first messages from a small basement office. When James Casey moved business headquarters to New York, his mother remained in Seattle. The Annie E. Casey Foundation, named by the family in her honor, developed the park as a gift to the city. A contemporary contrast to Pioneer Square's historic buildings, it is a pleasant oasis for a work- or shopping break.

5.   Lou Graham's Place
SW corner of Third Avenue and Washington Street
Go one block north, then one block east

In 1889 Lou Graham opened Seattle's first opulent bordello--one that rivaled the famed parlor houses in San Francisco. To staff her establishment, she imported cultivated, charming "ladies of the evening" to entertain local and visiting dignitaries. Her first floor parlor was for patrons seeking a quiet drink and pleasant companionship with women who could carry on discussions ranging from opera and literature to politics and economics. If a customer wanted more intimacy, he could rent an elegant upstairs suite, either by the hour or overnight. Other attractions were one of Seattle's finest dining rooms and a dance floor.

When Lou's first building was consumed by the Great Fire of 1889, she paid cash to immediately rebuild the brick structure that today houses law offices. She made private booths and libations free to representatives of city government, anytime day or night. Many of Seattle's leading citizens welcomed the amenities, as well as her business's substantial contribution to the city treasury. Although Lou was anathema to proper ladies, she ultimately fueled their agenda as well. When she died intestate with no next of kin, she left approximately a quarter of a million dollars that the court awarded to the Common Schools of King County.

Additional information about Lou Graham is in the history of the Pike

Place Market by Alice Shorett and Murray Morgan. The late Bill Speidel--a lively, lusty and often irreverent chronicler of Seattle's past--also wrote extensively about the tenderloin and especially about Lou whom he calls "the Hostess with the Mostest." In his book THROUGH THE EYE OF THE NEEDLE, he provides convincing evidence about her extensive influence on city business and political leaders. A photo of Lou and "her girls" is at 610 First Avenue, near the ticket window of the Underground Tour, founded by Speidel. Seattle's underground came about when the city raised the streets several years after buildings in the area were constructed. The lighthearted historic tour leads through erstwhile ground floor establishments that have long been uninhabited and buried.

6. King County Courthouse
Block between Third and Fourth and Jefferson and James
Cross Second Avenue, then go right one block

Called the County-City Building in its early years, today's King County Courthouse was once the home of both county and city government. Suite 239 was the mayor's office which from 1926 to 1928 was occupied by Mayor Bertha Knight Landes, Seattle's first and only woman mayor. (Please see Chapter V, Wilsonian Hotel, home of Mayor Landes for further information.) Later political pioneers who held office in the building were King County Councilwoman Bernice Stern, Lois North and Rudy Chow. (Please see Chapter I, Ruby Chow Park for further information.)

Women's most enduring saga in the building's history has been that of lawyers and judges, struggling to break the ranks of the judiciary. In 1914 Reah Whitehead moved into her chambers, as King County's and Washington State's first female justice of the peace. Following her term, other women--for years one at a time--have presided over the lowest court. Several made bids for higher judicial posts, but in the male-dominated milieu of politics and power, they ran into stiff resistance. In 1970 Nancy Ann Holman made history when Governor Dan Evans appointed her to the bench of the King County's Superior Court. As the women's movement of the 1970s and 1980s gained momentum, a groundswell of public support finally broke the barriers, admitting female elective and appointive judges at every judicial level in the county, state and nation and rendering the "token woman" a phenomenon of the past. Following are brief stories of struggles and achievements of some of King County's pioneering women lawyers and judges. (For further information, please see Elected Washington Women's video, "Her Day in Court," produced by historian Susan Starbuck.)

Reah Whitehead

Seattle's first female justice of the peace served from 1914 to 1941. In 1924 she entered the race for King County Superior Court Judge, stating her position to the SEATTLE STAR:

> There is no sex in brains....the state of Washington and King County in particular should have a woman superior court judge to even up matters. Don't get the idea that I think that I or any other woman can do judicial work better than a man. That's just the point at issue. It's that a woman's viewpoint plus a man's viewpoint equals the human viewpoint. And that is what our courts need.

Judge Evangeline Starr

In 1941 Evangeline Starr succeeded Rhea Whitehead as King County's lone female justice of the peace, then served seven elective four-year terms until her retirement in 1971. Even before she was born, her father had planned that his child would follow him into law. On hearing that they had a baby girl, he declared to his wife, "Oh well, SHE can be a lawyer." Following her graduation with a cum laude degree in 1922, she worked as a prosecuting attorney until she was appointed to the bench.

Judge Starr was a lifelong activist in women's organizations, serving as president of: Phi Delta Delta Legal Fraternity (a women's honorary); American Association of University Women (Seattle branch); Washington State Federation of Business and Professional Women's Clubs; Seattle Federation of Women's Clubs; International

Toastmistress Club, NW Region; and Traveler's Aid. From 1961 to 1969, she was a member of the Governor's Commission on the Status of Women, serving under Governors Rosellini and Evans.

When asked for a general characterization of women's mission after 1920 (when the 19th Amendment to the U.S. Constitution was ratified), she said; "One of the things I've thought of with all of this women's work is their humility, their complete humility...wanting to make things better. There was never any feeling of command or demand until the era of NOW (National Organization for Women). It started in Washington, D.C. [A friend] wrote me a letter [to ask if] I would like to belong, and I sent my $5.00....That's when women started to demand, but before that they had been very humble...we just wanted to be better, to make things better, but then we began to say we deserve something too."

In 1970 a group of women met in Judge Starr's chambers to form the first local chapter of NOW. Other politically oriented organizations were soon chartered, including Washington Women's Political Caucus, Washington Women United, and Elected Washington Women, while many established federations lent their support. Contemporary women's activism gave rise to unprecedented opportunities for women in non-traditional fields, ranging from blue-collar trades to leadership positions in business and politics. No longer the token women justice of the peace, Judge Starr was elated to see the ranks of women judges swell as other women broke the barriers to the higher courts. As women broadened their power base, they were able to bring women's issues into the mainstream of political concern.

Carmen Otero

As King County's first Latina Superior Court Judge, Carmen Otero came to the bench in 1980 and in the next decade rose to Chief Criminal Judge, supervising a department of 22 other judges. In the October 1992 issue of NORTHWEST ETHNIC NEWS, she wrote about her saga which began in rural New Mexico: "This child was sent home from school because she couldn't speak English. She was born during the depth of the Depression; her mother, married at age

15, had a fifth grade education, and she was unbelievably shy."

At her mother's urging, she pursued her education, then married, had children, and became a school teacher. One day she decided she needed a change and by process of elimination, chose law school, where she said "something clicked." She excelled, winning a full scholarship. Her move to King County "without a job and only a Visa card" was another leap into the unknown. After a year of teaching in Redmond, she passed the state bar exam, then accepted a position in

Women of Japanese descent had clubs and clubrooms at the downtown YWCA. While their mothers take classes or socialize, these girls in supervised day-care are at play on the roof.
(Courtesy of the Washington State Historical Society, Photo by Asahel Curtis #29753)

the Attorney General's Office as a trial attorney. Reflecting on how a shy young woman could do that, she wrote, "I guess I just plunged forward with my heart in my throat..."

She notes that changes have occurred during her tenure: "The judges are more accepting to change...Judges are now coming on the bench with diverse backgrounds, from a former nurse to the son of a migrant farmer. The court is a friendlier place and I believe our community is well served." A member of several committees, including Washington State Juvenile and Family Law," she says: "Because of the work I do in court, I now look at children with fear but also with optimism. Fear based on the poverty, crime and violence I see in our community today; and optimism and hope for their future based on my experience that this can change."

7.   Nippon Kan Theater
628 South Washington Street
From the underground station at 3rd and James, take the bus to the International District station at 5th and King. Go north to South Washington, then turn right

In 1909, the same year as the Alaska-Yukon-Pacific Exposition (AYP), "Japantown" was experiencing its own cultural awakening. Seattleites of Japanese descent numbered 6,000, the city's largest non-white population. Thanks to the tradition of arranged marriages, the ratio of men to women narrowed to two to one during the teens. When he had saved enough money, a lonely bachelor often asked his family in Japan to find him a wife. Sometimes men returned to their homeland for the wedding, but about one-third of the marriages were by proxy, involving an exchange of photos and information. On reaching an agreement, the man sent a one-way ticket to his "picture bride," then arranged for their marriage on the day of her arrival in America.

Perhaps it was the influx of picture brides, many of whom were schooled in traditional arts and culture, that prompted the community to build its own Nippon Kan (Japanese Hall). Perhaps it was the Japanese government's extravagant participation in the AYP. Or perhaps it was a proud reaction to Seattle's theaters that restricted non-whites to balcony seats. In any case the Nippon Kan filled a void as a community center where families enjoyed classical Japanese dance, Kabuki theater, Sumo wrestling, political debates and visiting evangelists.

On Women's Rights

A memorable program at the Nippon Kan in 1938 was the lecture by Waka Yamada, a famous crusader for women's rights in Japan. When she spoke about exploitation of Japanese women, men in the audience at first jeered. Her frank response was: "I dare to say these things because I myself had a hard experience!: Her story quickly brought the jeering to a stop. As an idealistic young woman, she had immigrated to America, only to fall into the hands of unscrupulous procurers who gave her the name of "Arabian Oyae," then forced her to serve American men in a Seattle brothel. After a harrowing escape, she was recaptured and landed back in the business in San Francisco, where she again escaped and found her way to a settlement house for Asian women. There she met her husband and returned with him to Japan, where she became a leading advocate in the emerging women's rights movement.

Historian Kazuo Ito who included Yamada and other Japanese prostitutes in his book ISSEI, said: "...we cannot criticize all of those girls who were brought in groups as prostitutes....It was 1956 when the anti-prostitution law was first passed in Japan." Ito says that in 1911--just after Washington women won the franchise--the Japanese Association launched its own efforts to rid the community of "pink hotels" (a euphemism for Asian brothels), deporting prostitutes and their pimps back to Japan.

Classical Dance

According to Tama Tokuda, who studied dance at the Nippon Kan, there were three dance schools, each of which was directed by its own teacher. One was Madame Nakatani who had learned to teach the exacting classical dance through a traditional apprenticeship program in Japan. Her entire repertoire was committed to memory and students learned by watching, then imitating her. She taught them one at a time, playing the samisen [a stringed instrument] herself to accompany them.

Tokuda remembers the space beneath the Nippon Kan's auditorium which contained a makeup room, a long pole with wigs hanging from it, and Mr. Hayashi's costume rental. In preparation for recitals, dance students squatted down in front of a long mirror, while the teacher carefully applied their makeup. When they were ready, they went to a special area to pose for the photographer.

For students and their families, classical dance was a serious commitment. Pupils went from public school to Japanese school and then on to their dance class, often arriving home after dark. Recitals at the Nippon Kan were family oriented and an important part of community life.

Preservation of the Theater
The Nippon Kan continued to flourish until members of the community were forced into exile in 1942. Thanks to the efforts of Edward and Elizabeth Burke, the theater was recently restored and once again stages lectures and performances, including Kabuki and Japanese dance. Prominently situated on a hillside, it serves as a reminder of Seattle's earlier Japantown, an area that spread from Second to Twelfth Avenue South between Yesler Way and South Jackson Streets.

8.   Tanaka Dressmaking School
600 South Washington Street
The building next door to the Nippon Kan was once home to the Tanaka Dressmaking School, where community women--often with young children in tow--learned to make Western clothing for themselves and their families. Mannequins modeled student-made dresses in the display window. After two years of training, graduates received their diplomas at the annual commencement ceremony and in subsequent years, they met for alumni reunions. In factories, shops, or at home, many used their sewing skills to supplement the family income.

9.   Goon Dip Building/Milwaukee Hotel
South King Street and 7th Avenue South
Go one block south

In the first decade of the twentieth century, Chinatown took root in the King Street area where Tongs (family associations) erected substantial buildings with ornate balconies on the top floor. By 1910 the population numbered 720 with only 16 families and a male-female ratio of thirteen to one--a consequence of the Chinese Exclusion Act of 1882. Designed to preserve jobs for Americans, the act did not apply to Chinese scholars or merchants and their families.

A member of the prominent merchant class, Goon Dip brought his family to Portland, then to Seattle where he served as Chinese Consul. In 1911 he dedicated his new building, the largest in Chinatown, which housed the consulate. In accord with upper-class Chinese tradition, Mrs. Goon Dip was rarely seen in public--her primary obligation being to home and family. When she appeared at official functions, such as the Lewis and Clark Exposition in Portland, she maintained an aristocratic bearing and wore richly embroidered silk robes with substantial integration of the color yellow to symbolize her high station.

Another cause for her reclusiveness was her four-inch-long bound feet, also an aristocratic symbol. Her grandson, Willard Jue, said that one of her greatest joys was raising daughters free of this restrictive cultural tradition. Unlike their mother, the daughters went to the university, entered business and professional careers, and participated in community organizations, including the YWCA. One of the daughters, Lillian Goon, earned an MA from the University of Oregon, only to find that schools would not hire her because of her race. She opened her own western dance studio in Seattle and also performed with the popular Seattle ballerina, Mary Ann Wells. At a time when the city had only a handful of Chinese families, these public-spirited women helped lay the foundation for a strong community.

Mrs. Goon Dip poses with her daughter Martha and son Daniel
(Courtesy of the Willard Jue estate)

10. NORTHWEST ASIAN WEEKLY
(formerly THE SEATTLE CHINESE POST)
414 8th Avenue South
Go west, then south

For half a century, the Pacific Northwest did not have a Chinese newspaper. That changed in 1982 when Assunta Ng, a far-sighted immigrant from Hong Kong, decided that one was needed. To finance her plan, she went from door-to-door through the Chinese business community, persuading proprietors to buy advertisements and subscriptions. As one of the only women in the United States to found and publish a newspaper, she took on the doubly daunting task of producing two papers a week--one in English and the other in Chinese.

Along with reporting news and stories of interest to her readers, Ng's mission was to organize meaningful activities and events in the Asian community. Her paper sponsors children's arts and essay contests, debates, commemorative dinners, and the selection of Women and Men of the Year.

As her newspaper broadened its focus to the entire Asian community, Ng decided to change its name to the NORTHWEST ASIAN WEEKLY. The recipient of numerous awards, she continues to foster understanding and connections among Asians and also between Asians and other ethnic groups. The newspaper is appropriately located in the former home of the Wing Luke Asian Museum.

11.   Wing Luke Asian Museum

407 Seventh Avenue
Phone: 623-5124. Open Tuesday-Friday, 11 a.m.-4:30 p.m.;
Saturday and Sunday, noon-4 p.m.; and some evenings
Admission: $1.50 adults; $.50 children, students, and seniors
Walk east one block

The nation's only museum preserving the entire spectrum of Asian-American cultures offers permanent and changing exhibits and sponsors a variety of cultural events. Unlike more traditional art and historical museums, its focus is not on priceless artifacts from Asia. Instead it interprets the experience of a quarter of a million Asian Americans from 30 different ethnic groups who today make Washington State their home.

Museum Director Ron Chew enlists the help of community volunteers to discover parts of our history that have not been told, documenting stories of community building, family life, work and play, and the history of racial discrimination. Widespread participation has paid off with donations of numerous diaries, photographs, artifacts, and ephemera. While older people share their stories--sometimes for the first time--younger generations are learning about their roots. Visitors of diverse cultures are getting to know their neighbors. In a May 1993 interview with the SEATTLE POST INTELLIGENCER, Chew summed up the museum's mission as involving people "in developing a community vision." It has become an important cornerstone of Seattle's revitalized International District.

From the beginning, women staff members and volunteers have played critical roles. The PI quoted Sudha Shetty, an Indian immigrant who said: "The most important thing is that our children come to this museum and know that their future is their past....To know what it is and to be proud of it."

12. Northwest Asian American Theater Theater Off Jackson
407 Seventh Avenue South
Phone: 340-1445

The Northwest Asian American Theater is an outgrowth of the earlier Asian Multi Media Center which in the 1970s had programs in photography, graphic arts, silkscreening and drama. When the AMMC folded, only the drama program survived. Now in its twentieth year, NWAAT owes much of its success and its survival to Bea Kiyohara, who as a single mother of three small children moved her family from Kansas to Seattle to accept the job of secretary for the AMMC. A month later when she found a better paying job, she joined the board. With a passion for drama, she began acting, directing and producing, and for fifteen years served as the theater's artistic director.

In NWAAT's 1993 twentieth anniversary booklet, DREAMS AND PROMISES, Mayumi Tsutakawa, who worked with the AMMC, credits Bea with: "recognizing local Asian/Pacific American talent and bringing legitimate and innovative Asian/Pacific American drama to the stage in Seattle." She notes, "Bea has helped to organize numerous progressive political shows uncovering the history of women and Japanese Americans in Washington."

Kiyohara, herself, wrote:

My vision of Asian American Theater has always been to use

the stage as an educational vehicle, to tell <u>our</u> story,...to influence our young so they could be proud of where they came from and who they are.

In her efforts to establish NWAAT, Kiyohara reached out to the broader artistic community, earning widespread respect as a member and chair of the King County Arts Commission.

In the early 1980s NWAAT went into partnership with the Women's Theater, where Mary Montgomery took the lead in securing their own 153-seat Theater Off Jackson. The women's troupe has since folded, leaving NWAAT to go it alone. To survive the company continues to expand its network. Its actors perform with most of Seattle's other major theaters. It also rents its own stage to other companies. One is the gay and lesbian Alice B. Theater, founded in 1984 and named for Alice B. Toklas, a graduate of the University of Washington who attracted public attention as Gertrude Stein's long-term companion.

Located in its own space, the 153-seat Theater Off Jackson in the heart of the International District is one of only a handful of small theaters that have become mainstays of Seattle's cultural life.

13.   Chong Wah Benevolent Association
522 Seventh Avenue South

The two-story benevolent association hall and school combines architectural features from both Chinese and Western cultures. Its impressive form appropriately symbolizes its political and cultural significance. According to Frank Chin, a contributor to the state centennial history WASHINGTONIANS, Seattle's Chong Wah board is the only one in the world with female members. Please see Ruby Chow Park in Chapter I for the story of how she and other Chinese-American women won their elections to this power center of the community.

14.   Union Pacific Railroad Station
Travelers Aid Society

503 Fifth Avenue South
Go west on King Street

In 1921 the Seattle Federation of Women's Clubs provided funding to found the local Travelers Aid Society. The chair of the all-female board of directors was Blanche Mason, head of the Women's Division of the Seattle Police Department. While the Union Pacific Railroad donated free office space, the King Street Station contributed $50 per month. On duty 18 hours a day every day, society volunteers offered information regarding community services and facilities, dealt with language barriers, and provided emergency relief.

Nationally and locally, Travelers Aid was a spin off of an earlier YWCA program that placed depot matrons at train stations and docks "to guard and guide young women traveling alone." Beginning as a protective service for young women, the society expanded its mission to serve immigrants, refugees, and defense personnel in transit, and to intercept and care for runaway children. From its present headquarters at 909 Fourth Avenue, and at Sea-Tac International Airport, it continues to provide information, referral and emergency services for travelers.

15. Bemis Brothers Bag Factory/Bemis Company Inc.
55 South Atlantic Street
Continue west, then go south on 1st Avenue South to South Atlantic

As part of the early twentieth century crusade to improve the lot of working women, union women, the YWCA and other supportive organizations urged employers to improve conditions at the worksite and many responded. A 1912 YWCA newsletter notes:

> The Bemis Brothers Bag Factory are putting in a cafeteria, for the benefit of the employees. This is a move in the right direction, and we wish every firm in the city might do the same. The young ladies of this firm have a flourishing club [in the YWCA's Federation of Industrial Clubs]. The Public

Library has offered to put in a branch in the rest room of the factory. This firm is making its cafeteria and rest room a model place for its employees. They also have a fine pianola in the cafeteria.

By the teens the YWCA had a network of industrial clubs, representing businesses and factories throughout the city. Members met at the downtown "Y" for weekly dinners and programs. In addition the "Y" coordinated intramural sports activities and sent instructors to the worksites to offer lunch hour classes.

16. Coast Guard Museum Northwest
Pier 36, 1519 Alaska Way South
Phone: 286-9608. Open Monday, Wednesday, Friday, 9 a.m.-3 p.m.; Saturday and Sunday, 1-5 p.m. Nearby is the Vessel Traffic Center where you can observe Coast Guard personnel guiding traffic. On weekends they offer guided tours of ships in port.
Free
Go north one block; turn left on Brougham Way, then left on Alaska Way South

In 1942 Congress opened the American military to career service women, making them eligible for rank, pay and benefits for the first time in the nation's history. Earlier generations of women had served their country as volunteers, predominantly in nursing and clerical capacities. The United States entry into World War II drew millions of Americans into overseas combat zones, severely depleting both civilian and military operations at home. Like private industry, the military turned to women to fill non-combat job vacancies.

The Coast Guard Museum includes interpretive historical exhibits relating to the SPARs (acronym taken from the Coast Guard motto "Semper Paratus,"--Always Ready) who were the first American women admitted to a military academy. Between 1942 and 1945, more than 700 future SPAR officers trained at the Coast Guard Academy in New London, Connecticut. Although no SPARs were assigned to ships, patriotic women who enlisted were considered daring for their time, somewhat rebellious and hungry for adventure.

In her book WOMEN IN THE MILITARY, Major General Jeanne Holm (USAF) wrote:

> There can be little doubt that women proved their value early on. The record of World War II is replete with testimonials attesting to the excellence of the women's contributions, their disciplined characters, and the overall positive effect on all the services. Commanders who in 1942 had cried, "Over my dead body will I take military women," were soon asking for their "fair share".

Nonetheless, the attitudes of military men continued to be the dominant factor influencing the acceptance and morale of the women individually and collectively. There was a constant, all-pervasive awareness that women had invaded a male preserve.

The museum's exhibits also document the work of the volunteer Coast Guard Auxiliary. In their book, WINDS OF CHANGE: WOMEN IN NORTHWEST COMMERCIAL FISHING, Charlene Allison and her co-authors note that in the 1950s the Auxiliary was predominantly male and that women sometimes encountered extra obstacles as they worked to pass 12 qualifying exams in skills such as piloting and navigation. They interviewed Lois Engleson, who fishes commercially and who was admitted to the Auxiliary in 1955. She recalled that men hid the charts to prevent her from taking her piloting exam, and that she had to reschedule it at a later date.

As an Auxiliary member, Engleson has participated in numerous search-and-rescue operations, taught classes in marine skills, and helped boaters with both mechanical and navigational problems. In an oral history interview, she described her duties:

> Being qualified you can be called at any time for patrol duty, or for search-and-rescue and things like that....except we're

not paid....For instance, one morning I was busy....scrambling eggs in a frying pan. The phone rang, and [this guy] said, "Lois, can you....get your boat over here? We're on search-and-rescue." I took my frying pan with me and I went, lit the stove on the boat, and then finished my breakfast out there. We're dedicated to....preservation of life and property.

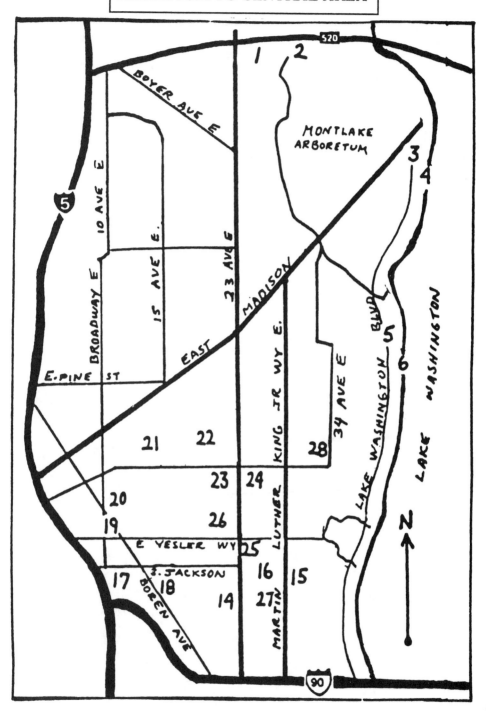

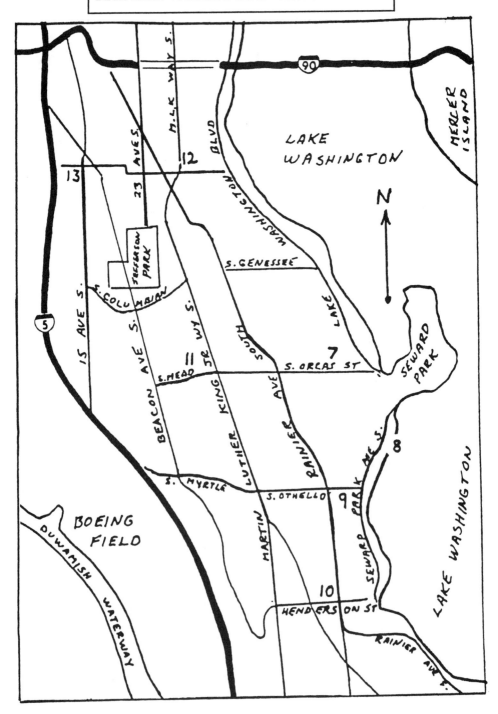

IX. LAKESIDE TO CENTRAL SEATTLE

Montlake to Rainier Valley to Central Area

This tour begins at the Museum of History and Industry with an exploration of permanent and changing exhibits from King County's most extensive historical collection. Your route through the Arboretum and along the shore of Lake Washington offers numerous opportunities for walking, bicycling or picnicking. From one of Seattle's most affluent districts, you continue into culturally diverse neighborhoods to explore a rich array of women's legacies. Included in the tour are sites connected with women from a variety of socio-economic, religious, ethnic and political orientations.

1. Museum of History and Industry

2700 24th Avenue East
Phone: 324-1125. Open 10 a.m.-5 p.m. daily.
Admission: $3 adults; $1.50 children and seniors; free on Tuesdays
Turn east on East Hamlin Street which is just south of the Montlake Bridge

November 13, 1911 was the sixtieth anniversary of the arrival of Seattle's first settlers. (Please see Birthplace of Seattle, Chapter XI.) On that date Emily Carkeek, a transplanted Englishwoman with a strong sense of heritage, invited several women friends to a Founder's Day luncheon to form a local historical association. Dressed in pioneer costumes, they dined on chowder made from Puget Sound butter clams. The elegant Carkeek mansion subsequently became the setting for annual Founders' Day celebrations of the Seattle and King County Historical Society.

Initially, members--both women and men--formed committees to research local history and gather artifacts and memorabilia, which they stored in their basements and in a fireproof building at the University of Washington. Until her death in 1926, Emily Carkeek led the society in its efforts to found a museum. Ten years later, the Carkeek's only daughter Guendolen Plestcheeff (Please see Plestcheeff Institute for the Decorative Arts in Chapter X) was elected president and served until 1952, when her mother's dream finally came true.

Locating the site for the museum was Plestcheeff's major achievement. Her parents had initially planned to establish it on the 35 acres at Sand Point on Lake Washington that they had given to the city for a park, and county officials had actively promoted the idea. But in 1926 the Navy acquired the property for an air station. The Carkeeks then replaced it with another site in north Seattle overlooking Puget Sound. While space in Carkeek Park was allocated for a museum, the trustees rejected it since they thought the location too remote.

When she learned that the site at the north end of the Arboretum belonged to the federal government, Plestcheeff flew to Washington D.C. and effectively lobbied to have it returned to the County, which subsequently deeded it to the City of Seattle. She then negotiated a trade with the City Council for the site in Carkeek Park. In 1952 at the formal dedication of the Paul Thiry-designed building, Plestcheeff presented the key to Mayor William O. Devin. Today the museum houses one of the largest historical collections on the West Coast.

2.   Foster Island
Washington Park Arboretum
Follow directions from the Museum parking lot

A half-mile nature trail with floating spans, docks, bridges, and interpretive signs leads through the marsh to Foster Island, which is connected to the Arboretum via a footbridge. The island has been preserved as a bird sanctuary, thanks to the Seattle Audubon Society. Founded by Minnie M. Crickmore in 1916, it affiliated nationally and eventually had a jurisdiction that encompassed western Washington.

From the start, the society regarded birds as vital components of the ecosystem. Not only were they aesthetic treasures for nature lovers;

they also devoured insects, protecting vegetation and crops. Audubon Society members, for the most part women, took "nature walks" with note pads in hand to study and document bird life. Hazel Wolf, a leading member of the Seattle Society since the 1950s, sees the bird song as an appropriate symbol for the spirit of the walks. She explained, "Bird song is like a symphony. At first it's a big hullabaloo; then you hear the parts." The society shares its interests with schools, teaching children about birds and showing them how to build birdhouses and feeding stations.

Another priority is lobbying for bird and wildlife sanctuaries. In the 1920s, the finely focused Seattle society dropped its membership in the Women's Legislative Council of Washington, so that it could raise funds to establish the bird sanctuary on Foster Island.

3. Junior League of Seattle
4119 East Madison Street
Go south through the Arboretum, then left on Madison

From temporary quarters in prestigious downtown hotels, the Junior League of Seattle moved to the Madison Park district in the 1950s, where it recently purchased its own building. Unlike most early women's clubs which have declined in membership, it is flourishing as one of the county's most significant voluntary service organizations. With 600 active members and 1,000 alumnae known as "sustainers," the greater Seattle association is one of the largest in the country.

Turn-of-the-century social reform movements prompted a group of affluent young women in New York City to want to help less fortunate slum dwellers of the lower Eastside. This was the beginning of the Junior Leagues which realized from the start that effective voluntary service required training programs. The Seattle League was formed in 1923 by an eager group of young women to support the Seattle Day Nursery. When Children's Orthopedic Hospital asked for volunteers, the League readily responded.

A major project that began in the 1930s was children's theater. As script writers, set and costume designers, and actors, members planted the seed for a new organization called Junior Programs. From the Great Depression through World War II and into the fifties, the volunteer troupe performed in housing projects and toured to rural community schools, often giving children their first taste of theater.

In the 1960s, the erstwhile bastion of society ladies began to accept working women as members, accommodating their schedules with evening meetings and training seminars. Today's members have a wide choice of placements, including child education programs in the new Seattle Art Museum, promotion of literacy and the rights of the differently abled, managing the Wise Penny Thrift Shop at 4744 University Way NE, and publishing PUGET SOUNDINGS MAGAZINE. In 1993 the League published its second critically acclaimed regional cookbook, SIMPLY CLASSIC.

4.   Pioneer Hall

1642 43rd Avenue East
Phone: 746-6305.
Open second Sunday of each month, 1-4 p.m.
Continue on East Madison, taking the loop to the right to 43rd Avenue East on the shore of Lake Washington

The King County Pioneer Association was founded in 1871 to preserve and record unique stories of adventure and settlement for future generations. It later merged with the Pioneer Association of the State of Washington with membership open to anyone whose family had arrived by 1889--the date of statehood. In 1910 Sarah Loretta Denny of the pioneer Denny family left a bequest of $20,000 to build Washington Pioneer Hall, the triple-arched brick building where the association continues to hold meetings and events.

A related organization is the Daughters of the Pioneers, founded in 1911, with the stringent requirement that members trace their Washington roots to before 1870. With a mission to "perpetuate the sentiment relating to pioneer days," the Daughters have collected biographies and artifacts, placed markers at historic sites, and successfully lobbied the legislature to require a course in Washington State history as part of the public school curriculum.

In the mid 1950s, the Daughters moved into Pioneer Hall, then in a state of deterioration, and set about cleaning and restoring it. Today, they continue to manage daily operations, including an impressive archival and genealogical collection that is available to researchers. Meeting space in the hall doubles as a museum with a pioneer portrait gallery and exhibits of vintage clothing and artifacts. This monument to Washington's pioneers is listed on the National Register of Historic Place.

5. The Bush School
(formerly called Helen Bush/Parkside School)
405 36th Avenue East
Hefferman House
408 Lake Washington Boulevard
Take East Madison to Lake Washington Boulevard; turn left, then right on East Republican; The entrance is on the left

The buildings on 36th Avenue East were erected between the 1930s and the 1960s. Historic Hefferman House now serves as a teachers' residence, while the large garage is used as a kindergarten.

In 1924 when Helen Taylor Bush was 44 years old, her husband suddenly lost his hearing and had to retire from banking. A Phi Beta Kappa graduate of the University of Illinois, she was faced with the unforeseen challenge of having to support the family. Knowing that she had "a way with children," she decided to open a school with progressive teaching techniques to make education fun and stimulating. From the playroom of her home in the Denny Blaine neighborhood, she soon moved her school to its current site. Two of her first six pupils started as kindergartners and remained until they finished high school.

A member of the Audubon Society and an avid gardener, Bush wrote in the 1928 catalog:

Nature study makes a universal appeal to children. They enter school equipped with an inquisitive intelligence, and the objects of their keenest interest are people, animals, plants....They learn to observe, to make their own deductions....

Field trips to the nearby park were frequent. In addition, Bush sought out talented artists and performers who could offer children opportunities for self-expression. A supportive Mothers Club contributed to the school, and students in turn did community service work, such as tutoring younger children in a nearby public school. Bush wrote: "This school subscribes to the philosophy of 'learning to do by doing.' As far as possible the children are allowed to set up their own goals--with the understanding that one of the functions of the teacher is to help them to evaluate these goals and to help them create new ones." Today the school with a student body of 520 boys and girls continues to aspire to the vision of its founder.

6. Viretta Park
Lake Washington Boulevard and 39th Avenue East
Continue south on Lake Washington Boulevard

When they developed the Denny Blaine neighborhood in 1901, Charles Denny and Elbert Blaine, both decendents of early pioneers, reserved this parcel for a public park. Viretta was Denny's wife. The nearby Minerva Fountain is named for Blaine's wife.

7. Congregation Bikur Cholim--Machzikay Hadath Mikva (Ritual bath)
5145 South Morgan Street
Continue south on Lake Washington Boulevard; turn right on Orcas Street; then left on Wilson Avenue South; then left on South Morgan

Since 1970 Cecilia Etkin has supervised the women's mikva. While men make daily visits to the men's bath, the ancient ritual for married women takes place monthly. From the beginning until seven days after the end of her menstrual cycle, a woman and her husband are required to abstain from physical intimacy. At that time she prepares for her mikva by bathing, washing her hair and removing all make-up, including fingernail polish. In the steamy bath, which combines rain water with scalding water, she immerses herself three times, symbolizing her commitment to ritual cleanliness, modesty and sanctity of the family.

In an April 23, 1993 interview with the JEWISH TRANSCRIPT, Etkin said: "When the women leave they are very happy. It is like a honeymoon....This is what makes the mikva important for the family and the couple." While the ritual bath is an Orthodox tradition, members of the Reform and Conservative Jewish communities often use Seattle's only women's mikva.

8. Martha Washington School for Girls (site)
6612 57th Avenue South
Go south on 52nd Avenue South; then left to the foot of South Holly Street

From the turn of the century, Seattle's indigent and delinquent children were housed in parental schools, first located in the dilapidated basement of a rooming house. After winning the vote in 1910, women tackled the issue of juvenile justice, promoting the establishment of juvenile courts and sex-segregated reform schools, one of which was the Martha Washington School for Girls. Supervised jointly by the King County Juvenile Court and the Seattle Public Schools, it operated from 1919 through the 1950s. The recently demolished buildings were located on this spectacular nine-acre lakeside site, which is listed on the Seattle Register of Historic Places.

As the court's first female referee for girls, Francette Plummer Maring befriended her charges, seeing several through their return to regular schools and business college. SUNSET MAGAZINE profiled her in its September 19, 1920 issue, noting that "Success has attended all communities where women have an official interest in delinquent girls, and many of those unfortunates, through the understanding of women, have been made self-respecting members of society."

9.   Kline Galland Home
7500 Seward Park Avenue South
Return on South Holly to Seward Park Avenue South and turn left

On her death in 1907, Caroline Kline Galland left a substantial bequest for construction of the Caroline Kline Galland Home for the Aged and Feeble Poor. Still in operation today, its original mission was to serve people of the Jewish faith and members of the Society of Universal Religion. For more about this caring philanthropist, please see Chapter X, Caroline Kline Galland House.

10.   Florence Crittenton Home
9236 Renton Avenue South
Continue south on Seward Park Avenue; turn right on South Kenyon Street; then left on Renton Avenue South

In the 19th century, proper townsfolk looked askance at the unwed mother-to-be, branding her a social outcast. Deprived of needed guidance and support, she suffered deep humiliation in a Victorian moral climate. Harriet Parkhurst recognized the problem and learned how to help from New York evangelist Charles Crittenton. In memory of his daughter who died at age four, he had founded a mission in 1883 with the purpose of rescuing the unwed mother and her baby.

In the late 1890s, Parkhurst enlisted several women friends to form a Seattle branch of the Florence Crittenton Rescue Circle. With support from Seattle businessmen the board purchased a handsome two-story building at 9259 50th Avenue South in Georgetown, the former home of Seattle Baptist University, which was a seminary for women.

Florence Crittenton Home not only cared for girls in their "hour of need;" its staff also provided counseling, child care instruction, and vocational training to prepare young mothers for their return to society. Of the board members who directed the home, a 1904 article in the SEATTLE MAIL AND HERALD said, "The home is blest of the love of holy womanhood for the fallen ones. In this work good women are devoting their lives to the care of those whom society has made outcasts, and doing everything within their power and means to save from evil ways those who come under their care."

In the 1920s with increasing demand for its services, the home moved to the larger campus on Military Road--now Renton Avenue South--where it could accommodate up to 70 unwed mothers at a time and serve nearly 140 per year. Due to changing social mores that resulted in fewer clients and decreasing contributions, the home could no longer meet expenses and closed in 1973. Today, the facility houses the Thunderbird Treatment Center for Alcohol and Drug Abuse.

11. Radical Women
New Freeway Hall
5018 Rainier Avenue South
Go north on Rainier Avenue South

Radical Women (RW) was founded in 1967 at New Freeway Hall in the University District, headquarters of the Freedom Socialist Party. (FSP) Members, who call each other "comrade," describe themselves as Trotskyists, modern-day disciples of Leon Trotsky whose dream of a worldwide workers' revolution was crushed by Josef Stalin. One of the founders, Clara Fraser, describes the organization as "the feminists in the radical movement and the radicals in the feminist movement." RW is made us largely of working-class women--many of whom are members of trade unions--who link racism and sexism with economic exploitation.

In addition to an ambitious schedule of programs, RW sponsors political candidates and has several publications and a small bookstore. In 1985 the FSP and RW purchased the building in the Rainier business district which now serves as their headquarters. For detailed historical analysis, read founding member Gloria Martin's book SOCIALIST FEMINISM: THE FIRST DECADE, 1966-1977.

12. El Centro de la Raza
2524 16th Avenue South
Go west on South Alaska Street which merges with Columbian Way; then right on Beacon Avenue South; then right on 16th Avenue South

Like many of the center's clients, Stella Ortega, Director of Community Services, grew up in a household where her mother refused to speak Spanish to her children. She told them that they were as good as white people, but that to succeed they could never talk with an accent. A fourth generation Texan, Ortega was the first member of her family to graduate from high school. After attending business school, she held good jobs, had a new car and nice clothes. She also got her first taste of politics, volunteering to work with Chicano youth and becoming involved in the new Chicano awareness movement. At a 1972 conference, she met some people from Seattle who had an action plan.

At age 22 she used her vacation to join the peaceful, but illegal occupation of an abandoned elementary school on Beacon Hill. It was simultaneous self-discovery--feeling that she belonged and no longer needed to wish she was white--and discovery of her mission. She returned to Texas to sell her belongings, resign from her job, and move back to the unheated, dilapidated school for the remainder of the winter. During the occupation, she fell in love and married one of the leaders, Roberto Maestas. After four months, the City of Seattle and the school district agreed to lease the property to El Centro de la Raza for $1 per year, whereupon Maestas became executive director.

In 1988 Jennifer James-Wilson and Brenda Owings-Klimek interviewed Ortega for their book, MAKING A DIFFERENCE: A CELEBRATION OF WASHINGTON WOMEN. She said, "I joke that El Centro is a women's organization because the majority of the workers are women." From its stormy beginnings, the center has worked to create a positive environment for women by eschewing sexist and racist behavior and by fostering mutual respect. Ortega notes that the atmosphere "has made it possible for women to become more confident. It has given women who didn't go to school for economic or other reasons an opportunity....We have learned administrative, negotiating, decision making and sharing skills, as well as leadership." Reaching out to thousands of needy people, Ortega oversees programs that offer health care, emergency housing, employment services, senior and youth services, and a food bank. Today, a primary motivation for Ortega is her two daughters who, she says "have a much greater sense of possibility than their mothers before them....They are our seedlings of hope."

13.   Jefferson Park Ladies Improvement Club, Clubhouse
2336 15th Avenue South
Go east one block, then north

In 1883 when pioneer Judge E. A. Turner built this home for his family, it stood alone on the wooded crest of Beacon Hill, far removed from the city. The next owner added the striking Queen Anne style architectural features including the tower, verandas and leaded-glass windows. When the Jefferson Park Ladies Improvement Club purchased the building in 1923, members renovated it as a clubhouse, then made it a community center.

Founded in 1910 by Gertrude Spencer, the club's goal was to establish a "real community center backed by real community spirit." Initially, members worked to establish a kindergarten at the neighborhood school and the Beacon Hill branch of the Seattle Public Library. In the late nineteenth century, Seattle's city fathers had designated remote Beacon Hill as a site for isolation facilities for some of society's outcasts. The women's club campaigned to get rid of the dilapidated pesthouse where patients with contagious diseases had once been confined. In 1915 when the Seattle Park Board agreed to burn down the structure, a crowd turned out to cheer as Mrs. Spencer lit the torch.

Another building that they happily saw go up in flames was the abandoned City Stockade--also known as the Lazy Husband Ranch-- which was located on the site of the baseball diamond at Beacon Hill School. In earlier years, a man convicted of neglect had served his sentence at work in the Stockade while his wife received his earnings. In recessionary times, desperate husbands had sometimes asked to be sentenced, so that their families could have a meager paycheck.

From their clubhouse, the women's club worked to upgrade neighborhood streets and sidewalks, enhance schools, and improve conditions for local working women. An activity center for youth groups and other organizations, the old house was popularly known as the Beacon Hill Clubhouse. After more than 50 years, the women's club sold the property to the Washington Federation of Garden Clubs which today maintains it in keeping with its designation on the National Register of Historic Places.

14. Rainier Elementary School
23rd Avenue South between South King and South Lane Streets
Go east to 23rd Avenue South, then turn left

Nationally, the General Federation of Women's Clubs and the Parent Teachers Association joined forces to promote environmental conservation, parks and gardens. In Seattle the Leschi Heights Woman's Improvement Club and the PTA worked with faculty and pupils at Rainier School to begin the local school garden movement, which quickly spread to other city schools. Each child was given bulbs and seeds and a window box or plot near the school. The program's objective was threefold: give children wholesome exercise, teach them the rudiments of horticulture, and beautify the city.

In his HISTORY OF SEATTLE, Clarence Bagley, who observed the activity first hand, noted that competition among the schools was keen. In 1914 Seattle Garden Club adjudicators proclaimed the five best gardens at Rainier, University Heights, Cascade, Interlake and Fauntleroy Elementary Schools. When America entered World War

I, the program expanded its objectives, encouraging children to grow "victory gardens" of fruits and vegetables and join in the nation-wide patriotic commitment to conservation.

During Wartime emergency, Seattle hospitals hired their first Black nurses who formed the Mary Mahony Club (Courtesy of Esther Hall Mumford)

15. Seattle Association of Colored Women's Clubs, Clubhouse (now a private residence)
161 30th Avenue South
Go north on 23rd Avenue South; turn right on South Jackson Street, then left on 30th Avenue South

In 1983 an aging and dwindling membership reluctantly voted to sell the building that had been its clubhouse for 20 years. In its heyday it was a hub of Afra-American social, cultural, educational and community service activities. The Seattle association traces its history to 1917 when local clubs were among charter members of the State Association of Colored Women's Clubs. Initially, they raised funds to purchase the Sojourner Truth Home, a Victorian house that once stood near 23rd and Union. In addition to a meeting place, it was one of the state's first residential hotels for black women. (Please see #23, this chapter, Phillis Wheatley Branch of the YWCA for related information.) In 1948 and again in 1978, the Washington Association hosted the national convention in Seattle.

16.   Flo Ware Park
NE corner of 28th Avenue South and South Jackson Street

When Florence "Flo" Ware died in 1981, she left a legacy of humanitarian activism that spanned more than 50 years. Members of the community signaled their appreciation by urging the city to name this neighborhood park in her honor.

The mother of 20 foster children, she was a founding member of the Central Area School Council and the Seattle/King County Equal Opportunity Program. With support form the Model Cities Program, she helped establish the county's first group home for young people and the Central Area Senior Center. Beyond her local activities, she served on the White House Conference Board of Nutrition and Health. Her radio program, "What's Going Down," on former radio station KRAB helped keep the public, especially residents of the Central Area, informed.

17.   Victorian Row Apartments
1234 South King Street
Go west on South Jackson; turn left on 12th Avenue South

When octogenarian Stacia Champie offered co-ownership of her building to Historic Seattle, she also ensured the restoration and preservation of the city's only unaltered pre-1900s apartments. Champie and her husband purchased the building in 1949. As its manager, her door was always open to the tenants, some of whom raised their children there and stayed for more than 20 years. Despite her efforts, the building fell into disrepair with crumbling back porches, frayed wiring and broken pipes.

Thanks to Historic Seattle's $1.5 million restoration, the 1891 structure with Victorian fishtail shingles and decorative spindlework looks much as it did when it was built. When it reopened in 1993, Champie joyfully moved back to manage the apartments, now designated as rentals for low-income families. The building is a City of Seattle Landmark and is listed on the National Register of Historic Places.

18.   Neighborhood House/Settlement House (site)
14th Avenue South and South Main Street
Go two blocks north to South Main, then right

The story linked to this historic site and the building that once occupied it is about a neighborhood and a city in transition. Shortly after the turn of the century, waves of southern and eastern European immigrants arrived in Seattle--among them Russian Jews who had been persecuted, denied an education, and ultimately forced to leave their homeland. Seattle's pioneers already included prominent, educated Jews who had left Europe in an earlier emigration for a better life in the "goldeneh Medinah" (land of gold). Among them were Babette Schwabacher Gatzert, Mina Eckstein, Rose Morganstern Gottstein, and Esther Levy, some of the charter members of Seattle Section of the National Council for Jewish Women. Sensitive to the plight of new immigrants, the organization founded a nondenominational facility modeled after Jane Addams's Hull House in Chicago. Settlement House opened in 1906, offering instruction in English, Americanization, sewing, and religion. The trustees soon added employment services, youth programs, legal advice, and social clubs. Since most of the neighboring homes lacked bathrooms, Settlement House offered free baths. Medical care was available from the start with doctors and nurses volunteering their services.

With the opening of the Panama Canal in 1914 and the outbreak of war in Europe, Settlement House prepared for a new wave of immigrants fleeing the turbulent Balkans. The board launched an ambitious capital drive to raise funds for the stately, three-story, brick building, designed by B. Marcus Pritica, that the JEWISH VOICE called "a monument to women's energy."

The Seattle Public Library contributed a reading room, while the Ladies' Musical Club and Cornish School established a Settlement Music School. In addition to teaching classical and American music, the school encouraged immigrant groups to preserve and perform their traditional music and dance. It was a give-and-take effort to promote Americanization while fostering improved intercultural understanding.

As the program grew, it attracted a wider clientele, including the local poor. Reflecting its changing role in the community, the agency changed its name to the Education Center in 1917 and later to Neighborhood House. Today it maintains several child care facilities and community centers, bringing needed services to the poor in Seattle and King County. The executive office is at 905 Spruce, near the site of the former building.

19. Women's Home of the Japanese Baptist Church (site)
1102 East Spruce Street
Go west; turn right on Boren Avenue; turn right on Spruce

When the Rev. Fukumatsu Okazaki founded Seattle's first Japanese Christian church in 1899, his wife Yoshiko turned her attention to the needs of Issei (first generation) women and children. Responding to her appeal for assistance, the Baptist Women's Home Commission in New York sent Nellie Fife, who called a meeting of representatives of Puget Sound's Baptist churches to form a board of directors.

Historian Kazuo Ito, author of ISSEI, said that the "Fujin Kai" (Women's Home), which opened in 1903, became "a light in the hearts of the Japanese in Seattle." It provided temporary accommodations, classes, counseling and safe haven for newly arrived girls and women, orphans, and women escaping from abusive husbands or from pimps who had forced them into prostitution in the red-light district down the hill.

Fife, like all of her successors, was a single white women who had lived in Japan, spoke Japanese, and had a deep appreciation for the culture. Ito quotes Tsuyako Uchida who said:

> As soon as I arrived in Seattle [in 1911], I was taken to the Home on 11th Avenue operated by Miss Fife....She taught us new arrivals manners, English, piano, sewing and cooking....She was very pro-Japanese. She planted a cherry tree in the yard, and during the season when it blossomed she held 'Japan Day' in the home inviting home economics students from the University of Washington to come. We enjoyed the entire day, playing shamisen (a stringed instrument) and arranging flowers and so on.

When time permitted, married women in the Japanese community came to the home to participate in classes, Christian education and socializing. Baptist and other Protestant churches offered different kinds of support, with members sometimes inviting residents to their homes for a family dinner or barbecue.

When residents of Japanese descent were evacuated from the West Coast during World War II, the home's director, Esther M. McCollough, moved to live near Camp Minidoka in southern Idaho, where she continued to teach classes and offer whatever services and encouragement she could. The home served the community for 60 years until it closed in 1963.

20.   King County Harborview Hospital
(now Harborview Medical Center)
325 9th Avenue
Go one block north; turn left

A public health nurse, Elizabeth Sterling Soule was statewide head of the Red Cross and the Tuberculosis Association in 1920, when she joined the University of Washington (UW) faculty. To meet professional qualifications, she earned BA and MA degrees in Sociology and Education. Originally hired to teach hygiene and health classes in the Home Economics Department, she developed the new School of Nursing. She considered her greatest achievement to be the alliance that she forged with the new County Harborview Hospital, which retained control over nursing services, while giving the responsibility for clinical nursing education to the university. Following its successful inception in 1926, the program quickly spread to other Seattle hospitals.

In 1940 in recognition of her contribution to the health of the state's residents, Soule became the first woman and the third person to be named Alumnus Summa Laude Dignatus--the highest award that the UW can bestow on one of its graduates. Under her creative direction, the School of Nursing was ranked among the nation's best.

During the World War II crisis, Harborview Hospital again made history as the first Seattle hospital to hire trained black nurses. To provide mutual support, they formed the Mary Mahoney Club which continues to meet today.

21.   Seattle Milk Fund/Ladies Fruit and Flower Mission

1316 East Columbia Street (original site)
Go east to 13th Avenue, then turn left; Hospital Central Services Industry is located on the site

In 1907 a group of women met at the home of Georgia Willis in this then-prestigious residential area, where they organized the Ladies Fruit and Flower Mission to provide assistance to needy children and adults of all faiths. They began by taking fruit and flowers to the infirm poor. Renamed the Seattle Milk Fund, the organization, now headquartered at 311 First Avenue West, continues to pick up the slack when children need milk, shoes or toys. With a membership of

Seattle's Providence Hospital designed by Mother Joseph in 1881
was replaced by the building at 500 17th Avenue
(Courtesy of the Sisters of Providence Archives)

almost 1,000 women belonging to more than 30 circles, it assists needy families with utility bills, food vouchers and college scholarships. The Overlake Services League, described in Chapter IV, is an outgrowth of this altruistic organization.

22. Demonstration Project for Asian Americans
Filipino Youth Activities Center
Filipino American National Historical Society
810 18th Avenue
Phone: 322-0203
Go east on East Columbia, then left on 18th Avenue

Located in the former Immaculate Conception School, the Demonstration Project for Asian Americans (DPAA) has been ably directed by Dorothy Laigo Cordova since its inception in 1971. It began with a two-year grant from the National Endowment for the Humanities to conduct nationwide research and create media products on the little-known heritage of Filipino-American and Korean-American pioneers. The project has produced exhibits, radio shows, lectures and a book, FILIPINOS: FORGOTTEN ASIAN AMERICANS, A PICTORIAL ESSAY, 1763-1963 by Dorothy's husband Fred Cordova.

Dorothy, Jeanette Castillano Tiffany and Nancy Ordona Koslosky have created local and national exhibits on Pinay (Filipina American Women) heritage and written a forthcoming book on the history of Pinays in Washington State. The 1920 census revealed that there was only one Pinay to 100 Pinoys in the United States--a ratio that because of restrictive immigration laws did not change until the influx of war brides after World War II. Strong women, they often raised large families, worked in family businesses, and traditionally controlled the purse strings. A daughter of one of these pioneers, Dorothy wants her own eight children and their peers to know about their female forebears. Interpreting their significance, Fred wrote in his book: "Pinays have been the yeast that set their men and children rising and the leaven that got their communities producing."

Shortly before they founded DPAA, the Cordovas organized the Filipino Youth Activities Program which is also housed in the old school. For years, Dorothy and other Pinay mothers trained, costumed, and shepherded the popular Girls Drill Team to parades and festivals in the Seattle area and as far away as Washington D.C. Programs like this have given young people understanding and pride in their heritage and a sense of commitment to the future. They have also helped foster cross-cultural awareness in the broader community.

Through the years, the Cordovas and their co-workers have amassed an impressive archival collection of national significance that is available to researches by appointment. With Dorothy as executive director, the office recently became headquarters for the new Filipino American National Historical Society (FAHNS). It has produced a video, "Filipino Americans: Discovering Thier Past for the Future," that documents their history from 1587 to 1965.

23. Phillis Wheatley Branch of the YWCA (now a private home)
1807 24th Avenue
Go north on East Cherry; turn left on 23rd Avenue, then right on Howell, and left of 24th Avenue

"Did you know that before August 15 there was no first-class, respectable place where a girl coming to Seattle alone might find lodging--if her skin happened to be dark?" With this lead sentence, the SEATTLE POST INTELLIGENCER reported the opening of the Phillis Wheatley Branch of the YWCA in 1919.

Seven years earlier, Corrine Carter, wife of the pastor of Mt. Zion Baptist Church, had called together some 50 Afra-American girls to organize the Culture Club which became part of the Seattle YWCA. Although they could participate in most of the association's programs, here--as in YWCAs throughout the nation--there were restrictions based on race. The new Phillis Wheatley branch (named for a famous Black poet of the Revolutionary War era) was the first of its kind in the Northwest, providing social, educational, and employment programs to 150 members. Girls who had not been welcome in the downtown YWCA hotel could find lodging at the branch. "We teach the girls, whatever they do to do it well," Carter said in her interview with the PI. "When they do that they remove the prejudice against our race....Already this association has created a better feeling among our people." The branch was a popular meeting place for weddings, dances for young people, and meetings of Black women's organizations. Now housed in its own brick building at 2820 East Cherry, it continues to play a vital role in the community. Its former home at 24th Avenue and Howell has long been a private residence. (Please see Chapter VII, the downtown Seattle YWCA sub-section on "Commitment to Racial Justice" for further information.)

24. The Pitter Home

1532 24th Avenue
Go south on 24th Avenue

Edward Pitter, King County deputy sheriff, and his wife Marjorie, a dedicated crusader for civil rights, bought this elegant 15-room house, complete with servants' quarters, in the 1920s. Their three daughters were raised in Seattle's middle-class Black society with supportive family, school, church, and community organizations. In 1981 Juana Royster Horne made the sisters the subject of her UW doctoral dissertation, entitled THE ACADEMIC AND EXTRACURRICULAR UNDERGRADUATE EXPERIENCES OF THREE BLACK WOMEN AT THE UNIVERSITY OF WASHINGTON, 1935-1941.

When the UW refused to admit black women to the nursing program, Maxine Pitter Haynes pursued her studies in New York and California. Prior to World War II, Seattle hospital administrators refused to hire a trained nurse if she was Black. The wartime emergency began to break down discriminatory barriers with Black nurses gaining a permanent foothold in Seattle hospitals. Responding to the demands of Afra-American students, the UW later recruited Haynes to serve on the faculty of the School of Nursing.

Constance Pitter Thomas graduated from the UW in 1939 with degrees in drama and speech pathology and a teaching certificate, but because of her race, the Seattle school district refused to hire her. She moved to New York City to pursue an acting career. In the late 1940s, the Seattle Public Schools began to hire Black women teachers. When Thomas returned home a few years later, she was finally accepted.

On enrolling in her chosen course in 1935, Marjorie Pitter King was told that the UW College of Business and Economics had never graduated a Black and had no intention of so doing. After earning her degree at Howard University, she returned to Seattle and in 1965, accepted an appointment to complete the unexpired term of a King County legislator. The first Black women to serve in the Washington

State Legislature, she has been a long-term leader in the Democratic party.

25.   Seattle Public Library
Douglass-Truth Branch
23rd Avenue and East Yesler Way
Go west one block to 23rd Avenue, then south

Thanks to Seattle's Delta Upsilon Omega chapter of the national Alpha Kappa Alpha Sorority, this community library has the largest collection of African and African American material in the Northwest. An example of the sorority's many important contributions is the 17-volume Schomburg Collection of Nineteenth Century Black Women Writers.

The library was originally named for Henry Yesler, Seattle's first mayor. In the 1960s the Black Friends of Yesler sponsored a contest to give the library a new name that would reflect the community's racial demographics. The two most popular nominations were Frederick Douglass and Sojourner Truth, both of whom had escaped slavery to become leading abolitionists. Both also spoke eloquently in favor of suffrage at some of the nation's first women's rights conventions.

26.   Odessa Brown Clinic
2101 East Yesler Way
Go west on East Yesler

As social unrest swept the nation, a Black woman in poor health and without insurance captured the attention of the community. Well known for her commitment to voluntary service, Odessa Brown helped organize the Central Area Motivation Program, then zeroed in on the health care crisis of her neighbors, many of whom had never had a medical or dental exam. Until her death in 1969, she served on the Model City Health Care Task Force that persuaded the all-female board of Children's Orthopedic Hospital (COH) and the city to establish services in the Central Area.

The Odessa Brown Clinic opened its doors the next year with an advisory board composed of community residents and hospital representatives. From its inception the clinic has benefited from dynamic and devoted Afra-American leadership. Founding medical director, Dr. Blanche Lavisso, formulated the motto, "Quality Care with Dignity." Until her death in 1984, she drew needy patients into "their" clinic, while continuing to expand its services.

Her successor   Dr. Maxine Hayes, a pediatrician, has broadened the clinic's focus to include social and health care issues, such as hunger, teen pregnancy, foster child health care, and AIDS among minorities. A strong advocate of public education as a catalyst for change, she said in an April 10, 1988 interview with the SEATTLE POST INTELLIGENCER, "I truly care about these kids, and feel and hurt for them....I believe that if I can articulate well enough and make people aware of these problems, they'll address them."

In recent years, Children's Hospital and Medical Center (formerly COH) has worked with the cities of Bellevue, Federal Way and Renton to establish satellite clinics modelled after Odessa Brown.

27. Alvarita Little Girls Club of Puget Sound
708 Martin Luther King Way
Go east on Yesler, then left on Martin Luther King Way

The Girls Club was a dream come true for Alvarita Little who solicited donations of sewing machines and cookware, persuaded friends to volunteer as instructors, then raised the necessary funds to purchase the clubhouse. Her goal was to foster self-esteem and confidence for inner-city black girls by offering them a variety of educational and recreational opportunities. Today, the club has more than 500 members with a second clubhouse located in West Seattle.

28. Phillis Wheatley Branch of the YWCA
2820 East Cherry Street
Go south on Martin Luther King Way, then left of East Cherry

In the wake of World War II, the downtown association and the branch raised funds to erect this badly needed new building. As in the past, the branch is a center of community services and activities. Please see the Phillis Wheatley Branch of the YWCA, described at its first location in a house at 24th Avenue and Howell.

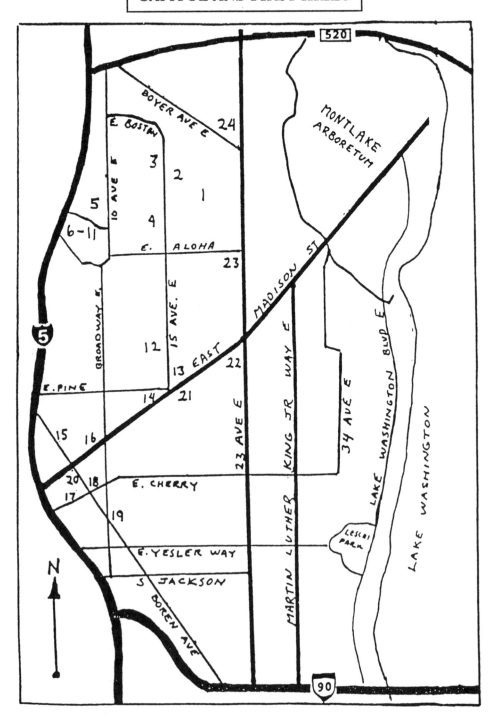

X. CAPITOL AND FIRST HILLS

Between 1900 and 1910, Seattle's population exploded from 80,671 to 237,174, spawning the rapid development of new suburbs. Two of the most prestigious were Capitol and First Hills which became home to some of the city's leading families. Your tour begins on Interlaken Boulevard at the former Forest Ridge School, a site chosen by Catholic Sisters who wanted a location "far from the wickedness of Seattle." The serpentine road continues through wooded Louisa Boren Park to one of the city's most spectacular viewpoints.

Although you may plan to drive the entire route, sites two through nine make a delightful walking tour from a pioneer cemetery, through Volunteer Park, and on to the venerable Harvard-Belmont District, which is listed on the Seattle and National Registers of Historic Places. Here gracious homes and elegant women's clubhouses have been carefully preserved. The route continues into the area popularly known as "Pill Hill," where modern hospitals and medical centers have inundated a once-prestigious residential neighborhood and where only scant vestiges of the past remain. The conclusion takes you down Madison Street to the east side of Capitol Hill, then west on Boyer Avenue East to St. Demetrios Greek Orthodox Church, located just below your starting point.

1. Forest Ridge School of the Sacred Heart
Seattle Hebrew Academy
1617 Interlaken Drive East
Take I-5 to the East Roanoke Street exit; go east following the arterial, then turn right on Interlaken Drive East

In 1910 just three years after they opened their school for girls in a large Capitol Hill home, the Sisters of the Sacred Heart of Jesus moved to their new campus, located "far from the wickedness of Seattle." They chose the name Forest Ridge in part to distinguish the school from their orphanage (Please see Chapter V, Villa Academy), and in part because it suited the spectacular setting high above

Portage Bay.

Up to 100 boarders lived at the school, while girls in the neighborhood enrolled as day students. One who later became famous was author and literary critic, Mary McCarthy, whose books included the spicy 1963 novel, THE GROUP, the 1957 autobiography, MEMORIES OF A CATHOLIC GIRLHOOD, and its 1987 sequel, HOW I GREW. She wrote, "I was 11 years old, a seventh-grader, when I was first shown into the big study hall in Forest Ridge Convent and issued my soap dish, my veil and my napkin ring."

In the post World War II era, enrollments escalated, forcing the sisters to consider expansion. In 1971 they moved their school to its striking new campus at 4800 139th SE on Bellevue's Somerset Hill. In the contemporary facilities, the dedicated order continues its tradition, providing high quality education to girls, grades five through twelve.

Designated as a Seattle Landmark, the neo-classical brick and sandstone buildings on Interlaken Boulevard now house the Seattle Hebrew Academy.

2. Louisa Boren Park
15th Avenue East and East Garfield Street
Continue northeast on Interlaken; turn right on East Galer, then right on 15th Avenue East

Louisa Boren, one of Seattle's founding pioneers, has always captured the imagination and hearts of local history buffs. When the Denny party boarded four covered wagons in Cherry Grove, Illinois to head West, her best friend, Pamelia Dunlap, gave her the parting gift of seeds from her sweetbriar rose to plant in a distant garden as a lasting bond.

During the first weeks of the journey, the women clung to the trappings of civilized life, serving meals on clean, ironed tablecloths and making beds with linen sheets. When she later described the journey to her daughter Emily, Louisa noted that the niceties ended in

Missouri, as violent weather and the "grinding and bumping of wheels" made them "glad to rest in the easiest way possible."

Louisa was the only woman in the Denny Party to have the good fortune of being young, single and without small children. A schoolteacher, she had developed a love of science and got into the spirit of the adventure, sometimes riding out to marvel at spectacular rock formations or at new species of fauna and flora, and sometimes attracting unwanted attention. On one occasion her traveling companions had a tough time convincing a native suitor that she was not for sale and that even the fine string of horses that he offered in trade was unacceptable.

The pioneers turned out for Seattle's first wedding on January 23, 1853, when Louisa married David Denny. At the cabin on their remote, forested homestead (now the site of Seattle Center) the newlyweds cleared a garden area, where the "Sweetbriar Bride" planted the treasured seeds that Pamelia had given her. As the population grew, her exuberant garden helped foster community spirit. She and David contributed the first public park to the city, along with a site for the Orphan Home--later renamed Seattle Children's Home.

Louisa Boren Park extends down the ravine past Interlaken Boulevard. A highlight is the sweeping viewpoint on 15th Avenue East that encompasses both Lake Washington bridges. Random sandstone blocks echo Lakeview Cemetery across the street where many of the pioneers are buried.

3.   Lakeview Cemetery
15th Avenue East north of Volunteer Park
Across from Louisa Boren Viewpoint

A walk through Lakeview Cemetery takes visitors to the tombstones of many of Seattle's pioneers, including Arthur and Mary Boren Denny and their decendents. As historian Roger Sale observes in his book SEATTLE, PAST TO PRESENT, cemeteries also provide "glimpses of the grimness of frontier life." There are numerous tombstones of children and infants, next to parents who outlived them. Since mothers bore the primary responsibility for home- and childcare, they often suffered the double pain of loss and guilt.

Catherine Maynard

For more than thirty years she visited her husband's grave with the now-toppled tombstone that lies next to her own. Hers bears the inscription:

> Catherine Troutman Maynard
> One of the Founders of Seattle
> July 19, 1816
> October 20, 1906
> She Did What She Could

In 1850 when Catherine Troutman Broshears headed West with her husband and family, their party fell victim to the dreaded cholera. Recognizing their plight and also the attractive widow, Doctor David S. Maynard left his own party to join hers. After they arrived in Washington Territory, he petitioned the legislature for a divorce from his first wife, then married Catherine. Since there was no hospital in Seattle, she cared for his patients in their two spare bedrooms.

Some years later, Doc Maynard's first wife Lydia--thinking that she was still married--came from the East intending to ask for her half of their homestead claim. In the midst of legal discussions, the three apparently lived together in harmony, and the Doc at times strode through town with a wife on each arm.

Increasingly prone to tippling, the effervescent doctor died in 1873 and was buried at Lakeview Cemetery. Catherine lived on for another 33 years. As a member of the library association, she converted part of her home into a public reading room where the Seattle YMCA was founded.

Angeline

When she died in 1896, she was buried in a canoe-shaped coffin in the lot of her pioneer friends, Henry and Sarah Yesler. An overflow congregation turned out for her funeral at the Church of Our Lady of Good Help, and Seattle schoolchildren collected pennies and nickels to purchase her headstone.

Kick-is-on-lo Cud, the daughter of Chief Sealth, was a widowed grandmother who lived alone in a waterfront shack (near the present Pike Place Market). Thinking she should have a prettier name than "Cud," Catherine Maynard asked to call her Angeline, and because of her lineage, others called her Princess Angeline. During her lifetime, Angeline had witnessed the coming of the first pioneers and the exile of her people to reservations. Like her father, she had converted to Christianity and chose to remain in the city among early settlers who were her friends.

Even though they offered to help her, she accepted little and sometimes earned money doing washings. If anyone dared to criticize her work, she walked out, hurling profanities. If young boys taunted her, she pelted them with rocks or clam shells. Undoubtedly the most photographed person in Seattle, she counted Presidents Hayes and Harrison among her visitors.

In her book, PIG-TAIL DAYS IN OLD SEATTLE, Sophie Frye Bass told about an extraordinary conversation with Angeline shortly before her death. Visiting at the Frye home, she sat on a stool in the center of the room:

> and when we gathered about her, she began to talk in her native tongue....She spoke of her childhood days, her father and her tillicums. We knew by the tone of her voice that she was greatly moved and as we listened, we regarded her with awe and a different feeling. We forgot her ugliness and her grumpiness and realized, as never before, the tragedy of her life and that of all the Indians.

> Mother, who understood Indian, interpreted for us. She who had had plenty--her father's daughter, the pet of the tribe--had lost all at the coming of the white man. She told of her happy,

carefree childhood, how the white man had taken over or destroyed their berry patches, their camp-sites, and fishing grounds that had been theirs for generations. She told of the rudeness of some of those white men and their cruelty to the Indians. Now she was often cold and hungry, yet she had some good friends who were kind to her and helped her when she went to them.

In addition to her gravestone, Seattle has commemorated Angeline in other ways. A street in Columbia City and Georgetown is named for her. In 1986 the YWCA established Angeline's Day Center for Homeless Women, a safe haven that provides shelter and services for up to 100 women a day. They are treated as people and with dignity-something that Angeline always demanded.

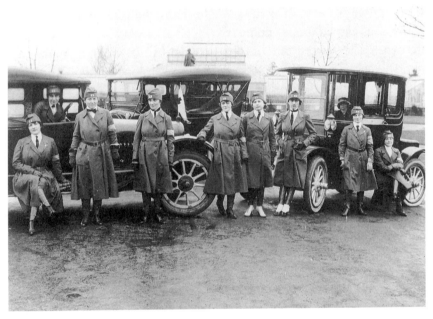

Members of the Red Cross Motor Brigade pose in front of the Conservatory in Volunteer Park. Each had a telephone and drove her own car. 1917.
(Courtesy of the Seattle/King County Chapter of the American Red Cross)

4. Seattle Art Museum
Volunteer Park
1400 East Prospect Street
The entrance to the park is adjacent to Lakeview Cemetery at 15th Avenue East and East Galer

In 1932 Margaret Fuller and her son Dr. Richard Fuller built the Seattle Art Museum, which they presented to the city, along with their impressive collection of oriental and Northwest art. From the start, Dr. Fuller received the credit, being honored as King County's First Citizen. In an interview housed in the University of Washington's Manuscripts Collection, arts patron Joanna Eckstein was asked whether the accolades were appropriately directed. Her candid answer was: "Well, originally, I would say it was almost more his mother than it was Dr. Fuller. People seem to have more or less forgotten about her...."

Another whose name has been obscured is Emma Baillargeon Stimson who was linked romantically to Richard Fuller for many years. A supporter of promising artists in what became known as the Northwest School, she was often the bread and butter for Mark Tobey, Morris Graves, Kenneth Calahan and others. She traveled with the Fullers to Asia, using her keen sense of art to select some of the museum's finest acquisitions. During the 1950s as head of the museum, she bore the major responsibility for its development.

When the new Seattle Art Museum opened in 1992 in downtown Seattle, Priscilla Bullitt Collins, Emma's niece, asked that something in it be named for her aunt, but nothing was. Collins says, "Aunt Em was a very sophisticated and learned person, ahead of her time, but when her name showed up in the newspapers, it was usually for pouring tea at the Sunset Club."

The building in Volunteer Park is currently undergoing extensive restoration as a permanent home for SAM's 7,000 piece Asian art collection--one of the most important in the nation. Margaret and Richard Fuller, Emma Stimson, and others who shared their foresight would no doubt be pleased.

5. Eliza Ferry Leary House/Diocesan House

1551 10th Avenue East
Phone: 325-4200. Tours by arrangement.
If on foot, walk west through the park and one block; If driving, go to the north exit, then west on East Prospect, then right on 10th Avenue East

In 1869, 17-year-old Eliza "Lizzie," the second of 11 children, ventured West with her family from Waukegan, Illinois to Olympia via rail and then steamer. With a presidential appointment, her father, Elisha Ferry, served first as surveyor general of Washington Territory and then from 1872 to 1880 as governor. Following his second term of office, the family moved to Seattle where in 1892 Eliza married their neighbor, John Leary, a prominent real estate developer and one-time mayor of the city.

The spirited and socially polished Eliza quickly became one of Seattle's leading women. When she and John Leary decided to build a suburban estate on the undeveloped crest of Capitol Hill, wealthy Seattleites quickly followed, establishing one of the city's most fashionable neighborhoods. After her husband's death in 1905, Eliza forged on to complete the magnificent 14-room Tudor mansion that they had envisioned. Alfred Bodley from England was her architect; the Olmsted brothers designed the landscaping; Stanford White carved the Italian dining set; and Louis Tiffany crafted the stained-glass windows and lampshades.

A gracious hostess, she opened her home for charity balls and other fund-raising events to support her many social causes. She was a stalwart Episcopalian and a founding board member of the Seattle Children's home, the Rainier Chapter of the DAR, the Sunset Club, Children's Orthopedic Hospital, the Pioneers of the State of Washington, the Seattle Red Cross, and the Seattle YWCA. An avid cyclist, she often rode to her meetings on her bicycle.

While she backed numerous programs to create better opportunities for women, she was nonetheless the local representative for the National Association Opposed to Woman Suffrage. Like many of her peers, she maintained that the sleazy backrooms of politics were no place for a lady. Since she waged no campaign, she endeared herself to friends who were impassioned suffragists.

After her death in 1935, the local American Red Cross acquired the home for its center of operations. Since 1948, it has served as headquarters for the Episcopal Diocese of Olympia, which offers tours to the public by appointment. The house is listed on the Seattle and National Registers of Historic Places.

6. Harvard-Belmont Historic District
Boundaries: East Highland Drive on the north, East Roy Street on the south, Broadway on the east, and Belmont Avenue and the bluff on the west side

This venerable neighborhood is listed on the Seattle Landmarks Register and on the National Register of Historic Places. Most of the elegant mansions with their beautifully landscaped gardens and dazzling views were built between 1905 and 1910. Picturesque apartment buildings, including some designed by Fred Anhalt, made their debuts in the 1920s, along with clubhouses for two of the city's prominent women's organizations and Nellie Cornish's arts school. The district was home to some of the city's leading families. While many of the men headed businesses, industries, and banks, the women were leaders in Seattle's social, educational, charitable and cultural circles.

The district's residents also included cooks, domestics and nursemaids who lived and worked in the mansions. By the mid-teens, matrons were sending their household employees, many of whom were members of the newly organized Domestic Workers Union, to the YWCA for training. To further address the complaint that "good help is hard to find," the YWCA offered another course for matrons, teaching them reasonable expectations and respect for their maid's rights. (Please see Chapter VIII, the YWCA for further details.)

7. Plestcheeff Institute for the Decorative Arts
814 East Highland Drive
Phone: 543-2977
Go south on 15th Avenue East, then right one block on East Highland Drive

When Guendolyn "Guen" Carkeek Plestcheeff first saw the reinforced concrete "palace" that rises out of a forested ravine, it was dark, damp, musty and in a state of deterioration, having stood vacant for several years. In the depths of the Depression, her husband Theodore--an exiled Russian prince who was once in the inner circle of Czar Nicholas and Empress Alexandra--said, "We'll take it." While it reminded him of his family's hunting lodge in Russia, she took a second look and began to cry. In subsequent years, she used her considerable design talents to restore the home to and possibly beyond its former glory.

The legendary Sam Hill built the dramatic edifice in 1909, adding it to his other legacies including the Peace Arch at Blaine, Maryhill Museum at Goldendale, and thousands of miles of Washington highways. During and after the Alaska-Yukon-Pacific Exposition, he entertained many a distinguished guest in the home, one of whom was Queen Marie of Romania.

Like Hill, Plestcheeff has elegant and exotic tastes. To admit more light, she had larger windows cut through the concrete walls, added crystal sconces, and the third-floor penthouse and ballroom. She furnished the house with her collection of priceless antiques, including Russian porcelain, French furniture, and English needlework. It became a centerpiece for Seattle society, where she and her late husband entertained in style.

Born in Seattle to Morgan and Emily Carkeek, Guendolyn grew up in her parent's mansion on First Hill--then the city's preeminent residential neighborhood. She began her European travels when her parents sent her to private schools in England and Switzerland. While living among aristocrats in Paris, Rome and Revel (Estonia), she collected artistic and historical treasures. An example is the exquisite porcelain covered teacup from which Czar Alexander III was drinking when Theodore Plestcheeff's grandfather requested his permission to marry. Signifying his approval, the Czar gave him the cup as an engagement gift.

In 1987 Guendolyn Plestcheeff willed her house and her entire collection to the University of Washington as an institute for the decorative arts. In addition to exhibits, the school will offer courses in conservation, identification and appreciation. The late Bill Alpert, who wrote about the institute in the Winter 1988 issue of the WASHINGTON ALUMNUS, said, "It will be a tribute to the far-ranging vision of a woman who believes in the role the decorative arts can play in our understanding of our past and ourselves." He quotes Plestcheeff who said, "They're really much more than objects. They're what people used, what they surrounded themselves with. I think some of these pieces have a great intimacy to them. You can't help wondering what secrets they witnessed, what events they shared."

The house is listed on the National Register of Historic Places. For more about Plestcheeff, please see Chapter IX, the Museum of History and Industry.

8. Cornish School of Allied Arts
710 East Roy Street
Go south to East Roy

In her autobiography, MISS AUNT NELLIE, Nellie Centennial Cornish (her middle name signifying the year of her birth) recalled the isolated eastern Oregon and Nebraska farmhouses of her girlhood where her parents struggled to make ends meet and where in the evenings her father instructed his children, determined that they learn to think for themselves, rather than simply memorize textbooks. His lessons stuck with her as she began to study, then teach music. Questioning traditional pedagogical techniques, she consistently sought out new ideas.

Photo is from an advertisement for Cornish School, placed in the
1916 Broadway High School year book.
(Courtesy of Seattle Public Schools Archives)

At the turn of the century, she moved to Seattle where she gave piano
lessons in a shared studio in the Holyoke Building. (Please see
Chapter VII, Holyoke Building for further information.) With money
borrowed from friends, she went to Boston to study the new Fletcher
Method of music teaching, based on Montessori techniques. She also
studied Calvin Brainerd Cady's ideas of unified education based on the
principles of music. In addition to providing a foundation for logic
and critical judgement, he maintained that the music lesson should
provide an opportunity "for spontaneity and for development through

intuition and inspiration."

In 1914 when she founded Cornish School in the Booth Building at Broadway and Pine, Seattle arts patrons readily enrolled their children. Women's post-war enthusiasm for the arts resulted in the founding of several of the nation's major arts institutes. In Seattle patrons contributed generously, so that in 1921 Cornish School moved into its own picturesque, Spanish-baroque building on East Roy Street. When neighbors objected to the noise and sued to have the school closed, the judge suggested that they move to the country.

Nellie Cornish created a school where students could experience the interrelatedness of the arts, including all branches of music, drama, the visual arts and dance. She maintained that creativity should be developed in the average person, as well as the talented, and further, that art's ultimate purpose was enrichment for everyone--not just the privileged elite.

With an uncanny instinct for quality and originality, she hired both famous and unknown artists for her faculty. Before he had gained even local recognition, she invited Mark Tobey to teach painting in his own manner. Her mentor Calvin B. Cady joined the faculty. She regularly engaged Ellen Van Volkenburg Browne who with her husband Maurice had founded the Little Theater movement.

Sensing an enormous and unusual talent, she arranged a solo performing debut for one of her avant-garde dance instructors, Martha Graham. Composer John Cage and dancer Merce Cunningham taught at the school, as did ballerina Mary Ann Wells and theater directors, Burton and Florence Bean James. When White Russian artists fled their homeland in 1917, Nellie Cornish went to New York to recruit them for her drama, ballet and music programs.

Known affectionately to her students as Miss Aunt Nellie, she often invited them to meet informally with famous guest artists over coffee and home-baked cookies in her apartment at the school. She was also quick to help with tuition costs, since she thought it wrong for artists to have to justify themselves economically. With wealthy benefactors who repeatedly bailed her school out of debt, she could afford to be generous.

Had it not been for friends including Jeannette Skinner, Agnes Anderson, Harriet Stimson, Anne Ames, Katherine Kerry and others, Cornish School might not have survived the Great Depression. An organization of women called the Seattle Music and Art Foundation assumed ownership of the school in the 1950s to put it on an even financial keel.

Today the school is managed by a board of both women and men and according to past president Jeannette Edris Rockefeller, its financial condition is excellent. In recent years, Cornish Institute has expanded its facilities adding new subjects to the curriculum to become one of four accredited schools of visual and performing arts in the country.

9.   Daughters of the American Revolution
Rainier Chapter House
800 East Roy Street

Across Harvard Avenue East from Cornish School is the DAR House, built by the Rainier Chapter in 1925. The exterior is a replica of George Washington's home at Mr. Vernon, while the interior is furnished with elegant antiques, including the crystal chandelier that was 100 years old when the building was erected.

The Rainier Chapter was founded on September 24, 1895, when the national association was just five years old. Early members included: Angie Burt Bowden, well-known writer of Northwest history; Elinor Ingersoll Thorne, teacher and writer with a degree in the new field of applied psychology; and Eliza Ferry Leary (Please see #5 in this chapter).

With a mission to perpetuate patriotism and the memory of their ancestors, membership was open to descendants of veterans of the war for independence. Of particular interest were the heroines of the war, most of whom had already fallen into obscurity. Recognizing the importance of historic preservation, the early DAR began its extensive collection of biographical sketches of pioneers and records of historic homes, buildings and events.

When University of Washington history professor, Edmond Meany, decided that a statue of George Washington should greet visitors to the 1909 Alaska-Yukon-Pacific Exposition, he turned to the Rainier Chapter. Among its schemes to raise $20,000 for the project, it declared Washington's Birthday as Monument Day, asking schoolchildren all over the state to contribute one, but not more than five pennies. Today, visitors still pose for pictures with sculptor Lorado Taft's heroic bronze statue that since 1909 has maintained its vigil at an entrance to the university campus. (Please see Chapter V, the Henry Gallery, for directions to the statue.)

In 1914 the state DAR sponsored a contest to create a Washington State flag. The winning entry was by Wenonah Blackwell of the Rainier Chapter whose design was accepted by the legislature as the state's official symbol.

Today, members of the Rainier Chapter continue to meet at their Capitol Hill headquarters. To maintain their building, they rent it out for special events such as weddings, receptions, chamber music concerts, and corporate Christmas parties.

10. Women's Century Club/Harvard Exit Theater
807 East Roy Street

While the Rainier Chapter of the DAR watched its replica of Mt. Vernon emerge, the Women's Century Club was building its own stately brick clubhouse on the corner across East Roy Street. The Century Club was founded in 1891 by an impressive group of women, determined to civilize the "sordid atmosphere" of their rapidly developing city. Their mission was to prepare women for full participation in the twentieth century which they also called the "women's century." Among the charter members were: President

Carrie Chapman Catt who later gained international prominence a leading suffragist; Alice Jordan Blake, the first female graduate in law from Yale; Julia C. Kennedy, Seattle Superintendent of Schools, the first women to hold the position; Sarah Kendall, M.D., and Marmora DeVoe Moody, M.D., two of the first women to graduate from medical school; and Celeste Slausson, founder and director of the Seattle Conservatory of Arts.

Twelve different departments met weekly to study their respective interests and to foster community improvements. The club paid the salary of the city's first librarian, helped found the Martha Washington School for Girls, led the fight to raise the age of consent, and in 1907 successfully lobbied the city council to pass a law prohibiting spitting in public.

In 1896 the club hosted a reception for Susan B. Anthony, then in her seventies, on her second visit to the Northwest. They decorated the Seattle Theater where the nation's leading suffragist gave an extemporaneous speech that, according to the SEATTLE POST INTELLIGENCER, was "so thoroughly interesting that the silence which it commanded was rarely broken even by applause." The club's political activism peaked in the mid-1920s when 350 members and juniors in training campaigned to elect a former president, Bertha Knight Landes, as Seattle's first woman mayor. (Please see Chapter V, Wilsonian Hotel--Home of Mayor Landes.)

Once a bastion of women's social and cultural life, the club gradually became a victim of its own success. As women gained access to government and the workplace, it no longer served as their primary power base. Faced with a declining membership and increasing maintenance costs, the club sold its building in 1968 with the provision that it could continue to use it for meetings.

Today some 40 members, most of whom are elderly, continue to meet twice a month in the velvet curtained parlor of the building that now houses the Harvard Exit movie theater. The leisurely meetings are reminiscent of a bygone era, complete with luncheons served on delicate bone china. The major order of business is allocation of the $4,000 per year scholarship fund, earned from the sale of the building. Beneficiaries have included the University of Washington Medical School, the Seattle Youth Symphony, and Woodland Park Zoo.

11. Seattle Federation of Women's Clubs Clubhouse (site)
232 Harvard Avenue North
Go south three blocks on Harvard

Prior to planning its own building, the Women's Century Club worked with the Seattle Federation of Women's Clubs (SFWC) to raise funds for a clubhouse for women throughout the city. Now a vacant lot, it once was a center that coordinated the work of the SFWC with its state and national affiliations. From an original 18 clubs in 1898, the SFWC grew to 45 by the 1920s, representing more than 4,000 women. As a good clubwoman and editor of the SEATTLE MAIL AND HERALD, Louise C. Beck wrote in the December 17, 1904 issue:

> ....while laboring upon altruistic, ethical philanthropic or aesthetic lines women are acquiring what they greatly lacked, the beautiful spirit of comradeship. We are learning to stand and fall together, as men have done almost from the beginning of time....

The SFWC took a lead in successful campaigns to promote juvenile courts, pure food and sanitation laws, and playgrounds for children at schools and in public parks. The predominantly white, middle-class, Protestant organization joined union women in a vigorous campaign for protective labor laws for working women and children. In the late teens, it joined forces with the state's Federation of Colored Women's Clubs to lobby Congress for passage of an anti-lynching bill.

In 1926 United States Secretary of Commerce Herbert Hoover appointed Helen Zednick to chair Seattle's Better Homes in America, Inc. program. Her clubsisters mobilized, enlisting support from the business community and city government--then headed by Mayor Bertha Landes--to organize annual home tours and related events, including competitions among women architects to design affordable model homes. In an interview with the SEATTLE POST INTELLIGENCER, Zednick explained:

> The future history of America will be shaped in a large measure by the character of its homes....This means that our homes must be convenient and comfortable; that, however modest they may be, they must be places of beauty; that they must represent to individuals and families the center of their affection and loyalty.

As noted in several other items in this guidebook, communities throughout King County have been enriched by legacies of clubwomen. Two that began as statewide projects are Federation Forest State Park (Chapter I) and the University of Washington Women's Building/Cunningham Hall (Chapter V).

Although no longer in its heyday, the General Federation of Women's Clubs remains an active international organization where women volunteers participate in community, state and world affairs. With the motto "Unity in Diversity," member clubs, including several in King County, maintain their individuality while working together.

12.   Elizabeth Ayer, Architect
1315 East John
Go east one block, then right on Broadway East, then left on East John

When she took down her shingle in 1970, Elizabeth Ayer ended a 50-year career as the designer of some of Seattle's and the region's most appealing traditional homes. In 1916 as the first woman to enter the University of Washington's School of Architecture, she attracted the attention of the UNIVERSITY OF WASHINGTON DAILY which printed the perfunctory boxed statement on the first page: "ARCHITECTURE IS NOT FOR WOMEN." With determination, ability, and a keen sense of humor, she won the respect of her male professors and colleagues, while opening the doors for other women. As the first female architect licensed by the state, she worked with male partners and later on her own.

In 1891 the Seattle Chapter of the American Institute of Architects Senior Council, then presided over by Jane Hastings, honored Ayer as a pioneering woman architect who left a legacy of handsome, traditional houses and a strong role model for later generations of women in the profession.

13.   L. Jane Hastings, Architect
1516 East Olive Way
Go south to East Olive, then left

Like Elizabeth Ayer, L. Jane Hastings was at one time the only woman in her class at the University of Washington. In the post-World War II era, a faculty member told her that she was wasting the taxpayers' money and taking space that could be used by a returning serviceman. As a young girl, Hastings had decided that she wanted to be an architect. The first member of her family to go to college, she had to support herself, taking seven years to graduate. She later recalled the encouragement of Elizabeth Ayer who invited her and other "girls" in the school for tea.

Like Ayer, Hastings, who owns her own firm, has received numerous awards for her residential designs. Unlike Ayer, she has ascended to the top of her profession, holding the prestigious position of Chancellor of the College of Fellows of the American Institute of Architects. She is past president of Seattle's Senior Council of the AIA and past vice president of the Union Internationale des Femme Architectures. In a profession that is still more than 90% male, she remains at the forefront of the AIA's commitment to diversity, easing the way for other women and minorities.

14.   First African Methodist Episcopal Church
1522 14th Avenue

In 1889 women in Seattle's small Black community organized the Ladies Colored Social Circle which sponsored literary, musical and social events, using the proceeds to purchase the site for Seattle's first Black church. According to Esther Mumford, author of SEATTLE'S BLACK VICTORIANS, "The work of women in both the A.M.E. and the Baptist Church sustained the financial stability of those institutions through the early years." The church became the Black community's center for religion, culture, education, recreation, and politics.

In the early 1890s, women in the A.M.E. Church organized the Frances Harper Unit of the Women's Christian Temperance Union with former slave, Emma Ray, as president. Members went into the city's red-light district, intent on redeeming society's victims. They spent time with the down-and-out, cooking, cleaning, washing their clothes, and sometimes holding prayer meetings. In some cases their new friends became converts and joined them in church.

Although the unit received high praise from leaders in the predominantly white WCTU, their pastor criticized them, maintaining that their altruistic work should be under the aegis of the church. For a time the unit disbanded with Emma Ray continuing on as the lone Black woman attending city and regional meetings. When the national convention was held in Seattle in 1899, Lucy Thurman, a nationally prominent Afra-American leader, urged Emma Ray and others to reorganize their unit. With support from their new pastor, the Frances Harper Unit of the WCTU continued its work well into the 1900s.

The original church was torn down and replaced by the present structure in 1912. It is listed on the Seattle Register of Historic Places.

15. Sunset Club
1021 University Street
Go east on Pike, then left on Boren; The clubhouse is at

In 1913, 28 of Seattle's well-to-do matrons formed the Sunset Club, their purpose being predominantly social and cultural. They engaged Somervell and Cote, well-known architects, to design the luxurious clubhouse that opened in 1916 in what was then one of the city's most prestigious residential neighborhoods. Today the building nestles among modern medical centers and apartment buildings, providing a welcome contrast and a reminder of yesteryear. As in the past, membership is exclusive and a prospective member may have to wait several years for her name to reach the top of the waiting list.

16. Jewish Family Service
1214 Boylston Avenue
Go one block east on Boren; turn left on Seneca, then right on Boylston

Jewish Family Service traces its beginnings to the Ladies' Hebrew Benevolent Society, organized in 1889 by a group of women, determined to help families in the wake of the great Seattle fire. the first president was Esther Levy who was succeeded by her daughter Lizzie Cooper. To support their wives' efforts and to perpetuate their names, Aubrey Levy and his son-in-law/business partner, Isaac Cooper, established a trust for needy children and their families. They also left sizable bequests to the Jewish Family Service.

Members of the LHBS worked with the Seattle Federation of Women's Clubs and other like-minded organizations to promote woman suffrage and temperance. Under the leadership of Mina Eckstein, they were instrumental in helping establish the Seattle Juvenile Court and related rehabilitation programs for troubled youth.

17. Charles and Emma Frye Art Museum
704 Terry Avenue
Phone: 622-9250. Open Monday to Saturday 10 a.m.-5 p.m. and Sunday noon-5 p.m. Call first to arrange a guided tour. Free.

Continue southeast on Boylston; turn right on Broadway;
turn right on Cherry; The Museum is at Cherry and Terry

Unique in King County, the Frye is completely self supporting with no need to charge admissions or solicit donations. This gift to the public is the legacy of Emma and Charles Frye. While he operated a meat packing business, she studied art with a special emphasis on 19th-century European painting. On their several trips to Europe, they amassed their collection of then-unfashionable pastoral and portrait paintings, primarily from Germany and France. Through the years, the paintings have become valuable and are a lasting tribute to the Fryes' discerning taste. In addition to their paintings, the Fryes left a substantial endowment to pay for a new building, its operations and continuing acquisitions.

A mainstay has been Ida May Greathouse, the wife of the Fryes' attorney who was founding director of the museum. She began working there on opening day in 1952, served as director from 1966 to 1993, and continues as a member of the board of directors. During her tenure, she acquired some of the museum's strongest holdings, including the $1 million"Snow on Marly" by Impressionist Alfred Sisley and notable American and Russian paintings. To accommodate its growing collection, the Frye expanded in 1983, tripling its exhibit space. On her retirement on August 14, 1993, a reporter from the SEATTLE POST INTELLIGENCER asked Greathouse what she was proudest of, to which she replied: "I kept the museum opened, I kept it free, and I didn't steal a thing."

18. Stimson-Green Mansion

1204 Minor Avenue
Phone: 624-0474. Call to schedule a tour.
Go northeast on Cherry; turn left on Minor Avenue

In the 1980s, Patricia "Patsy" Bullitt Collins bought the showplace Stimson-Green mansion, which is listed on the Seattle and National Registers of Historic Places. Designed by renowned architect, Kirtland Cutter, the half-timbered structure with stables in the rear was built in 1909 for Collins's grandparents, C.D. and Harriet Overton Stimson, and was the girlhood home of her mother, Dorothy Stimson Bullitt. From 1914 to 1975, it was owned by Joshua Green, and then by Historic Seattle and Preservation Authority which rescued it from demolition after Green's death.

C.D. Stimson was engaged in the timber industry in Michigan and Minnesota. When clear-cutting threatened the survival of Midwest forests, the family decided to move West, arriving in 1889, the year of the great Seattle fire. Unlike most earlier women pioneers, several who came in the 1880s were educated, trained in the arts, and veterans of women's organizations--a new phenomenon in the city and one that the newcomers were quick to introduce. Accustomed to social and cultural amenities, they were determined to recreate them in their new hometown.

In a recent interview Collins made some astute observations about her grandparents' influence on the development of Seattle. She said: "Grandfather came to cut down the trees and Grandmother came to plant them; he came to settle; she to civilize. He brought the old Ballard sawmill and built the Stimson Mill Company; she was a founder of the Seattle Symphony, Children's Orthopedic Hospital, the Visiting Nurse Service, and a primary benefactor of Cornish School." Collins noted that the business enterprises started by C.D. Stimson are long gone, but that her grandmother's legacies are still here and still strongly supported by younger generations of women. She said, "He made the money; she put it to use," noting that while men built the city, it remained for women to civilize it.

Today, the Stimson-Green Mansion is one of only a few reminders of yesteryear's gracious First Hill, where matrons received their women friends during calling hours, where rose gardens proliferated, and where a neighbor, Agnes Healy Anderson, held onto the past until 1935, departing punctually at ten each morning in the city's last horse-drawn brougham. As owner of the mansion, Collins runs a catering business, hosting weddings, Christmas parties, and receptions. Tours, which are available by appointment, conjure up images of the age of elegance, leading from servant quarters in the basement to richly-paneled drawing rooms lined with framed portraits and photographs of the Stimsons.

Following their mother's death, Collins and her sister, Harriet Bullitt, sold KING Broadcasting Corporation, pledging the proceeds--estimated at $100 million--to preservation and revitalization of the Northwest's environment. The Bullitt Foundation is headquartered in the former carriage house behind the mansion. (Please see Chapter VI, King Broadcasting Corporation for further information.)

19. Childhaven (formerly Seattle Day Nursery)
302 Broadway
Go southeast on Minor; turn right on Broadway. Childhaven is at Broadway and Boren

In 1909 the dynamic Reverend Mark Matthews met with a committee of 12 women at First Presbyterian Church to organize the Seattle Day Nursery. It was to be a home during working hours for children of mothers (and some single fathers) forced to earn a living--usually in low-income jobs such as factories, laundries, or domestic service. In an era when most women did not work for pay if their husbands could afford to support them, women in the church considered it a privilege to serve others who bore the double burden of breadwinner and homemaker.

In 1911 the Seattle Day Nursery Association incorporated as a separate non-sectarian body, then moved out of the church's Sunday School rooms into the former Kenney residence on Broadway. The home was torn down in 1921 and rebuilt, so that it could accommodate up to 60 children ages two to nine. Two years later the all female board added a second two-story structure at 1320 Valley Street with a nursery, kindergarten and play area. The home has always operated on a sliding fee scale that in the depths of the Depression ranged from 10¢ to 25¢ per day. Through the years the program has added professional staff and other branches located in neighborhoods throughout the city.

20. Cabrini Hospital/Columbus Hospital
Southwest corner of Madison and Boren
Go northwest on Boren

In 1916 Mother Frances Xavier Cabrini founded Columbus Sanitarium which became Columbus Hospital and later Cabrini Hospital. It was renamed as a memorial for the leader of the Sisters of the Sacred Heart who during her lifetime founded 67 American institutions, the last of which was the Seattle hospital. The sisters continued to operate the small hospital until 1990, when increasing medical costs forced them to close their doors. They could no longer provide quality service to patients, regardless of their ability to pay.

Having immigrated from Italy in 1889, Mother Cabrini was the first United States citizen to be canonized and elevated to sainthood by the Roman Catholic Church. The Patron Saint of Immigrants has her name engraved on a plaque at the foot of the Statue of Liberty. Today, the former Seattle hospital is known as the Perry Building. A corner commemorative plaque bears the names Cabrini Hospital and Columbus Towers. (Please see Chapter V, Villa Academy for further information.)

21. Caroline Kline Galland House
1605 17th Avenue
Go northeast on Madison. The house is at 17th Avenue and Madison

Twice widowed, Caroline Kline Galland emerged at the turn of the century as one of Seattle's foremost philanthropists. Her dignified Georgian Revival mansion, designed in 1903 by architect Max Umbrecht, is a vestige of bygone days, when homes of similar stature lined Madison Street, the cable car route from downtown to Lake Washington. Born in 1841, she immigrated to Seattle from her native Bavaria to marry a successful clothier, Louis Kline. Her second husband, Bonham Galland, was a retired merchant who had made his fortune in San Francisco.

With no children and substantial income from downtown properties (including the Caroline Kline Galland Building directly south of the new Seattle Art Museum), she turned her attention to charity, contributing substantial funds to her synagogue, Temple de Hirsch, and providing assistance to numerous individuals, small businesses and social services. Her major legacy was for construction of the Caroline Kline Galland Home for the Aged and Feeble Poor, located on Seward Park South. (Please see Chapter IX, Kline Galland Home.) The mansion on Madison Street, now listed in the National Register of Historic Places, has been home to different social and health services, including the New Memorial Hospital, the Charles Segal Hospital, and the Seattle Mental Health Institute."

22.   Planned Parenthood of Seattle-King County
2211 East Madison Street

In 1935 Jeanne L. Percy picked up the gauntlet thrown down by Margaret Sanger, founder of the national Planned Parenthood movement. A trained nurse, Percy shared her compassion for young women who committed suicide or died from self-inflicted abortions because they lacked access to birth control. With moral support from the Church of the People, she began advising patients in her home and when necessary made referrals to cooperative physicians. In 1940 interested citizens formed a city-wide board to open Seattle's first birth control clinic at 516 Broadway. Until 1967 when the board hired Lee Minto as its first executive director, volunteers kept the agency alive, frequently relocating the clinic that for decades was the Northwest's only birth control resource for low income families.

In 1970 Planned Parenthood members and friends worked for passage of State Referendum 20 which at that time was one of the most liberal abortion laws in the country. In addition to parent education programs, the agency provided volunteer speakers in the public schools. The county wide program was credited with a 37% reduction in teen pregnancies between 1971 and 1982, a period when there was a statewide rise of 12.5%. While establishing clinics throughout King County, the agency has expanded to other western

Washington communities and has established sister projects in Mexico and Nepal.

In the late 1980s, the Seattle Clinic moved into the building on East Madison, where it began offering confidential abortions. When United Way responded by dropping it as a member agency, there was a public outcry that resulted in a new direct donor designation, ultimately increasing contributions to Planned Parenthood's coffers.

In a recent discussion of the agency's success, Lee Minto attributed it to the commitment and professionalism of volunteers and staff. She noted, "We are respected by the Federation for our successful volunteer program and our expertise in public affairs, counseling and education, and quality control."

Holy Names Academy on Capitol Hill, 1908
(Courtesy of Special Collections Div., University of Washington
Libraries, Neg. #9168)

23. Holy Names Academy

728 21st Avenue East
Continue on Madison; turn left on 21st Avenue East

In the 1880s, the Sisters of the Holy Names of Jesus and Mary came to Seattle, bringing with them a piano and a mission to establish an academy for high school girls. According to their leader, Sister Superior Francis Xavier, the piano was symbolic of their devotion to music, one of their most important subjects.

From humble beginnings in a leaky, rat-infested building, the Sisters attracted students and gained a reputation for providing a high quality liberal arts education. Within three years, the academy was able to move into its own distinctive building at Seventh and Jackson. Holy Names gradually expanded its curriculum to include a kindergarten through eighth grade program and a normal school for teacher training.

When city engineers began the Jackson regrade project to make the hill less steep, the Sisters were forced to abandon their building. In 1908 they constructed the handsome Romanesque edifice on Capitol Hill where they continue to provide four years of basic education, preparing girls for both college and careers.

24. St. Demetrios Greek Orthodox Church

2100 Boyer Avenue East
Go north on 24th Avenue East; turn left on Boyer Avenue East

Each fall Seattleites flock to the church's three-day festival to feast on authentic Greek cuisine and celebrate Greek culture. The month preceding the event is a beehive of activity in the church kitchen where dedicated women (most of whom are grandmothers) bake more than 100,000 pastries including honeyed baklava, delectable spinakopita and buttery koulourakia.

In response to public requests for recipes, the women formed a

Cookbook Committee that selected the best authentic Greek concoctions, then translated the dashes of this and pinches of that into standard measurements with directions that even a novice cook can follow. Churchwomen, who had learned cooking from their mothers in Greece, submitted their favorite traditional recipes. Each was thoroughly tested and when there was a question about which version to use, the women brought their preparations to church for a cook-off with members of the congregation eagerly giving taste tests, then casting their votes.

The church's dedication to GREEK COOKING IN AN AMERICAN KITCHEN is:

We dedicate this book to the mothers and grandmothers who are
affectionately called
"Ta Koritsia Mas" -- The Girls.
Through their cooking they have helped keep alive our traditions
and the Greek spirit in America.

First published in 1982, the cookbook has been reissued in several editions and continues to enjoy steady sales. Its proceeds help support the church's Hellenic Cultural Center.

In the September 1981 issue of ELDER AFFAIRS, Dorothy Mootafes, a member of the Festival Committee, wrote: "Few functions would be successful at St. Demetrios without the church's senior women; in fact they would likely never take place at all." In the old church, built in 1921, and in the present beautiful edifice, built in 1963, women have kept their cultural traditions alive, preparing hundreds of Greek dinners throughout the year, making dance costumes, and creating traditional artwork and embroidery for the church boutique. As members of Philoptochos (friends of the poor) and the Daughters of Penelope, they continue to reach out with programs to assist the sick and needy in the greater Seattle community.

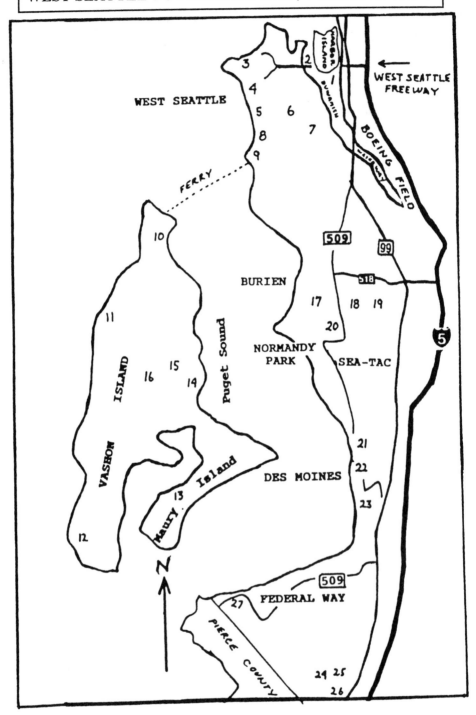

XI. ALONG THE SOUND

West Seattle to Vashon Island to Federal Way

The last of your tours is also the most nautical with stunning views of Puget Sound and multiple opportunities to explore forested parklands and saltwater beaches. It begins on one of Washington's ill-fated bridges in an historically industrial area. Only recently connected to the rest of the city by freeway, most of West Seattle was for decades primarily a settlement of summer vacation homes and popular resorts, accessible only by ferry. Although it was the landing place of Seattle's first pioneers, most of them quickly moved to the sheltered harbor across Elliott Bay, where they staked their claims and founded their city.

As in the past, the ferry transports you from West Seattle to still rural Vashon-Maury Island. Relax and take in the captivating scenery on the way to this historic haven of farms, vacation homes, artists' retreats and summer camps. A major industry was the now defunct shipyard at Dockton on Maury Island. Now a moorage for pleasure and fishing boats, several of the buildings retain their turn-of-the-century character, including the Dockton Store, described in this guide.

Back on the mainland, continue south through Burien, Seahurst, Sunnydale, Des Moines and Federal Way. Explore vestiges of this burgeoning metropolitan area's rural past, when farms, logging camps, beach homes and small towns dotted the landscape. Of special interest is Des Moines Memorial Way that honored deceased veterans of World War I, including women volunteers. The tour ends in Federal Way which incorporated in 1989 to become Washington's fourth largest city. Thanks largely to women, visitors can still find wildlife sanctuaries and a loggers' cafe turned into a community center, that preserve the area's heritage.

1. West Seattle Bridge
West Seattle Freeway, crossing the Duwamish Waterway
Take Exit 163 from I-5

In the pre-dawn hours of Sunday, June 11, 1978, the freighter Antonio Chavez rammed the West Seattle Bridge, wrenching the east end into a permanently upright position and damaging the span beyond repair. Senator Warren Magnusson tapped federal emergency funds for a whopping $110 million and the city quickly allocated the balance of the $142 million budget to tear down the old structure and rebuild it.

But City Councilwoman Jeanette Williams, then chair of the Council's Transportation Committee, was not satisfied and demanded that consultants be hired to reevaluate the design. When they recommended a more expensive bridge that would rise above harbor traffic, Williams swung into action and within three weeks raised the requisite additional $30 million dollars.

Suggestions for naming the most expensive public works project in Seattle's history included the Jeanette Williams Bridge and the Warren Magnusson Bridge, but the geographic moniker won out. Under Williams's leadership, the West Seattle Bridge was completed on time, within budget, and according to Affirmative Action regulations.

2. Elliott Bay Yacht and Engine Company
West Waterway at 1710 West Spokane Street (now the route of the West Seattle Freeway)

In the 1890s, the Corps of Engineers channeled the Duwamish River into East and West Waterways around the mound of ballast that later became man-made Harbor Island, the heart of the Port of Seattle. Some of the city's most enduring businesses began in the area, including The Boeing Company, Todd Shipyards, Lockheed Shipbuilding Company, Fisher Flour Mills, Bethlehem Steel, National Fruit Canning Company, and others. Until World War II, most of the women employees worked in low-status, low-paying jobs in offices and canneries.

An exception was Nellie E. Morrow, proprietor of the Elliott Bay Yacht and Engine Company. When she and her husband established the business in 1910, Nellie brought their three small children to work, taking care of them while managing the office. As the war in Europe escalated and as business boomed, her husband decided to found a larger shipbuilding company on property about a mile away. Wanting a business of her own, she persuaded him to legally transfer 99% of the stock in the original company to her.

By 1917 after the first year, her assets had mushroomed from $100,000 to half a million dollars with work booked months ahead. Having studied drafting with her husband, she personally made estimates on ship repairs, hired and supervised employees, and purchased new equipment. A September 1918 profile of her in SUNSET MAGAZINE notes that Nellie kept "the home fires cheerfully burning for her big-business husband and their three children." She explained, "I think that a woman in business is healthier than one who is kept at home continually....She has broader interests and an opportunity to keep in touch with the outside world. If she is capable in business, and enjoys it, I think that she can keep up her home life and still work." Of her job she said, "I am a shipyard proprietor simply because I love the work."

3. "Birthplace of Seattle"
Alki Avenue SW and SW 63rd Avenue
Continue westbound on SW Admiral Way; turn right on SW 63rd Avenue

The inscription on the monument begins: "At this place on 13 November 1851 there landed from the Schooner Exact the little colony which developed into the City of Seattle...." Engraved are the full names of twelve children and eight adults. The remaining members of the Denny party were four married women, acknowledged after their husbands' names simply as "and wife." When Lenora Denny, one of the children, presented the monument to the Washington State Historical Society on November 13, 1905, social conventions allowed a wife's identity to fade into obscurity. For the record, Seattle's first married women were Mary Ann Boren Denny (wife of Arthur), Mary Boren (wife of Carson), Lydia Colborn Low (wife of John), and Sarah Ann Bell (wife of William).

When the Denny party arrived at Alki, the only shelter awaiting them was the roofless, shoreside cabin that served as the first home for all 24 people. A Mrs. Alexander who remained aboard the Exact recalled their departure:

> I remember it rained awful hard that last day--and the starch got took out of our bonnets and the wind blew, and when the women got into the rowboat to go ashore they were crying every one of 'em,...and the last glimpse I had of them was the women standing under the trees with wet bonnets all loping down over their faces and their aprons to their eyes.

The reluctant pioneers quickly dried their tears and set to work, trying to create comfortable homes for themselves and their loved ones. As the pioneers cleared land and erected cabins, more than a thousand native people gathered nearby, building longhouses and setting up camp. In and out of their homes, the newcomers lived under the constant scrutiny of curious onlookers. Too weak from illness and from recent childbirth to produce milk, Mary Denny was grateful when a native woman recognized her problem and introduced her to clam nectar as a nutritious drink for baby Rolland.

When women in the Denny party prepared meals, they used produce, raised by pioneer farmers in the Duwamish valley. They also cultivated relationships with their Indian neighbors, trading pieces of cloth and trinkets for labor, duck down to fill quilts, and additional food supplies. Native women introduced them to unfamiliar roots, berries, and shellfish, teaching them what was edible and when. While Louisa Boren, Mary Denny and Lydia Low each reported hostile encounters with native men, their contacts with women seem to have been peaceful and often mutually supportive. Within a year of their arrival, the Dennys, the Borens, and the Bells moved to isolated homesteads east of Elliott Bay, leaving Lydia Low as the lone woman settler at Alki. (Please see Chapter X, Louisa Boren Park for further information.)

4. Weather Watch Park
End of SW Carroll Street on Beach Drive SW
About a mile south of the Alki Point lighthouse

This jewel of a beach-front park was designed and developed in the 1990s by Lezlie Jane, a West Seattle native and sculptor who conceived the idea, then got the community involved. A bronze relief map, inlaid into a curved concrete bench, identifies the craggy Olympic peaks and islands that stand in sharp contrast to the Sound. More than 500 bricks, engraved with names, quotes, and historic anecdotes form a half-moon deck area. Topped by a whimsical weather vane, a triangular column displays etched bronzed historical photos, taken nearby, and captions. An inviting path lined with a variety of saltwater tolerant plants leads down to the driftwood beach.

One of the photos, dated 1899, is of Native Americans on the beach. Another shows the little steamer Eagle which from 1907 to 1920 stopped at the site to transport passengers and parcels to the downtown Seattle waterfront. The dock was later dismantled with the sloping lot left vacant. Thanks to Lezlie Jane and the community, an abandoned lot has been restored as a pristine viewpoint with historic, environmental, and artistic interest.

5. Emma Schmitz Memorial Overlook and Me-Kwa-Mooks Park
Beach Drive SW and SW Oregon Street
South of Weather Watch Park

In 1945 Emma Schmitz made a gift to the city of nearly 1,000 feet of Beach Drive waterfront with sweeping 240° views. From the streetside promenade and benches, visitors can walk down a staircase to investigate tide pools on the beach below. Overlooking the park from across Beach Drive is the site of the former hillside estate of Emma and Ferdinand Schmitz, who immigrated from Germany in the 1880s. Damaged beyond repair by the 1964 earthquake, the luxurious mansion and grounds live on only in memories. The city later purchased the site for a park, creating the shaded green meadow at the base of the steep wooded hillside and adding tables for picnickers. The park is named Me-Kwa-Mooks after a native village that was once nearby. In the Nisqually dialect it means "shaped like a bear's head," which also describes the shape of the area that includes Alki Point and the Duwamish Head.

The Schmitzes' property also included the irreplaceable tract of old-growth forest at Southwest Admiral Way and South Stevens Street which they gave to the city in 1908, stipulating that it be preserved in perpetuity in its natural state. Thanks to their vision, visitors to Schmitz Park can still experience the wilderness and giant trees that greeted the pioneers.

6. Mount Saint Vincent Nursing Center and Retirement Apartments

4831 35th Avenue SW
At the south end of the park turn left on Jacobson Road; turn left on 49th SW; turn right on SW Alaska Street, then right on 35th SW

In 1924 the Sisters of Providence built this imposing four-story brick structure as a convalescent home for infirm elderly of all faiths. In the 1960s, they expanded the original space, adding the entire wing of 150 retirement apartments and the new building that houses infirm Sisters, along with those who work at "the Mount."

Today, the beautiful grounds and parts of the buildings are alive with a new kind of vitality. On weekdays, parents drop off some 60 preschoolers for daycare. Trained staff and an abundant supply of "grandparents" have found the mingling of young and old to be a great benefit for both.

7. **Louisa Boren Junior High School**
5950 Delridge Way SW
Go south on 35th Avenue SW; turn left on SW Juneau Street; turn left on 30th Avenue SW; turn left on SW Brandon Street, and right on Delridge Way SW

Please see Louisa Boren Park located on North Capitol Hill and the "Birthplace of Seattle" on Alki Beach for information about the school's namesake. When the school opened in 1963, Victor Denny, her grandson, presented the portrait of his grandmother that now hangs in the library.

8. **Kenney Home**
7125 Fauntleroy Way SW
Return to SW Juneau Street and continue west; turn right on Fauntleroy Way SW

Samuel Kenney, born in North Ireland in 1829, sailed to Scotland as a young man to marry Jessie Allen. After learning the tailoring business together, they immigrated to Seattle. As their business prospered, they invested in real estate, including the ten-acre site in West Seattle where they built cottages to serve as retirement homes for the elderly. When Samuel died in 1895, he willed his property to "my beloved wife who knows my plans and hopes for founding, with her, a home for the aged." Jessie died five years later, leaving their substantial estate in the care of trustees of the First Presbyterian Church with directions to found the Samuel and Jessie Kenney home.

Designed as a replica of Independence Hall in Philadelphia, the three-story building "in the woods" was dedicated on Washington's Birthday, 1908, and was popularly known as "the finest retirement home in the Northwest." The first residents paid $2,000 for a lifetime membership, while bequests subsidized some of lesser means. In keeping with the Kenneys' dream, the trustees sought to provide a complete and pleasant home environment. Faced with growing demand, they solicited additional donations to purchase lots in front of the building for expansions in 1958 and again in the 1980s.

9. Lincoln Park

Fauntleroy Way SW
Continue southwest on Fauntleroy

In 1970 the Federated Women's Club of West Seattle was named "Most Outstanding Club in the United States" by the General Federation/Sears Roebuck and Co. Improvement Program. Corrine Wing and Helen Sutton represented their club at the annual convention in Texas, where they stood before the throng to accept the bronze plaque and the $10,000 award. In the community history, WEST SIDE STORY, edited by Clay Eels, Sutton recalled the proud moment: "When our club was announced the winner, the Montana delegation rang cowbells and the Californians popped pop guns....I felt like I was at the Miss America pageant." True to its prize-winning character, the club used the money to buy playground equipment for three sites in Lincoln Park and at Fairmount Elementary School.

10. Betty MacDonald Farm

Vashon Island
Board the ferry at the south end of Lincoln Park; The beach-front farm is located on the east side of the island about a quarter of a mile south of Dolphin Point which is just beyond the ferry landing; From the road high above, visitors can easily spot the huge red and white barn

Her first book, THE EGG AND I, rocketed to the best seller list in 1945, shortly after Betty and Donald MacDonald and their family moved to Vashon Island. In the wake of World War II, the hilarious backwoods stories about her adventures as a farmer's wife in Chimacum Valley (near Port Townsend) were a welcome breath of fresh air for readers around the world. While some of her former neighbors resented the parallels to Ma and Pa Kettle, the book was eventually translated into 30 languages.

Fifteen years earlier at age 18, Betty had married her first husband and moved to the Chimacum farm that had neither plumbing nor electricity. Whatever money they made had gone to the chickens that

Betty so eloquently hated: "Even baby chickens. Their sole idea in life is to jam themselves under the brooder and get killed; stuff their little boneheads so far into their drinking fountains they drown, drink cold water and die....and peck out each other's eyes." After four years, Betty left Robert Hesket, taking their two daughters, Anne and Joan, with her. On return to her family home in Seattle, she worked at different jobs, keeping her sense of humor even when tuberculosis forced her to spend a year at Firland Sanatorium north of Seattle. Later, that experience became the subject of her book THE PLAGUE AND I.

Ironically, when the MacDonalds moved to Vashon Island, the family was back in the chicken business, marketing eggs on the island and at the Pike Place Market. But their major source of income was Betty's writing. Her bestseller, ONIONS IN THE STEW, told about their life on the island. Inspired by children who were her constant companions, she also wrote the still-popular MISS PIGGLE WIGGLE books. In 1958, two years after they left their island home, Betty died of cancer at age 49 in Seattle.

The imposing barn that the MacDonalds built "in the style of the 1900s" is now painted red and white and has been remodelled as a residence. Adjoining it is the former chicken house, where Betty loathed some 4,000 hens at a time. As in Betty's time, the neighborhood is rich in orchards, woods, and luscious garden, fronted by beaches piled high with driftwood.

11. Matilda Jane Redding Carmen Proper holdings
Cove, Vashon
Take Westside Highway SW

In 1884 Matilda Jane Carmen, the mother of six children, moved her family to Vashon Island, where she paid $725 to purchase the 80-acre tract at Cove that Michael Racine had preempted just four years earlier. After logging off his claim, Racine sold it to Mary A. Bright who in turn sold it to Matilda.

In an era when most women followed their husbands, Matilda was independent, enterprising, and adventuresome. Four of her six children bore the name Redding from her first husband who was killed in an accident at their home in Missouri. She had packed up the family's belongings, moved to California, and married Aaron Carmen, a teamster who later found work in Seattle.

Preferring island life to the squalid city, Matilda took the children to Vashon where Aaron visited on his days off. By 1886 when he was killed in an industrial accident, she had expanded her real estate holdings down to the beach of Colvos Passage and north and south from 168th Southwest to Southwest 160th. She continued to buy and sell neighboring properties, so that today nearly every home between the towns of Cove and Colvos is on land that she once owned.

In 1888 Matilda was married again, this time to a 21-year-old named Peter Lester Proper. Some of her Redding children acquired parts of her property as indicated by Reddings Beach at Cove. Matilda later moved to Everett where she died in her home at age 86.

12. Camp Sealth/Camp Fire Girls and Boys
Camp Fire, Seattle/King County Council
Continue south past Paradise Cove to the island's southwest shore

Groups of Camp Fire Girls began to organize in King County in the early teens, shortly after the national association was chartered. Their mission was to "perpetuate the spiritual ideals of the home" and to develop health and character. Members made their own ceremonial gowns, beads and leather badges that they earned for community service and for outdoor survival accomplishments, such as frying an egg on a rock or swimming a mile.

In Seattle the different groups banded together under the leadership of Ruth Brown who helped them acquire and develop a campsite. In 1921 thanks to generous donations from the Kiwanis, they purchased the 159-acre Luceta Beach Resort on the southwest end of Vashon

Island. The camp included five streams, one mile of beach, an orchard, wharf and 17 cottages, each with a fireplace and running water. In subsequent years, the board acquired neighboring property, increasing the camp to 400 acres.

Shortly after it opened, National Field Secretary Edith Kempthorne visited Sealth and proclaimed it a model for the entire country. Under Ruth Brown's direction, camp life included morning dips, horseback riding, canoeing, singing, hiking, crafts, cookouts, team sports and more. In the process the girls learned self-reliance skills, made friends, and developed commitments to serving their communities and protecting the natural environment.

In her book, THE PAST REMEMBERED, Blanche Hamilton Caffiere tells of island residents turning out to greet the steamboat Virginia IV on Sunday evenings when girls left camp singing "Till We Meet Again." One of her interviewees recalled watching as they paddled their mammoth canoes to Lisabuela (a community to the north on Vashon) on day trips--"always singing THAT song."

For more than 70 years, camp life at Sealth has in many ways remained the same, but the middy and bloomer uniforms are gone, and the former all-girl organization now includes approximately 25% boys. Today, almost 2,000 kids go to summer camp at Sealth and an additional 5,000 participate in other programs throughout the year.

13. Dockton General Store and Post Office
Dockton, Maury Island
From Camp Sealth drive north, then turn west on 232nd Street SW, follow signs

Recently designated as King County Landmark, the building's history is intertwined with that of the Berry family. In 1912 Dockton residents celebrated the wedding of Rosie Bussanick and Theo Berry, the boy next door. With income saved from his fishing, they purchased the building in 1919 which they expanded and developed into the island's principal store and only post office. While Theo served as postmaster, Rosie worked at his side, all the while caring for their three daughters, Katherine (Peterson), Mary (Johnson), and Rose (Carcick).

In an interview quoted in Caffiere's THE PAST REMEMBERED, Katherine recalled, "I must have been only about four, but I remember Mom bringing us all to the store and making a bed for us with a blanket on a little pile of gunny sacks where we could take a nap while she and Dad were busy with customers." She noted, "Dad gave Mom high praise for her work in the store, especially in the meat department." When the girls were old enough, they also helped out, remaining in the business long after all three married local men. The Berrys were active in their community's civic, social and religious life. They offered their home for the first Catholic Mass and were prime movers in the fund-raising drive to build little St. Patrick's Church.

14.   Chautauqua, Madrona Lodge
Return to Vashon Island, then go north along the east shore past Ellisport

The Methodist-Episcopal summer education programs that swept rural America began at Chautauqua Lake, New York in 1874. Like its namesake, the Vashon Island camp began with the purpose of training Sunday school teachers and church workers, then expanded its program to general adult education in the arts, sciences, and humanities. The popular Chautauqua lecture series provided traveling speakers and vaudeville acts to small towns and rural areas throughout the country. Crusading suffragists, temperance workers and other social reformers were always present to deliver their message through this important informal network.

Families flocked to the Vashon Island site, filling the Madrona Lodge and a cluster of cottages and pitching tents in the woods. Entertainment and lectures were enhanced by the magnificent backdrop of Puget Sound and Mt. Rainier. The official season lasted for three weeks with visitors often prolonging their stay. In the early twentieth century as the Chautauqua movement began to fade, the event evolved into the island's ever-popular annual strawberry festival, where local women continue to play leading roles as organizers and hosts.

15. Beall Family Home
91st Avenue SW and SW 185th Street
Go west to Vashon Highway SW, turn right, then left on 185th

In 1899 Jennie Beall, Lewis Cass "L.C." Beall, and their four children headed west from the estate in Maryland where members of the Beall family had made their home since the mid-1600s. On Vashon Island, Jennie worked with a local builder to design a replica of her childhood home in Georgia, which she had watched burn to the ground in the wake of Sherman's March. An ardent Confederate, she regaled her grandchildren and neighbors with stories of the Civil War until the day she died. In 1925 she wore her wedding dress, as she and L.C. welcomed more than 200 friends to their home to celebrate their fiftieth anniversary.

The Beall family made important contributions locally and internationally to floriculture and poultry breeding. By the 1930s when members of the second generation managed the business, the Beall Greenhouse Company was the largest of its kind in the Northwest, featuring prize-winning orchids, roses, carnations, camellias and gardenias. During World War II when the English sent out an urgent plea to American nurseries to help save their outstanding rare orchids, the Bealls purchased thousands of cuttings. In subsequent years, the family expanded the business with greenhouses in the southwestern states and South America. Because of the high cost of labor, they closed down the business on Vashon Island in the mid 1960s. Their rose plantation in Bogota, Columbia is still in operation and is connected to Beall's Roses retail stores in Seattle and Kirkland.

Jennie Beall's southern mansion has been preserved largely through the efforts of her female progeny. On her death in 1942, her daughter Connie Beall Howe and her husband moved into the family home.

Page 301

Jennie's granddaughter Virginia Beall Bonner (son Wallace's daughter) and her family moved in in 1973. The home remained a center of family activity from its construction in 1899 until Virginia sold it to the present owners in 1986. Thanks to these three generations of women with a sense of heritage, Jennie Beall's dream house has remained largely unchanged. It is listed on the King County and Washington State Registers of Historic Places.

A more recent addition to the King County Register is the 15½-acre Harrington-Beall Greenhouse Company Historic District which includes 59 greenhouses, workers' residences, a log cabin that belonged to company founder, Hilan Harrington, and the Beall family home. Nancy and Chuck Hooper recently purchased the plant from Tom Beall Jr. Relying on her experience as a florist and his as an architect, they plan to restore the greenhouses from a tangle of blackberry vines and broken glass to their former productivity. Hoping to sublease some of the buildings to other growers, the Hoopers have renamed the complex Beall Road Greenhouses Inc.

16. Mukai House, Garden, and Cold Process Fruit Barrelling Plant
18017 107th Avenue SW and 18005 107th Avenue SW
Go north on Vashon Island Way; turn left on Bank Road; go one-fourth mile, then left on 107th Avenue SW; The property is on the right side

The Mukai agricultural complex is historically significant as one of few intact legacies of Japanese-American heritage in rural King County. The family's American saga began in 1885 when 15-year-old Denichiro "B.D." Mukai immigrated to California with the ambition "to make money." While working at different jobs and then in his own business, he gained crucial fluency in English. He married Sako Nakanichi, who according to the family may have been a picture bride, (Please see Chapter VIII, Nippon Kan Theater for further information.) then moved to a strawberry farm on Vashon Island in 1910. When their son Masahiro "Masa" was still a small boy, Sako died of cancer. B.D. married her sister Kuni who was working for a

Chiyeko (left), son Milton and Kuni Mukai on top of the island in their garden
(Courtesy of King County Parks, Planning and Resources)

Seattle doctor's family as a domestic. As their only child, Masa always called her "Mother" and years later when B.D. returned to Japan, Kuni remained with Masa and his family.

In the mid 1920s at age 15, Masa purchased the 40-acre strawberry farm that became the family home and business. Unlike his Asian-born parents, who could neither become citizens nor own land, he was an American. B.D. and Kuni financed construction of the two-story gabled house, the formal garden and the Mukai Cold Process Fruit Barrelling Plant--the first on the island. The plant took care of the Mukais' and their neighbors' overproduction strawberries, opening up worldwide wholesale markets.

While B.D. and Masa were the buildings' architects, Kuni designed the expansive formal garden that blends traditional Japanese and American landscaping. With help from laborers, Masa and B.D. constructed the garden with a centerpiece of artfully arranged raised rockery, bordered by curved ponds, a large circular lawn, and narrow flower beds for perennials and annuals. Kuni chose a unique variety of plants including flowering Kanzan cherries, feathery Japanese maples, Sawara cypress, local rhododendrons, junipers and wisteria that cascaded across a natural trellis of moss-covered fallen trees. She graced the ponds with water lilies and koi (Japanese ornamental carp). Near the back of the house, she designed a separate kitchen garden. Until the outbreak of World War II, the garden attracted visitors from on and off the island. A social highlight was Kuni's annual spring tea party at cherry blossom time.

In the early 1930s Masa married Chiyeko Wakasugi whose family grew strawberries on Bainbridge Island. Like Kuni, she was involved in the family business, hiring, supervising and sometimes firing members of a large labor force that included Native Americans, Filipinos and whites. Some 35 women, under supervision of a matron, sorted berries on conveyor belts in the processing plant. During the Great Depression, the Mukai enterprise prospered, providing seasonal jobs for almost 500 workers.

World War II spelled devastation for West Coast people of Japanese descent. With the exception of the Mukais, those living on Vashon Island were given two weeks notice of their enforced evacuations, the Mukais were allowed to leave voluntarily and moved to a farming community in Idaho where Chiyeko's brother lived.

In the post-war period, many of the younger families resettled in other areas, but several from the immigrant generation returned to Vashon. The Mukais found their house rented and the garden suffering from neglect. Wanting to avoid further conflict, they moved into another house and resumed farming and berry processing, then finished building the smaller new house on their property that became their home until the 1980s when they moved to West Seattle.

In 1993 the 11-acre house, garden and barrelling plant area--now subdivided with two different owners--was designated a King County Landmark. The owner of the barrelling plant is rehabilitating it for artists' studios and commercial space. The house is a private residence. Funding is being sought from King County to support restoration of Kuni's garden under the direction of Masa and Chiyeko.

17. Ruth School for Girls/Ruth Dykeman Children's Center
10th Avenue SW and SW 152nd Street
From the ferry dock go west to State Route 509, then south to 152nd Street, then west

In 1932 the 11-year-old Ruth School for Girls moved from temporary quarters in north Seattle to the picturesque former country estate on Lake Burien. Its charges were wards of the juvenile court--troubled and delinquent teen-age girls, thought by the judge to be in danger of drifting into serious trouble. In accord with social mores of the day, girls who were pregnant or afflicted with a social disease were not admitted, and those found guilty of criminal acts were sent to the State School for Girls at Grand Mound in Thurston County.

The school is named for the daughter of King County Juvenile Court Judge King Dykeman who played a major role in its founding. It was governed by an all-female board of 20 trustees from Protestant churches in the greater Seattle area. Support came from church guilds, auxiliaries, and several secular organizations, including Business and Professional Women, the Soroptimists, the Kiwanis, Rotary, Camp Fire Girls, Girl Scouts and others. When the school moved to its Lake Burien campus, donations ranged from livestock and farm equipment to volunteering to plant fruit trees or clear brush for a playground. The Capitol Hill Auxiliary held a "hen party," where each member donated a live chicken. The formal dedication ceremony attracted more than 1,000 people, and Ruth Dykeman was on hand to pour tea.

Residents of the school were housed in the stately Colonial mansion, surrounded by sweeping lawns, flower and vegetable gardens, fruit orchards, and a barnyard with chickens and milk cows. Girls who arrived underweight and anemic quickly regained their health. The Seattle Public Schools provided a teacher for academic instruction, while clubwomen volunteered to teach music, art, sewing, cooking and gardening.

Today, the institution's mission has changed, as reflected in its name, Ruth Dykeman Children's Center. It offers a variety of services for severely stressed children and their families. The mansion, built by former owner George Albee, still stands as does the picturesque water tower.

Planting memorial trees
(Courtesy of Everett Public Library)

18. Des Moines Memorial Way South
Monument at Sunnydale School
Des Moines Memorial Way South and South 156th Street

On Armistice Day, November 11, 1921, members of the Seattle Garden Club, led by President Lillian Gustin McEwan, planted the first 25 elm trees along Des Moines Way South--the beginning of a living memorial to "American men who gave their lives for their country during World War I." Eventually a continuous arch of 1400 majestic elms extended from the Seattle City limits to the Kent-Des Moines Highway. In 1963 changing needs dictated removal of some of the trees including those in front of historic Sunnydale School at 156th Street. Their replacement is an expansive pink granite monument, engraved with a bas-relief sculptured American Elm, along with more than 1,000 names.

But like the elms--many more of which have been removed since 1963--part of the history of the Memorial Highway has been lost. While the Seattle Garden Club's membership was predominantly female, it remained for former service women to pay tribute to the female war dead. On February 22, 1922, the following announcement appeared in THE SEATTLE TIMES:

> DEAD SEATTLE EX-SERVICE WOMEN TO BE HONORED--Smiling faces and courageous hearts, tender hands and soft voices which ministered to the sick and wounded, cheered the gloomy and homesick, suffered and died in the cause of freedom--women 'soldiers' from Seattle-- will be honored tomorrow afternoon by the Ex-Service Women's Club, whose members will dedicate trees to their memory along Memorial Highway near Des Moines.

A February 26th article that covered the ceremony notes "the supports of the eight elm saplings....carry small silk American flags to mark them from their fellows which have been dedicated under auspices of the Seattle Garden Club to men who died in the service of their country." A photograph shows Miss Geraldine Doheny "who has just returned from three years' Red Cross service in France and the Balkans, affixing a flag to the support of Mrs. McDonald's tree." In the article we learn that Mrs. Lottie Brainerd McDonald attended Ballard High School, then joined the Northwest Division of the Red Cross when the United States entered the war. While serving in Siberia, she married an Army officer, but then contracted an illness and died in Shanghai. The article also includes stories and photos of the seven other memorialized women. Following the ceremony, 40 members of the Ex-Service Women's Clubs convened for a luncheon at the YWCA tea room, where they paid further tribute to "the women who died in the cause of freedom."

For years, Veterans have held Memorial Day ceremonies at the granite monument which bears all of the names submitted to the Garden Club, including those of a handful of women. There are other bronze plaques: two to the Unknown Soldier; another noting the dedication of the Elmer Noble Memorial Tree; and still another commemorating the dedication of a tree to the French "Blue Devils" regiment. Hopefully, at some future ceremony, visitors will find yet another commemorative plaque with the names of the long forgotten female heroes to whom ex-service women paid their own special tribute.

19.   Mrs. Kelly's Kitchen School/Sunnydale School
South 156th Street and 8th Avenue South
Same as above

In 1872 Jane Fenton, a member of a Duwamish Valley pioneering family, married Mike Kelly, an Irish immigrant. Together they founded the community of Sunnydale (now Burien). Jane taught the three Rs to her own and neighbors' children in what Mike affectionately called Mrs. Kelly's Kitchen School. In 1882, 28 pupils moved from her kitchen into a new log-cabin schoolhouse on the Kelly property. It was later replace by the historic Sunnydale School that is still in operation as part of the Highline School District.

Although Mike was a supportive husband who approved of Jane's teaching, he threatened to leave her in 1886 when Washington women won the vote. In her memoirs, published in Esther Balzarini's book, OUR BURIEN, Jane wrote: "Now this was getting serious, as my mind was fully made up to go [to the polls]. I did not argue, but I said to myself, 'No boy is coming over here from Ireland to dictate to me what I shall do politically.'" Hoping that the pen was mightier than the sword, she won him over by composing a poem:

A WOMAN'S SENTIMENTS ON WOMAN SUFFRAGE
Jane Fenton Kelly, 1886
>   Oh! Man! Why dost thou dread
>   To let woman with thee walk
>   In public as in private
>   And of our country's welfare talk?
>   Is it not she to whom
>   Your children come for knowledge
>   Long before they seek it
>   In public school or college?
>   Then if she should wish to step
>   Upon the round of fame
>   Give her a helping hand
>   And tarnish not her name!
>   Does she not bless your home,
>   And purify your life
>   Whenever she is with you
>   In pleasure, or in strife?

For three years Jane marched to the polls with Mike, confiding in her memoirs that she sensed he was actually proud of her. But her victory was cut short, when the Territorial Supreme Court ruled the women's vote unconstitutional in 1889. A year later, Jane and other Washington women regained the right to vote in school elections. (Please see Chapter I, Joseph and Martha Jane Steel Foster House for further information. The Fosters were Jane's grandparents.)

20.   Highline School District Museum at Lakeview School

Phone: 433-2272. Open Thursdays, 10 a.m.-noon and 1-2

p.m.; and on the 2nd and 4th Saturday of each month.
*Continue south on Des Moines Memorial Way South; turn
right on SW 158th*

This museum recently moved from its original quarters at Sunnydale
School. Among its exhibits is a replica of Mrs. Kelly's Kitchen
School, complete with the trappings of a pioneer kitchen.

21.   Des Moines/Zenith Historical Society Museum
728 South 225th Street
*Go south on Des Moines Memorial Way South onto Marine
View Drive South, turn right on South 225th Street*

The Des Moines/Zenith Historical Museum is appropriately housed in
the community's oldest clubhouse, built in 1912 by the Commercial
Club and later purchased by the Odd Fellows. Its exhibits and
archives shed light on important contributions of women's
organizations.

In 1900 Emma Van Gasken, a newly arrived bride, organized the
community's first musicales and literary readings. With other women
she founded the Booster Club (later renamed the Enterprise Club),
which was Des Moines' first service organization. Enlisting help from
their husbands, members raised funds to build board sidewalks, so that
women could walk to the post office and stores without dragging their
skirts in the mud. The club built its own clubhouse where it organized
the area's first public library. It also funded a comfort station at the
Vashon Ferry dock and rallied to Red Cross work during World War
I.

In the 1920s the club merged with the Men's Improvement Club where
it initially functioned as a ladies' auxiliary. According to Richard
Kennedy, author of ONE HUNDRED YEARS OF THE
"WATERLAND" COMMUNITY, "....women have been the
backbone of the Improvement Club. They maintained the clubhouse,
bought all necessary equipment, organized and furnished books and
shelving for the library until it became part of the King County

system....continuing at all times to work together for the improvement of our city." Prior to the city's incorporation in 1959, the club acted as a community council.

In 1978 the Improvement Club contacted local pioneers and their descendants, inviting them to a meeting to organize the Des Moines-Zenith Historical Society. Melanie Draper--long term volunteer librarian and author of the first history of Des Moines, TIMBER, TIDES AND TALES!--was chosen as director of the society's museum, a position that she still holds.

22. Daddy and Mother Draper Home/Draper Park
Now Des Moines Beach Park
Go north to South 222 Street, then left; The park is located at the mouth of Des Moines Creek

When Herman Draper and Annie Pacey were married in 1879, he held degrees and certificates from music schools in both England and the United States, including the prestigious Boston Conservatory of Music. Working at public schools and orphanages in Nebraska and Michigan, he taught music and organized the popular "Jolly Entertainers"--touring band that were a source of pride for their communities.

When Annie's sister died, leaving a daughter, she became the first of the Drapers' many children. In 1907 the family--including six adopted children from the original band--headed west to Washington State with "Daddy" at the wheel of their "house car," a precursor of the modern mobile home that was built on an old truck chassis.

The Drapers established their own Childrens' Industrial Home and Training School at 5517 22nd Avenue Northwest in Ballard. A year later, they decided to move to a tamer, less urbanized setting in Des Moines, where they purchased the 29-room Hiatt Hotel and the park below. After converting the hotel into a large family home, they turned their attention to the adjacent barn which became their "opry" house for musical and vaudevillian performances. The park doubled as a setting for outdoor summer concerts and a playground for their growing "family."

"Daddy" trained the spiffily uniformed Jolly entertainers, taking them on performing tours throughout King County and Washington State that culminated in a major tour of 38 states. The popular little band supported the home which at times housed as many as 47 children and which thrived for two decades without governmental or major charitable assistance.

All of the Drapers' children attended the Des Moines public schools, receiving private tutoring when on tour. In the fall 1981 issue of PORTAGE MAGAZINE, historian Charles Payton wrote:

> A non-sectarian love of God and country was instilled in the children, but above all, "Daddy" Draper taught by means of his music, which he well knew, acted as a refining influence, and helped instill self-discipline, cooperation, and self-sufficiency in the children.

While "Daddy" is well remembered, "Mother" has fallen into obscurity. With a three-story home, a family of 47 children, and a husband who took his band on tour, she must have been a strong partner, responsible for managing the household, caring for a sick or troubled child, and sharing her husband's unflagging devotion to their family. That the Drapers were always the guiding spirits of the home is without question. When they died within five days of each other in April 1927, others stepped in try to keep it going, but to no avail.

Today, all that remains of the home is the park, once called Draper Park. In 1931 when the property was sold to the Northern Pacific Conference of the Evangelical Covenant Church of America, it was renamed Covenant Beach and used as a Bible camp. The city later purchased it and renamed it Des Moines Beach Park.

"Daddy" and "Mother" Draper and their children: Harry (middle), Cecil, and Edith Mae "Birdie" (Courtesy of Melanie Draper)

23. Salt Water State Park
Marine View Drive
Two miles south of Des Moines Beach Park

In 1945 as president of the Des Moines-Zenith Improvement Club, Ruth Meenach Peeler brought Salt Water State Park's deteriorating sea wall and dilapidated community kitchens to the attention of the Director of State Parks in Olympia. When she learned that no state money was available, she effectively lobbied the legislature to include badly needed park maintenance funds in the budget.

Accepting an appointment to a six year term on the Washington State Parks and Recreation Commission, she saw a need for historical markers. Governor Arthur B. Langlie responded by appointing a Historical Advisory Board to assist her. By 1953 she had obtained and dedicated markers in 32 parks and recreation areas throughout the state.

In 1979 the Ginko Petrified Forest Vista, located near Vantage on the west side of the Columbia River, was renamed the Ruth E. Peeler Vista in her honor. A bronze plaque at the vista's museum enumerates her accomplishments. She and Pearl A. Wanamaker, former State Superintendent of Public Instruction, are the only women whose achievements are recorded in the time capsule that was sealed in Olympia during the State Centennial Celebration.

24. Brooklake Community Center
726 South 356th Street
Federal Way
Go south on I-5, then west at the South 320th Street exit; turn left on SR-99 (Pacific Highway South), then right on South 356th Street

One of Federal Way's oldest unaltered buildings opened in 1920 as the Wagon Wheel Inn. Catering to the whims of its logger clientele, it evolved into a brothel and speak-easy that was eventually closed by the county sheriff. Today, its setting remains virtually unchanged--a sharp contrast to nearby shopping malls, apartment complexes and gridlock traffic. Located in the woods, it overlooks the West Hylebos Wetlands and a stream that until three years ago was a route for spawning salmon.

In the mid-1940s, the Brooklake Women's Club, the Brooklake Community Club and the Brooklake Dance Club joined forces to purchase the building for a non-profit, private community center, to be governed by a board of trustees. Members sold shares of stock, raising additional funds to expand and renovate their clubhouse. Nellie Flemming, who belonged to all three clubs, says that the women's group was especially active. For women in the predominantly rural neighborhoods of Federal Way, it was the center of social and community life.

Members of the Brooklake Women's Club organized flower shows, participated in blood drives, sponsored guest speakers, and dressed up in costumes to perform at the clubhouse. A highlight of the year was the gala ball at Foster (now Tukwila), held by the consortium of 52 South King County Community Improvement Clubs. The state governor led the grand march and queen candidates from each club competed for the title of Miss South King County.

Flemming blames television for the demise of most social clubs, noting that the Brooklake Women's Club, which disbanded in the early 1980s, was never the same after TV took over people's spare time. She says, "We found an alternate form of entertainment, instead of getting together and gabbing....which was always a lot of fun."

In 1984 the Federal Way Community Center Association leased the property, which remains a popular venue for wedding receptions, meetings, classes, garden shows, teen dances, and other special events. According to its charter, the center cannot be sold to a business or commercial interest.

25. West Hylebos Wetlands State Park
34915 4th Avenue South
Go south on SR-99, then right on South 348th Street; The entrance is just past the two pioneer cabins

At its 1993 convention in Nebraska City, Nebraska, the National Arbor Day Foundation presented its Good Steward Award to Ilene Marckx, who led the effort to preserve and develop this remarkable 100-acre wildlife refuge into a state park. In 1955 Marckx and her late husband, Francis, founded Wetlands of the West Hylebos, Inc., beginning with their own 10-acre parcel. As neighbors contributed additional forested land, she platted the mile-long boardwalk that leads through the park. Visitors get an intimate but non-intrusive look at abundant varieties of foliage and animal life.

A retired school librarian with a B.S. in biology and botany from Washington State University, Marckx has identified more than 140 species of birds in the park. She publishes an informative newsletter which updates visitors on her finds and on park-related issues. Her signage has drawn admiration from the Washington State Park Board which recently commissioned her to compose a new interpretive sign system of the park.

26.   Spring Valley Montessori School
36605 Pacific Highway South (SR-99)
Continue south on SR-99

In 1951 Madeleine J. Justus founded Seattle's first Montessori school, then in 1960 moved it to its present location. The school adheres to the precepts of Maria Montessori, Italy's first female M.D. who pioneered her innovative pedagogical methods at the turn of the century, working with children in the slums of Rome. Justus learned the method while helping set up pre-schools for orphans during World War II, when Romania occupied her native Hungary. In 1950 as an immigrant in Seattle, she wanted to enroll her three-year-old son in a Montessori school, but found that none existed.

The program recognizes each child as a unique individual who grows naturally in the prepared environment, learning to solve problems and understand abstract concepts. The atmosphere is positive and enriching with an ultimate goal of developing sensitive and useful members of society. Parents are a vital part of the program and are encouraged to become involved.

While in Seattle, Justus took her children on outings to the lovely trout farm in Spring Valley. When she heard that it was for sale, she persuaded her husband to buy it, then set about converting it into a school for children, age three to seven. In response to parents' urgings, she added the next grade, continuing until the school reached eighth grade.

Campus I for preschool through second grades is in a park-like, 14-acre setting with spacious lawns, tall trees, a lake and a creek. It extends into the neighboring Hylebos Wetlands State Park which enhances the school's nature study and recreational program. The first campus was formerly a farm with many of the original buildings converted to classroom use. Staff members enjoy showing visitors the meat hooks in a closet of a historic building--reminders of its former use as a meat-packing plant. Located one mile to the south is Campus II, also known as the upper campus, for students grades two through eight.

Accredited by Washington State's Office of the Superintendent of Public Instruction, the school houses the state licensed Montessori Teacher Training Program, which Justus developed in cooperation with the University of Puget Sound. She has trained thousands of teachers and has also written several books on the Montessori method that are in demand throughout the world.

A pioneer of early childhood education in the state, she worked diligently in the 1950s and 1960s to promote regulations for pre-school and daycare centers, making almost daily trips to Olympia when the legislature was in session. Today, she continues to direct her school and serves on the board of the Washington Association of Independent Schools.

27.   Sisters of the Visitation Monastery
3200 SW Dash Point Road
Go north on Pacific Highway South; turn left on SW 356th Street; turn right on 21st Avenue SW; turn left on SW Dash Point Road

Located on a spectacular 12-acre site overlooking Puget Sound, the monastery was home to the Sisters of the Visitation from 1957 to mid-1993. Having come to the Pacific Northwest in 1891, members of the order taught, nursed the sick, and provided religious retreats for regional women. With fewer novitiates entering the convent, the community gradually dwindled to seven members, whereupon the order decided to sell the property and leave the Pacific Northwest. As the new owner, the City of Federal Way is making it available for symphony concerts, business retreats, regional conferences and weddings.

Mother Mary Ruth Dolch, the monastery's mother superior, was pleased to announce that two-thirds of the proceeds from the sale of the property and from the auction of many of its contents would go into a trust to care for the elderly. The remaining third was to be distributed among other Visitation monasteries, chosen by the seven nuns as their new homes.

SUGGESTED READING

Allison, Charlene J., Sue-Ellen Jacobs and Mary A. Porter
Winds of Change: Women in Northwest Commercial Fishing
Seattle: University of Washington Press, 1989. (Through 10
life histories, the authors document choices available to
women in commercial fishing.)

Andrews, Mildred Tanner, Washington Women as Path Breakers,
sponsored by the Junior League of Tacoma. Dubuque:
Kendall/Hunt, 1989. (An illustrated history that examines
women's roles in social reform crusades and in community
building.)

Armitage, Susan and Elizabeth Jameson, eds., The women's West.
Norman and London: University of Oklahoma Press, 1987.
(An anthology of 21 articles that creates a multidimensional
portrait of western women and gives direction for
researchers.)

Blair, Karen, ed., Women in Pacific Northwest History, Seattle:
University of Washington Press, 1988. (An anthology of eight
articles that interprets a wide range of women's experiences.)

Cochran, Jo, J.T. Stewart, and Mayumi Tsutakawa, ed. Gathering
Ground. Seattle: Seal Press, 1984. (An anthology of
writings and art by Northwest women of color.)

Miller, Page Putnam, ed., Landmarks of Women's History.
Bloomington and Indianapolis: Indiana University Press, 1992. (An
anthology with scholars from different backgrounds discussing the
urgency of identifying and preserving historic sites associated with
women.)

Mumford, Esther, Seven Stars and Orion. Seattle: Ananse Press,
1986. (Annotated oral histories of seven black women and
one man who lived in King County before 1940.)

Owings-Klimek, Brenda and Jennifer James-Wilson, A Centennial
Celebration of Washington Women. 2 vols. Olympia:
Superintendent of Public Instruction, 1989. (A collection of
biographical sketches with the theme of cultural pluralism.
Includes curriculum guidelines.)

INDEX

Note: Roman numerals are for chapters, followed by Arabic numbers for specific sites. This index does not duplicate the Table of Contents. Sites listed there are included only if they appear in other parts of the guidebook.

Chinese Americans: I, 24; V, 23; VII, 4, 17; VIII, 9-13
Chinese Girls' Drill Team: I, 24
Chow, Cheryl: I, 24
Chow, Ruby: I, 24
Clise, Anna Herr: IV, 11; VI, 10
Coast Guard Auxiliary: VIII, 16
Collins, Diana Borst: III, 4
Collins, Patricia "Patsy": VI, 13; X, 18
Conklin, Mary Ann: VII, 2
Cooper, Doris: IV, 17
Cooper, Lizzie: VII, 6; X, 16
Cordova, Dorothy Laigo: I, 18; IX, 22
Cornish, Nellie: V, 22; VII, 8; X, 8
Costie, Candy: IV, 3
Cotton, Jacqueline: II, 16
Cross, Virginia: I, 6
Cunningham, Imogen: V, 20
Currie, Myrtle: I, 11
Danish Sisterhood, Enumclaw: I, 3
DAR: IV, 14; V, 21; VI, 23; X, 5, 9
Daughters of Norway: VI, 2
Daughters of Penelope: X, 24
Daughters of the Pioneers: IX, 4
Davis, Georgina MacDougall: V, 18
Demonstration Project for Asian Americans: IX, 22
Dempsey, Bessie Leister: I, 22
Denny, Louisa Boren: VI, 9; X, 2, 3; XI, 3, 7
Des Moines/Zenith Improvement Club: XI, 21
DeVoe, Emma Smith: VII, 6
DeVoe, Helen: IV, 4
Domestic Workers: X, 6; XI, 16
Dougherty, Kate: III, 16; XI, 27
Duniway, Abigail Scott: VII, 11
Durham, Heidi: VII, 13
Duvall Women's Civic Club: III, 15
Duwamish Indians: II, 11, 12; III, 4; XI, 4
Duzanne, Zoe: V, 21

Gottstein, Rose: VI, 23; IX, 18
Graham, Martha: X, 8
Greathouse, Ida May: X, 17
Hadley, Deborah: VI, 17
Halibut Fishermen's Wives' Association: V, 32
Harrington, LaMar: IV, 22
Hayes, Maxine, M.D.: IX, 26
Health Care:
    Birth Control and Abortions: V, 24, 26; X, 22
    Hospital Founders and Administrators: I, 4, 20; V, 6; VII, 16;
        IX, 26; X, 20
    Midwifery: II, 8; IV, 5
    Nursing: I, 20; V, 6; VI, 8, 10; VII, 9, 16; IX, 20, 24
    Physicians: IV, 4; VII, 17; IX, 26; X, 10
Hiang, Cheng: IV, 4
Higher Education: II, 6; IV, 12, 25; V, 3, 14-21, 24; VI, 1; IX, 20, 24
Hill, Ada: III, 2, 3
Hjertoos, Bergette: III, 13
Hogan, Isabel: I, 17
Holman, Nancy Ann: VIII, 6
Hutchinson, Mary Gross: V, 16
Hutton, May Arkwright: VII, 6
Jackson, Sara Oliver: V, 22
James, Florence Bean: V, 22; X, 8
Japanese and Japanese Americans: I, 11, 12, 15; IV, 26; VII, 17;
        VIII, 7, 11, 12; IX, 19; XI, 16
Jeffs, Richard and Mary: I, 10
Jenkins, Rufina Clemente: VI, 4
Johnson, Agnes: IV, 10
Johnson, Lazelle: VI, 18
Joseph, Mother: VII, 16
Junior Programs: IX, 3
Justus, Madeleine: XI, 26
Kelly, Jane Fenton: XI, 19
Kendall, Sarah, M.D.: X, 10
Kennedy, Julia C.: X, 10
Kent Woman's Improvement Club: I, 17

Ray, Dixy Lee: VI, 15
Ray, Emma: V, 29; X, 14
Reitan, Rae: I, 13, 17
Retirement Homes: VI, 12; X, 21; XI, 7, 8
Ringdahl, Borghild: IV, 26
Rockwell, Kathleen "Klondike Kate": VII, 21
Ross, Zola Helen: IV, 25
Russell, Francia: VI, 17
Salvation Army: VII, 18
Sandall, Lois Beil: VII, 20
Satterlee Family: III, 11
Sam, Julia: I, 7
Schools:
　　　Establishment of: I, 21; II, 11; IV, 4, 29; V, 5; IX, 8; XI, 19
　　　Gardens: IX, 14
　　　Named for Women: IV, 26; V, 9; VI, 6; XI, 7
　　　Private: V, 13; IX, 5; X, 23; XI, 26
　　　Sports and Playgrounds: II, 5; X, 11; XI, 9
　　　Teachers and Administrators: I, 11; III, 2; IV, 4, 14, 29; V, 9,
　　　　　29; VI, 12; IX, 24; X, 10; XI, 17
Schultz, Cecelia Augsburg: VI, 23
Seagrave, Dr. Mabel: VII, 17
Seattle Audubon Society: VI, 1, 7; IX, 2, 5
Seattle Federation of Women's Clubs: V, 25; VIII, 6, 14; IX, 14;
　　　X, 11
Seattle Garden Club: IX, 14; XI, 18
Seattle Infant Development Center: VII, 20
Seattle Mountaineers: III, 1
Seattle Music and Art Foundation: X, 8
Seattle Office for Women's Rights: VI, 18; VII, 13
Seattle Public Library: VII, 15; VIII, 15; IX, 18, 25; X, 10
Seattle Rape Relief: 24, 5
Seattle Symphony: VI, 32
Shockey, Janet: VII, 13
Shumway, Carrie: IV, 14, 16
Sisters of Providence: II, 6; VII, 16; XI, 6
Snoqualmie Indians: III, 4, 5, 7, 10

NOTES

NOTES

NOTES

NOTES

NOTES

NOTES

NOTES